THE TIMELY RAIN

by the same authors

LONG MARCH TO FREEDOM

books by Stuart Gelder

THE EARLY LIFE OF D. H. LAWRENCE
(with Ada Lawrence)

THE CHINESE COMMUNISTS

FRONTISPIECE: Lhasa Valley from Sera Monastery

Grant
McClellan

Stuart & Roma Gelder

THE TIMELY RAIN
Travels in New Tibet

Foreword by
EDGAR SNOW

Photography by
STUART GELDER

MONTHLY REVIEW PRESS
New York

First published in 1964
by Hutchinson & Co. Ltd.
London

★

Published in the United States 1965
by MONTHLY REVIEW PRESS
333 Sixth Avenue, New York 14, N.Y.
Library of Congress Catalog Card Number 65-22568

*This book has been set in Bembo, printed in
Great Britain on Antique Wove paper by The
Anchor Press Ltd., and bound by Wm. Brendon
& Son Ltd., both of Tiptree, Essex.*

'Your will is like the gathering of clouds,
  your call like thunder,
'From these comes timely rain to nourish
  selflessly the earth!'

*From a hymn to Mao Tse-tung composed by
the fourteenth Dalai Lama Dantzen-Jaltso at
Norbulin-Shenfu Palace, Lhasa, 1954. It was
presented to the Chairman of the Chinese
People's Republic on the occasion of the Dalai
Lama's visit to Peking in 1954, and now hangs
in the Buddhist Temple of Broad Charity in
the Chinese capital.*

For Ann, Alison, David & Imogen

CONTENTS

CONTENTS

ILLUSTRATIONS

COLOUR

9

BLACK AND WHITE

FOREWORD

By EDGAR SNOW

When I met Stuart and Roma Gelder in Peking in the autumn of 1960 they urged me to join them in an attempt to storm Tibet. After fifteen years' absence from China the provinces alone seemed enough to occupy me during a brief visit, but who would count himself out on a possible view of the Potala? Just in case anything came of their petition to Premier Chou En-lai, I asked to be included. At that time the trip proved impracticable chiefly because of old man weather. Two years later Stuart and Roma quietly (that is, without a word to me) went back to China, made a second try and attained the unattainable. As a personal lesson, this book proves how mistaken I was in consoling myself, in 1960, that anyway 'I could have learned little' (as I wrote) by 'spending a few days in Lhasa as a guest of the Chinese authorities'.

Now to add insult to the professional injury of their 'we told you so', I have been asked to say grace for the banquet spread before us by this team of intrepid travellers. I cannot complain; I was fairly warned; I can now only applaud their achievment. And what a story it is! Here is a work superbly realized from an opportunity largely created by human persistency, and from rich materials woven together in a brilliant and vivid tapestry that brings to life the most remote and forbidden of all the highlands of the world.

We are fortunate that the Gelders were well prepared to understand so much of what they saw, to photograph its contrasts of beauty and pathos with fidelity, and to narrate the experience with honesty, humour and compassion. As a professional newspaper man for many years, Stuart's record establishes his credibility. He first went to India, a youthful journalist, thirty-eight years ago. On the staff of the *News Chronicle* of London for twenty years, he was its correspondent in India where he followed the ups and downs of the independence movement and became an admirer and friend of Mahatma Gandhi.

During World War II Stuart covered events in China, Burma and India; his documentary book *The Chinese Communists* reflected a foreknowledge of revolutionary victory. While a war correspondent he was the first Englishman to bomb Japan—as an observer with the 20th Bomber Command of the U.S. Air Force. Later, when chief correspondent of the *News Chronicle* in Washington, he and Roma came to know American politics and politicians and conceived a deep affection for the American people. Throughout the McCarthy years Stuart retained his faith and interest in both the United States and China, and the judgment he had formed of them. In their book *Long March to Freedom*, published following his return to China with Roma in 1960, he was able to report changes and great progress from pre-revolutionary memories of Chinese society which few Western visitors nowadays bring to that scene. A man of warm spontaneity and enthusiasm, once he has made a judgement, Stuart obviously lives with it; his marriage to Roma has lasted thirty-seven years, and children and grandchildren, as well as Roma's fortitude under the physical tests of Tibetan altitudes, attest to its continued durability.

Whether or not one agrees with the implications of this book, few will read it without recognizing that it is an honest inquiry made with no political commitments to any organized powers that be.

One is given ample space and air to read between the lines. It informs rather than indoctrinates. If it is contradictory in some respects, the facts themselves— or the elusiveness of facts—are often, as elsewhere on the China landscape, to blame. As a pioneer work *The Timely Rain* is both news and history to enrich man's knowledge of revolutionary Tibet. As a once-in-a-lifetime story, fellow writers will salute it with a much deserved well done.

EDGAR SNOW

St. Cergue, Switzerland

I

JOURNEY TO THE UNKNOWN

In 1960 we travelled more than 5,000 miles through seven Chinese provinces as freely as we wished, but our report was incomplete because we didn't see Tibet. We couldn't go there, said Foreign Minister Chen Yi, because in winter the return journey by land from Chengtu in Szechuan or from Sining in Chinghai could take more than a month and we hadn't so much time to spare.

We argued that even during a brief visit we could discover if Tibetans were victims of genocide by the Chinese who were accused of destroying them by starvation and murder.

In 1962 in his autobiography *My Land and My People*[1] the Dalai Lama wrote that:

Tens of thousands of his people had been killed, not only in military actions but individually and deliberately. They had been killed, without trial, on suspicion of opposing communism or for hoarding money or simply because of their position, or for no reason at all, *but mainly and fundamentally they had been killed because they would not renounce their religion.*[2] They had not only been shot but beaten to death, hanged, scalded, buried alive, drowned, vivisected, starved, strangled. These killings had been done in public; the victims' fellow villagers and friends and neighbours had been made to watch them; eye-witnesses described them to the Commission (of lawyers) who compiled stories of refugees. Men and women had been slowly killed while their families were forced to watch; small children had been forced to shoot their parents.

We asked if we could be flown in, but Prime Minister Chou En-lai said the government was short of suitable aircraft for this hazardous journey. We could not know if these were diplomatic

1. Weidenfeld & Nicolson
2. Authors' italics

evasions or genuine excuses, but we were promised that if we could
return in another year arrangements would be made for us to travel in
Tibet without restriction for as long as we liked. In 1962 we told
Peking we were ready and on 11th August we left London for Lhasa.

But it isn't Chairman Mao, Premier Chou or the Foreign Minister
who finally decide if you can go to the roof of the world. The last
word lies with another, entirely impersonal and non-political trium-
virate: an electro-cardiogram, a blood-pressure measuring kit and
an X-ray machine at the Fu Wai Hospital. And if they say 'No,' all the
personal influence in China won't get you a yard further on your way.

No Everest climbers were more searchingly tested by the relent-
less electric pens which recorded our heart-beats clanging in our
heads like steam-hammers, the fluoroscope in the dark-room which lit
up our insides like neon signs and the mercury pumping painfully in the
pressure tubes so that we were sure our arteries must be wafer-thin.
Only when medical certificates pronounced us fit to live and work at
altitudes of 13,000 to 15,000 feet was the rarest passport in the world
and the first to be issued to Westerners, placed in our hands.

We had asked Koo She-lone, the companion of our 1960 journeys,
if he could come with us as secretary-interpreter, and after the doctors
had worked on him for a week, getting down his blood-pressure to the
permitted level we left for Lanchow where we were received in one
of the 300 to 500-room hotels which the Chinese inexplicably build
for tourists who aren't allowed to visit them. Our suite of lounge,
bedroom and bathroom was deliciously perfumed and huge dishes
of water-melon were brought to wash the dust out of our throats. It
was our last luxury for five weeks. At three o'clock in the morning we
began the ascent on the single-track railway to Sining, gateway to
Lhasa.

The cries of people loading and unloading luggage and the squeaks
of little black pigs wakened us as dawn was slowly lighting a wide
valley, and bare, deeply cleft mountains which enclosed it loomed
through the last pale shades of the night. Between them and the railway
track peasants were already working on the stony earth behind wooden
ploughs drawn by donkeys, oxen and mules.

Men and women were winnowing grain by tossing it in the air
with forks. Every foot of fertile earth was growing cabbages, potatoes,
onions, buckwheat and soya beans. Women and girls were gathering
a colourful harvest of ruddy apples, plums and persimmons from
orchards near every village, whose mud houses might have been
anywhere in Mexico. Cézanne would have felt at home in this hard,
rolling, sunburned landscape. These might be the brown summer

mountains of the Route Napoleon and the skies of Provence over the baking fields. As we drew near to the city we saw on the horizon what appeared to be red cathedrals towering hundreds of feet into the morning sky. These were vertical rock formations sculpted by wind and water. Vast apses had been formed, heightening the illusion of human architecture where the rock had been most deeply eroded.

Great industrial areas are being developed in West China, but in this high hinterland more than six million peasants still live in the cottages and use the tools of their ancestors of the Chinese Middle Ages which politically ended here only thirteen years ago. The people still face a bitter unceasing struggle with Nature but no longer live in fear of War Lords whose avarice and cruelty can never be forgotten or forgiven.

2

GATEWAY TO LHASA

From Sining you can walk up the dirt road just beyond the only hotel, climb through the valleys on to the Chinghai uplands and travel cross-country over the Tibetan plateau without coming to another town in more than 2,000 miles. Until the Chinese occupied Tibet in 1951 this was the only way to Lhasa from the east. Now a road has been driven through the wild wastes and grasslands of the border 1,300 miles to the Tibetan capital. The only other highway to the Holy City runs 1,500 miles from Chengtu in Szechuan province, via Chamdo and over some of the most formidable passes in the world rising to 15,000 feet. This was hacked out of the vertical mountainside by Chinese and Tibetan labourers and Red Army soldiers who worked within inches of 1,000-foot drops to make the hard shoulders which would enable trucks to pass round hairpin bends.

Compared with the Szechuan route, the Sining-Lhasa road is a gentle undulating journey. But when we arrived in early September long stretches had been washed out by the heaviest summer rains for fifty years, so that it would have taken us one or two back-breaking weeks to cover the distance to Lhasa by jeep. The Chinese Government had given us the choice of going to Tibet by air or land, but because our time was limited, we had asked the Air Force to fly us in if the weather was favourable. We had hoped to stay only one night in the unlikely opulence of the hotel at the edge of this wilderness which had been built by the City Communist Council only a couple of hundred yards from the medieval mud homes of the local peasantry.

But Air Force radio operators above Lhasa were telling the Sining Commander that demoniac winds howling through the ice-cowled peaks would tear the wings off our aircraft like gossamer moth wings if we took off now. The China-Tibet mountain ranges aren't the highest in the world but here the weather can change from calm to furious storm and back to calm again within an hour so that for aircrews they are the most dangerous.

It wasn't surprising that the Buddhists, ignorant of meteorology, believe this violent world is in the power of malevolent demons in everlasting conflict with benevolent gods who have all their work cut out to maintain brief uncertain periods in which human and animal life can survive.

After dinner we stretched our travel-cramped legs by walking through the town. Main streets in China are the broadest in the world. There are no private cars and few motor vehicles of any kind but when they are mass-produced, tunnels will have to be driven to enable pedestrians to cross from one side to the other unless they are to be slaughtered by the thousand. Sining main street is one of the broadest of all. Now, with foot on accelerator and hand on horn, drivers can scatter jay-walking citizens to safety.

At first sight the female population seemed to be composed of black-cowled nuns. These were Moslem women. Their menfolk, in grey-white pill-box hats, might have been figures in any Middle East city. The new squat box-shaped shops and offices had no national identity and might have been thrown up overnight anywhere on earth where an oil strike or newly discovered mineral deposits had attracted a flood of immigrants. Only weirdly and wonderfully dressed Mongolians and Tibetans, wearing sheepskin coats, leather boots with upturned toe points and hats with outlandish ears, turquoise ear-rings and carrying rosaries twined round their wrists, reminded us that we had come to the country where two cultures meet.

At dawn Koo She-lone wakened us with a message from the airfield. We couldn't hope to fly for another twenty-four hours.

So we drove to Kumbum monastery of which Thubten Jigme Norbu, the eldest brother of the fourteenth Dalai Lama, was formerly abbot.[1]

Five hundred yards beyond the hotel the smooth macadamed road came to an abrupt end and we pitched into a curtain of dust thrown up by mule and donkey carts carrying vegetables into Sining over a deeply pot-holed dirt track. Between one gear change and another we had passed from the new sophisticated city into a countryside which was a few steps and a thousand years away. Here, for the first time in China, we saw men, women and children in rags. But, incongruously, some of them sat at the doors of their mud houses which were one-roomed huts, eating breakfast from beautifully shaped and decorated bowls,

1. Thubten Jigme went to India when the Chinese first entered Tibet in 1951. He now lives in the United States.

the designs on which have remained unchanged for centuries. Compared with this peasant ware, the expensive new crockery sold in town shops is crudely decorated and shoddily finished.

Tall poplars, lining the rocky way through the closely cultivated fields, again gave us the illusion that we were travelling through a southern French landscape until we were jolted back to China by frantic swerves to avoid vegetable carts coming at us straight down the centre of the track. With bruised bones we reached a long village where it was market day, and slowly brushing our way through flocks of chickens, goats, ducks, pigs and people came upon a row of white, blue and gold chortens, the pagoda-shaped memorials of holy lamas, guarding the way to the monastery.

Thirty temples, the houses of the Abbot, the Dalai and Panchen Lamas and high ecclesiastics, the cells and hermitages of the monks, barns and store houses lay within the folds of the sun-parched hills planted with cedars and juniper bushes. Thubten Jigme Norbu, like his brother the Dalai Lama, was born in a cow-byre at the small farmstead of their peasant parents in the poor village of Tengtser, two days' journey on horse-back from this great religious town.

In his autobiography *Tibet is My Country*[1] he has related to his friend Heinrich Harrer, author of *Seven Years in Tibet*[2], that when he was an infant, it became known to his father and mother that he was the reincarnation of a famous monk, Tagtser, and had inherited great wealth through his previous incarnations at Kumbum and from other monasteries besides.

When he was eight years old this peasant child was dressed in fine clothes and taken to his 'rich and splendid' inheritance. At Kumbum, like a prince in a fairy-tale, dressed in silk-embroidered robes of finest quality, he was placed on his throne to receive the homage of the Abbot and thirty other Rimpoches, the high dignitaries who were his fellow monastic aristocrats. The boy from the dark windowless cottage at Tengtser now ruled from a house filled with beautiful and valuable treasures which according to Buddhist belief had been left by himself to himself when he departed from his previous body. Now the child who had never seen a clock possessed fifteen, with little cuckoos to pop out and tell him the time and a collection of lovely musical boxes, from one of which a girl came out to dance to the music, carrying in her hand a smaller box from which another dancer appeared.

In his previous incarnation Thubten Norbu had achieved a great reputation as a healer which brought him a fortune. He had fled to

1. & 2. [Rupert Hart-Davis]

Mongolia from a tribal rebellion during which Kumbum was destroyed by fire and from there went to Russia, where his healing powers were in wide demand and he was handsomely rewarded. In middle life he returned to Chinghai with a caravan full of treasures including the cuckoo clocks and music-boxes. The wealth of this incarnation had been passed on to his successive reincarnations and increased by shrewd investment in property and land. The farms of the estates and monasteries yielded large revenues. They were leased to peasants under the ancient feudal system by which they gave up a percentage of their harvests to their landlord.

Five years after Thubten's birth another boy, named Lhamo Döndrub, was born to his mother in the cow-byre at Tengtser. When he was four, high lamas from Lhasa, disguised as merchants, came to look for the new incarnation of the thirteenth Dalai Lama, recently dead, in a house which had been seen, reflected in the waters of a lake near the Holy City, and under whose strangely shaped gutter pipes the Regent had dreamed he saw standing the fourteenth Incarnation.

There, in Tengtser village, was the identical house, the home of Thubten Norbu's parents. The 'merchants' told the housewife they were on their way to Chakhyung, and asked if they might rest awhile in her kitchen. The leader of the search party, Kyetsang Rimpoche, had dressed himself as a servant so that his companions appeared to be his superiors. In order to observe little Lhamo Döndrub more closely they asked if they might stay the night. They were made welcome and played with the infant until it was his bedtime. They were impressed by him but if he was truly the reincarnation for whom they were looking he must prove it by recognising certain objects which he had possessed in his former life.

Kyetsang Rimpoche carried among other things, the thirteenth Dalai's rosary. The boy claimed it as his own and moreover saw through the disguise and told Kyetsang he was a lama and, it is said, to the amazement of his parents and the visitors, addressed him in the Lhasa dialect, which had never been heard in Tengtser. He also recognised a walking-stick and a small drum which had belonged to his previous body. He took them in his hands and refused to part with them. Without revealing their identity the 'merchants' left before dawn, but returned to declare who they were. Now they carried with them the thirteenth Dalai Lama's silver pencil and eating bowl as well as indistinguishable replicas of them. The boy would have none of the imitations.

This time Kyetsang Rimpoche also wore the former Dalai's rosary round his neck and carried a replica in his hands but little Lhamo

Döndrub knew his own and tried to pull the genuine beads from the monk, crying out that it belonged to him.

The visitors also found, on examining the child's body, two marks on the shoulders, traces of an extra pair of arms, which all true incarnations possessed. There could now be no doubt that the fourteenth Dalai Lama was discovered.

The romantic story was complete. The peasant boy was taken to his capital where he would reign from the mighty Potala Palace until he died and was reborn to reign again. His father, who was made a duke and his mother now a duchess went with him to the Holy City, where the great ecclesiastical and lay lords received them with the reverence and high respect due to parents who had been chosen by the gods to bring back the Dalai Lama to the world from the 'Honourable Field'.[1] They were given lands and riches and their other children were ennobled and enriched likewise.

Until 1951, when the Chinese Communists came to Tibet, they lived happily ever after.

Thubten Jigme Norbu, who had been elected Abbot of Kumbum, was living the last chapter of his fairy-tale when Ma Pu-fang, Chiang Kai-shek's Governor in Sining, fled before the advancing Communist army, taking with him all the treasure he could pack into his private plane and abandoning his troops to rob the local peasantry of food and every valuable they could lay hands on.

Governor Ma had exploited Buddhism but he had not suppressed it. In a country where the oppression of corrupt officials was accepted with long-practised resignation, his behaviour did not occasion protest from the lay and ecclesiastical aristocracies even though the price of their peace was the payment of tribute when the governor's bank account was running low.

It was true that Thubten Norbu's little brother, Lhamo Döndrub, was found to be the Dalai Lama, but the boy had not been allowed to leave China for Tibet until a large sum of money had been paid to Ma Pu-fang. The monks who had discovered the Incarnation could not raise the money until a party of rich merchants, travelling to Lhasa, lent it to them. But the public practice of religious beliefs had never been forbidden nor had the local war lords been so foolish as to put out of business the monastic landlords who put such generous taxes into their pockets.

It was understandable that the Abbot and his monks should fear that Communists would seize their treasure and property and destroy their

1. Death.

religion as well. But if the Dalai Lama's brother was so ready to believe, even before he met them, that these godless men would be cruel and ruthless oppressors, they certainly outraged him as soon as they arrived by their total lack of sympathy with his religious outlook on social problems. Eleven years later we were well able to imagine his dismay when twenty monks, who had made it, proudly showed us a screen six feet high and eighteen feet wide, sculptured out of one and a half tons of butter. This depicted the wedding journey of the Princess Wen Cheng who went from Sian, China's ancient capital, to Lhasa in the seventh century to marry the King of Tibet and took Buddhism with her. The wedding coach, the escorting nobles on prancing horses, the border landscape with rivers, boats, trees and flowers, houses, deer and huntsmen with their hounds, were exquisitely carved and delicately coloured in the minutest detail by the artists, who began to learn this craft when they were boys. This fantastic piece of work had been completed in the previous January. Now it was slowly disintegrating. In the New Year they would begin another. Cut in stone in a Christian cathedral, it would be as renowned as the windows of Chartres. Here it was housed in a dilapidated barn for the folk from the surrounding country, who had donated the butter, to see. In early September a rancid stench advertised its presence.

In the winter of 1949 the new Communist Governor of Chinghai had lectured Thubten Norbu on his duties to the peasants, now liberated from feudal oppression by the People's Army. The lands of Kumbum, he said, should be distributed amongst the population, and monks should work, instead of idling around the monastery, wasting time praying and frittering away money on incense and wasting large quantities of butter in religious ceremonial. Beggars should be given jobs.

Wearily recalling this ordeal, the former Abbot wrote that they had been talking at cross-purposes.

If the Communist was being impossibly pompous the unhappy monk was naive in his simplicity when he complained that the Governor would not or could not understand that 'almsgiving was one of the fundamental obligations of our religion and that the beggars were therefore fulfilling a useful function in society'. He probably could not have astonished the Marxist more if he had given him a prayer wheel as a goodwill present.

But if Thubten Norbu was a little lacking in political sensibility he didn't lack courage, for when the Governor asked him to issue an immediate order forbidding the burning of any more butter the Abbot firmly refused and told him that if he wanted this done he must do it himself. Confounded by this brave resolution, the atheist soldier declared he had no such intention and conceded that the authorities would have to proceed to reform step by step. Eleven years after their conversation the sculptured butter screen confirmed that progress continued to move at an unforced unhurried pace.

Worshippers still come to the shrines, carrying their small butter lamps in their hands to burn in propitiation for their sins in this life and the hope of a more comfortable existence in their next, and the gold and jewelled Buddhas still sit, impassive and undisturbed, in the shadows cast by the soft light of hundreds of butter flames flickering from enormous bronze and silver vessels at their feet.

As we arrived at the first temple of the monastery, two Mongolian women and a small boy and girl appeared at the gates. Their long wild tangles of hair fell over their shoulders. They wore sheepskin coats stiff with grease and dirt, and skirts decorated with strips of brightly coloured leather. Round their necks, and from richly embroidered belts, hung long ropes of red and blue beads and large silver discs. In their hands the women carried tiny and beautifully wrought silver cups in which small butter lights were burning. Without a glance to either side, apparently unconscious of our presence, they walked slowly past us and disappeared silently into the shrine like apparitions from the lost world of Genghis Khan.

Now only 400 of the 3,000 men who were here before the Communists came remain to live out the quiet monotonous rhythm of the Buddhist Religious. The Chinese say that after the Tibetan rebellion in 1959, when the government decreed that all monks were free to remain in monasteries or go as they pleased, the monks of Kumbum, which is in China proper, were also 'liberated', and that those who went from here returned to lay life to marry and settle down as farmers, craftsmen, labourers and clerks. But it is also probable that, as Thubten Norbu reported, many fled before the Communists arrived because they feared they would be persecuted or killed. It is also likely that others went because they saw no future in a monastic life which Communist unbelievers might not destroy but could not be expected to encourage. And there would be more who, having been given to Kumbum as religious offerings when they were children, were glad to be quit of a life for which they had no vocation but from which their fears of heavenly retribution would not allow them to escape before.

Certainly Thubten Jigme Norbu and the departed monks never saw Kumbum in its present splendour.

The temple where we met the Mongolians might have been created by a monk designer for the delight and terror of children. For this quiet and sacred place was also a bizarre and barbaric setting for a play where one would not have been surprised to see outlandish pantomime characters come tumbling down the sanctuary steps to perform in the courtyard below. This was like an Elizabethan stage, flanked by galleries for an audience. Looking down from them now, as if they expected us to throw them titbits, were stuffed horses, bears, cows and impudent-faced monkeys occupying the vacant seats. The walls were garish with delicately painted pictures of exquisite torments suffered by the damned in manifold Buddhist hells. Immediately inside the temple entrance, where the placid deities gazed through a thin haze of butter smoke into the autumn light, the stuffed white horse of the eighth Panchen Lama, his neck garlanded with white hatas (good-luck scarves), stood waiting as if he expected the god to descend at any moment and ride off on his back over the mountains to the Holy City of Lhasa. The local taxidermist had a keen sense of humour for he had suc-ceeded in giving all his animals the expressions of comical human characters.

When we walked out of the village into Kumbum we stepped from reality into a child's dream world of gods and demons where good and evil spirits lived in stones and trees and animals were the souls of human dead who had returned to earth. If they were good bears, horses, cows and monkeys they might find redemption in the next round of existence as men and women again. According to the belief of Tibetan Buddhists, if you don't live virtuously in one life you may be punished by having to live again on a lower plane. If you are rich and powerful, but misuse your gifts, you might be chastened by being reborn poor and humble but if your misbehaviour is really serious you might not be reincarnated in human form at all but could reappear on earth as a mouse or a fly. So Tibetans have a special reason to be kind to animals. After all, if you beat your mare or dog you may be beating your aunt or grandfather, and personal sentiments apart, this could seriously prejudice your position in your next existence. Strangely enough, this situation causes no embarrassment in Tibetan social relations, for if one meets a poor ragged old monk like Lo Tsang Geng-den the keeper of this temple at Kumbum, it doesn't occur to one that he might have lived disreputably when he was on earth before nor did one assume that the more richly attired Chu Cheng Chien-chuo, who received us in the name of the senior Abbot, absent on a pilgrimage to Lhasa, was a more reputable charac-ter. For while to Tibetan Buddhists their religious belief is a convenient way of explaining the human dilemma in an otherwise inexplicable universe, they have been like other people in the world, rich or poor for much the same reasons.

Lo Tsang Geng-den came to Kumbum forty-six years ago as a poor boy without a dowry, and while he might now be advancing spiritually towards such perfection that dead, he might go straight to heaven and never have to return to endure human life again, he had obviously made no material progress here.

Chu Cheng Chien-chuo had come from a more prosperous family who could afford to pay an entrance fee to the monastery, so that he had got off to a better start. Unlike his poorer brother monk, he did not become a monastery servant but learned to read and write. So he was now well qualified to be Kumbum's representative on the Nationalities Commission, set up by the government in all parts of China where there are racial minorities, to protect their interests.

Although monks are not a racial minority, they form a separate community with a separate culture, and so have been given an official voice through selected representatives who see no conflict of interests between a government which doesn't believe in gods and monks who assume that spirits live in every juniper bush.

We at first mistook Chu Cheng Chien-chuo for a civilian, as he wore dark trousers, tunic and soft peaked cap, but when we said we wished to photograph him he changed into his best monks' clothes with gold-thread trimmings and the embroidered, thick-soled boots of a prosperous lama. In this more appropriate dress he escorted us through the steep narrow streets and courts of the monastery in which we should have been lost without a guide.

Newly gilded roofs and Buddhist symbols shone from every hill. Intricately carved eaves of temples were freshly painted in red, green, blue and gold, and everywhere walls were decorated with charmingly coloured ceramics in relief, of deer, pastoral scenes, monkeys and legendary animals and pious murals.

Chu Cheng Chien-chuo told us that the Peking Government had given 300,000 yuan[1] for restorations and redecorations since the monastery's lands and their revenue had been taken over by the state. The diminished community was no longer self-supporting. Aged and infirm monks were given small government pensions of a few shillings a month, presumably provided from the profits of confiscated manors. Younger, able-bodied men worked to grow food on land which Kumbum had been allowed to retain for its own use. But it was not forbidden to accept alms and the devout peasantry still made gifts of food

---

1. Seven yuan to £1.

and money to monks, who were also able to earn extra income by conducting special prayer services for the laity in their own homes and officiating at religious weddings and funerals.

Were the peasants still as religious as before?

'Yes,' said Chu Cheng Chien-chuo. 'A government can't destroy beliefs which have been a part of people's lives since they were children.'

But the people are no longer subservient to monastic secular rule and no longer dependent on Kumbum, of which they were tied tenants, for their livings. Religion is tolerated by the Communists and the faithful are not denied the right to practise it. Also they are no longer compelled to support it by taxation or induced to make gifts, by threats of ecclesiastics that they will suffer heavenly retribution if they don't. Kumbum is still a centre of devotion but no longer exercises political or economic authority over the neighbourhood.

We could hardly expect this young man who supported the new government, to express regret that this change has come about, for he now occupies a more important position than he held under the old order. But when we asked him what he thought of the new situation he showed no hesitancy or embarrassment when he answered: 'The majority of the peasants and the majority of the monks were poor before. Some monks and some laymen were very rich. I think the big change is that no one now is rich at the expense of others.'

But what about the impoverishment of religion?

He replied: 'The Communists don't believe in it, but they don't persecute it. You can't impoverish religion itself.'

Even if the Communists had wished to do so there was no need to persecute the few harmless monks in worn-out clothes, stiff with the dirt and spilled rancid butter grease of years, who shuffled round the silent streets and altars which had once been alive with more than a thousand men.

Perhaps if the buildings of Kumbum had been flaking and crumbling in decay they would have appeared less melancholy to us than they did in their fresh gay brilliance. The greatest religious foundation in China is now a splendid stage set for a majestic play which cannot be produced because only 400 of the cast of 3,000 who were needed to perform it are still there. Those who remain are figures in a small charade in which, lost among the colossal props, they can hardly be seen.

But there were some remarkable individual performances in the wings where monks mimed their rituals out of sight of any audience.

Before a lovely shrine, housed beneath a jade, gold and crimson roof, a tall bearded man was prostrating in penitential exercises before a row of images who smiled down on him with expressions of benevolent but faintly amused approval. He wore woollen pads on both palms to protect them from hot friction with two broad parallel strips of wood worn to glassy smoothness. He flung himself down and slid forward on his hands until his body, face downwards, was pressed close to the ground. Then, without bending his knees, he raised and lowered himself slowly, supporting his weight with rigid arms a dozen times before springing to his feet again. His breath softly whistling from his deep chest like a blacksmith's bellows, he was continuing this ceaseless rhythmic movement a half-hour later when we left him, and two hours afterwards we saw his figure slowly rising and falling as we passed through the court again. Chu Cheng Chien-chuo explained that this monk was gaining great merit by his strenuous devotions which he would probably continue until he was completely exhausted or even unconscious. Since a thousand prostrations counted only as one according to mystical Buddhist calculations, it obviously took superhuman endurance and resolution to make a reputable score in the eyes of the gods.

As we watched him, we remembered a confession by the former Abbot, Thubten Norbu, that he was quickly tired by these exercises and gave up after only a few prostrations. It was all very well for him. He had stored up a large credit of merit in his former lives so that he could now afford to live on his capital without further effort. Judging by his enormous exertions, the bearded monk must have dissipated his spiritual reserves in his previous incarnation and bequeathed to himself in his present life a load of debt which he was now working hard to pay off. With odds of a thousand to one against him, it didn't seem a very good bet that he would be in credit before he died, so perhaps if we returned to Kumbum twenty years hence we might find him in a new body, still sweating it out.

We should have been unimaginative travellers if we had felt no momentary nostalgia for the past, described with such evocative sympathy by the former Abbot, for an ordered world in which all men knew their places and were without envy of their neighbours, who were in better ones. Because, knowing they had brought their fates upon themselves by their foolishness in previous lives, the poor and oppressed and afflicted bore their adversities, not only without resentment but with hope because they were now being given another chance of a more joyful life when this unfortunate existence was mercifully ended and they were reborn. The rich and powerful could accept their good fortune as reward for their personal excellence. If they were momentarily disturbed by the sufferings and hardships of their lesser brethren they could instantly dismiss their qualms with the thought that but for the grace of their own superiority they would have been similarly punished.

Here was a security which could not be rudely disturbed by social change and progress. Inevitable discomfort ensued when men rashly brought it upon themselves to make their own justice instead of leaving its dispensation to the gods.

In such a world the people of Tibet and its monastic satellite societies, which the Dalai Lama has described as without envy, would become envious of others, like all who lived in foreign countries where freedom was synonymous with licentiousness when it preferred material progress to spiritual advancement.

Perhaps we should have sympathised less with the Abbot's comforting illusions if we had been Pa Tei Chiang Chu, the little monk in rags whose home was a stable on a hillside which he shared with a few chickens and pigs. We couldn't ask him how he felt about the disruption of the old unchanging life of the monastery where he had lived since he was eight years old, for he was a deaf-mute.

He gently pressed our hands in his and uttered unintelligible sounds which his poor neighbour, who lived in an earth cell next door, assured us was his welcome.

But perhaps Pa Tei Chiang Chu was the most fortunate monk of all. No one could tell him that he was living the life of a destitute tramp because he had misbehaved himself in his former life. So in his ignorance how could he by acts of contrition put himself right with the gods in the hope that they would give him a good pair of ears with his next body? Or in their inscrutable charity, had they already rewarded him at birth by blessing him with an affliction which also freed him from the fears which tormented his brethren, because he was innocent of any sense of guilt?

This was our first meeting with Buddhism and we had begun our journey in Kumbum a little self-consciously, fearful lest we might commit an irreverent act by speaking too loudly in a temple or forgetfully turning our backs on the gods as we walked out. The monks, who accepted cigarettes and struck matches on the pedestals of deities in the courtyards and lit up under their noses, put us at our ease. We had been even more nervous of personally offending these holy men in whose minds cleanliness had no connection with godliness and whose feet looked and smelled as if they hadn't been washed since they were born. So they might have thought us stand-offish but for the screen of tobacco smoke which now made intimate conversation possible.

The loneliest inhabitants here are the Buddhas in the great prayer house where every day they used to hear the voices of the great community chanting their office. Now there are long gaps which will never be filled in the low thick-carpeted benches covering the vast floor, which are the choir stalls.

Vivid banners hung from the immense walls. Tall pillars supporting the high roof, clothed in richly coloured overlapping scalloped tapestry, resembled rows of giant figures in Plantagenet costume.

Before we left we were offered tea from a small pitcher in a kitchen where it was once made for 3,000 monks and their guests on festival days. In former days food was cooked in three metal vats each of which could have concealed a dozen men.

Chu Cheng Chien-chuo suggested we should return next day to make more film if we were unable to leave for Lhasa. The weather report was still hopeless in the morning and we accepted his invitation.

Perhaps the prayers of our friend the bearded monk, who after a night's sleep was continuing his devotional exercises, might help to placate the furies over the mountains. At any rate, early on the third day the Air Force reported that they were quieter and we could make a dash for an intermediate airfield from which we should have a better chance of getting through to Tibet in rapidly changing wind and cloud.

Over the turquoise ice-shored lake of Koko Nor we flew into the back of the Chinghai beyond.

Potala Palace from the Norbulingka road at sunset

Lhasa Valley from a Potala roof

Detail of butter sculpture made by lamas at Kumbum Monastery, Chinghai. The entire work, 6 feet high and 18 feet long, was carved from one and a half tons of butter. This is the first colour picture to be taken of this fabulous Tibetan art

3

FLIGHT INTO DANGER

When we had asked if it was forbidden to take photographs during the air journey the Chinese authorities had replied, 'Only from the aircraft on the approaches to Tibet.' They could hardly have imagined that our cameras were filled with X-ray lenses which would absorb enough light to expose film through aeroplane windows opaque with frost at 22,000 feet. Or they were joking.

No one would take up the dreary underpaid job of spying if he were intelligent and energetic enough to make a living at any other trade. This is perhaps the reason why professionals usually appear even sillier than their fictional counterparts and why their government employers, who must justify the money they spend on Secret Services, disown them as soon as they are caught. They cannot admit they waste money on such dolts, especially since the really valuable information can always be had for nothing.

There has never been a shortage of scientists who really know how to blow the world to bits and are anxious to give their blueprints to an 'enemy' so that everyone will possess the deterrent which all will be afraid to use, and so save us all from destruction. But they can never persuade a professional 'enemy' agent to accept them for nothing. This would spoil the market. So they are soon inevitably caught as they almost certainly never would be if they were not forced to behave as spies are expected to behave. They usually have a few enemy pounds in their pockets, hardly enough to give them a decent week's holiday at the seaside.

If the Chinese are as inscrutable as they are supposed to be, they should be very good at this sort of thing. They are no good at all.

We were gulping oxygen through our masks and staring at a frosty blur of propellers thrashing the thin air over the mountains which school maps had told us forty years earlier were down below, when an officer came to see us. 'They' would be obliged, he said, if we didn't

c   33

report the name of the place where we would come down in a few
minutes. Since we couldn't keep a secret if we didn't know it, we asked
its name. He immediately told us, but we can't repeat it because we
have forgotten it.

We landed on a salt desert as empty as the surface of the moon,
enclosed by razor-edged ice and snow-covered peaks. The men who
maintain this staging post, an ice-box in winter, a furnace in summer,
live in a group of unheated wooden huts at the edge of the runway.

Now the mountain devils were whipping up such a furious storm
over the Tangla Range that we couldn't take off for Lhasa, and Roma,
shivering and shaking in her thick padded clothes, was ordered to
bed by a major-doctor. Our chief pilot said she would have time to
recover; some travellers had been held down here for weeks. Had we,
after all, turned our backs carelessly on some offended Kumbum god
who had now struck her down and conjured legions of demons to close
the gates of the Holy City when we were almost in sight of them? We
hoped the prostrating bearded monk was still interceding for us as he
had promised. Perhaps, with the clairvoyant powers sometimes attri-
buted to lamas, he had already sensed our plight and accelerated his
exercises to speed Roma's recovery. The doctor said it was a long warm
sleep and the effect of antibiotics which brought down her temperature
so that she was just well enough to stagger up for dinner. But when,
late that night, the meteorological officer reported that the new storm
was dying, we gave all credit to our protector in the monastery nearly
a thousand miles away.

No people are more practical than the Chinese and occasionally
none can be more inexplicably lacking in common sense. What is
surprising about their recent history is not that they have suffered
setbacks in their crash plan to industrialise China but that without
experience they have begun developing a modern state at unprece-
dented speed. They have organised a great steel industry. They have
designed and built huge hydro-electric and water-conservation schemes
of enormous complexity, yet you will be lucky if you are not kept
awake in the best hotels, whose food and service are usually excellent,
by dripping taps and water-closet ballcocks which don't work properly.
Millions of gallons of water must drip to waste every day.

The major-doctor, who was taking a turn as duty officer, served
us a dinner at the salt-desert airfield cooked by an Air Force chef who
would qualify for a job at one of Peking's best restaurants which are the
equal of any in France and better than most.

But the most nauseous lavatories in France, than which there are
few more repelling on earth, except at Kuwait Airport, where they

are rich enough to make them of gold, were fragrant bowers compared
to the nightmares into which we found our way through the night.
Unlike the wooden living huts, these massive structures were perma-
nent brick and concrete halls in which one squatted over troughs
constructed at such an angle that they were choked with the defecations
of previous visitors. Behind their rear walls, and running along their
entire length, were wide deep moats into which, presumably, this
horrific debris was washed down when the squatting platforms became unusable. Between these lavatories and the nearest mountains
was fifty or sixty miles of unoccupied plain, but it hadn't occurred to
the architect to have trenches dug, protected by canvas screens and
filled up and replaced by new trenches when necessary. Having put
up the brick and concrete monuments, the victims were stuck with
them, monstrous moats and all.

Later, in England, when turning out the contents of a desk, we
came upon a photograph of the first cottage in which we lived thirty-
five years ago in a Nottinghamshire village. The earth closet, a few
yards from the kitchen door, was emptied by the council night-soil
man twice a year. We endured it for one summer and fled. We determined then that we had made our last odious comparisons between
China and England or anywhere else.

Before dawn a gap opened in the weather, wide enough for us to
pass through safely. As we hurried to breakfast we saw our plane taking
off on a test run. To lose an engine at 23,000 feet over the wildernesses
of ice between here and Lhasa would mean our certain end. If we weren't
lucky enough to be killed outright in a crash there would be no hope of
rescue.

The cold bit through our layers of cotton, padding and fur, but
just before take-off soldiers came running with heaps of quilts which
they threw into the aircraft with warning shouts to us to keep warm.
We were the first from the West to go to Tibet for eleven years. We
weren't going to be the first to die getting there if they could help it.

We climbed in wide circles to reach 20,000 feet above the first
mountain barrier before we turned to cross it.

Now we flew south-west to Tan Hsiung, the highest airfield in
the world, 13,000 feet above sea-level.

Below the starboard wing, white reflected sunlight flashed from
the windscreens of trucks, traced for us the thin course of the Sining–
Lhasa road snaking through the Chinghai foothills to the north.

Our feet began to freeze in our wool-lined boots. Roma, masked
and encased in her padded coat and pants like a spacewoman, was
adjusting her oxygen control when a burst of hot air from the gaping

end of a flexible metal pipe lying on the floor blasted my ankles. It had been there yesterday, but probably, with the traditional Chinese aversion to making direct statements, the chief pilot hadn't cared to mention it until he was sure it would work. Better first to provide quilts and blankets. Now we threw them off, loosened the fastenings of our coats and relaxed in soporific warmth.

A few years ago this flight was thought to be impossible. The eastern air-route over the Himalayas between Chabua, Dinjan in Assam and Kunming had been pioneered by the American Air Force and the Chinese civil airline, when the Japanese overran the Burma road, to maintain the only link between India and China. Scores of planes disappeared in the mists of those borderlands. Climbing safely at 23,000 feet over the highest mountains on the maps, many had exploded into them a thousand feet below their peaks. I had made many of these blind journeys. After the first three or four you weren't afraid of being killed because you learned to die before you started and put your trust in the Douglas and Curtis factorymen who had made you good aeroplanes, the skill and guts of the American insurance clerks and farmers and students who flew them and the prevailing westerly winds which helped you into Yünnan. But from Chinghai you looked straight into the wind's teeth, dripping icy saliva on the edges of your wings.

While an army of soldiers and civilians began to dig out a 1,300-mile trace to Lhasa from Sining, a group of Chinese Air Force pilots and navigators began to grope a way through the high valleys. It wasn't a job for intrepid dashing adventurers. It was important to get as far as they could and survey the ground they could cover with meticulous accuracy, but it was more important to return with their marked charts. If they didn't they had only shown the way to disaster for another crew.

Everyone came back safely until the last, which was also the first aeroplane to land in Tibet, had the complete picture of the route. From that day on all aircraft had got through, but only because they didn't take off unless pilots and navigators could see most of the way with their own eyes.

We moved over glittering peaks and high snowfields which looked near enough to touch if one could have leaned out of the windows. Sometimes we passed so close that the slipstream of the propellers kicked up flurries of snow behind us. Then we were flying between ice gorges into fantastic bottomless valleys and turning again away from frozen walls through which there was no gap from one horizon to another.

I dropped my mask from my face to get a clearer view and was wakened half an hour later by a steep diving turn in which the pistons sounded as if they were bursting through the sides of the engines. We were screaming through blinding cloud and the altimeter needle was down to 14,500 feet. Koo She-lone's eyes glanced over his mask—a reassurance or a mute gesture of resigned farewell? Now Roma was waving a hand to attract my attention and pointing down. We were levelled out over a long green valley flanked by the shining icy heads of mountains whose shoulders were buried in vast capes of snow. Hundreds of animals were running from the noise of our motors which were now being throttled back so that I could hear her saying, 'They're yaks.'

We were on top of the world.

4

JOURNEY IN REVERSE

Soldiers with rifles stood every hundred yards on either side of the runway—guarding it from rebellious Tibetan saboteurs? We asked why they were there.

'To shoot yaks if they stampede and run in the path of a landing aircraft,' said the young officer who helped us with our luggage into a reception hut. 'The ground is too hard here to drive in fence posts and we had some nasty moments when the first flights came in before we had the sentries. It's a cold and lonely job but the traffic isn't heavy.'

An Air Force doctor came to measure our blood-pressures. They were above normal, but he reassured us: 'It happens to everyone. All the same, don't stay up here too long or you won't feel well. We'll try to get you away in half an hour.'

I had hardly assured him that I couldn't have felt better when my eyes began to lose focus and my head swam with nausea. Roma handed me a mug of tea. After a few minutes reclining in a chair the furniture came into sharp outline again and I noticed that she was quietly writing in her diary. Surely only sex prejudice or a feminine indifference to such impractical pursuits prevented a woman from being the first to reach the South Pole or the summit of Everest.

Our chief pilot came to tell us that if we had been an hour later taking off it would have been impossible to land. Cloud which had blinded our approach had now closed in over the last range and he and his crew were likely to be grounded for the rest of the week.

As he talked, his face receded until it was a small blur like my bedroom window, which in childhood fevers had become a small square of light at the end of a long grey tunnel, and then reappeared in normal size as though it was tied to my eyes on elastic string which stretched and shrank as they tried to keep it in its usual place.

A driver came to say he was ready. Someone heaved me to my feet and I floated into the yard to which I felt I was only held down by

38

the heavy cameras and tape-recording gear on my shoulders. It was ten o'clock when we rattled out on to the last stretch of the Sining–Lhasa road in a bus in which Keystone Comedy stunt-men would have refused to travel without danger money.

We had thought the city was vaguely round the corner until we asked what time we should arrive. The driver replied that he could make the journey in nine or ten hours if we weren't bogged down by floods, and the next moment crashed down screaming gears to stop in the middle of a rocky stream over which rode a cavalcade of Tibetan horsemen.

Dressed in bright embroidered boots, and fur hats with long-barrelled rifles, bows and quivers of arrows and gleaming swords slung from shoulders or belts, they turned in their saddles to stare in slow surprise at our white faces. We were a type of Chinese they had never seen before. They passed slowly by the windows to get a closer look at us, and then, shouting with laughter, galloped up a long slope towards a group of black yak-hair tents at the foot of a mountain. These were herdsmen who had come to take part in an archery festival at the weekend.

The driver of a lorry carrying petrol from Sining, which was half capsized in a ditch further up the road, helped to push us out of the water and we staggered on with our feet drumming on the vibrating floor which threatened to slide off the chassis, and us with it, at every pothole between which there were only brief intervals of solid ground. The last spring had stretched itself out and died a hundred journeys ago, and for all the buoyancy they gave the tyres, almost flat on the wheel-rims, would have been more useful as boot-soles. Within a few minutes Roma had discovered how to survive the next mile without a broken back. She held on to the top of the seat in front and rode the bus like a bucking horse, rising and falling and leaning with the jolts. Soon we all got into the rhythm. The vehicle, propelled by madly galloping passengers led by fair-faced demons from another world, may now be a legend in those wild lands.

The road-makers had cut the first highway through north-east Tibet parallel with the River Kyi, which raced and boiled in flood through a wide enchanting valley sheltered by the snow mountains and carpeted with small daisy-shaped, deep blue flowers.

Hundreds of inquisitive little brown mouse-hares popped out of holes in the ground when they heard us coming, took a quick look at us and popped down again out of sight of gliding eagles and huge hawks.

This was the edge of the lands of the nomads and the eleven and a

half million yaks and sheep which outnumber human beings of Tibet
by more than ten to one. Herds grazed between river and mountains
as far as we could see. Every few miles we came upon a camp of yak-
hair tents which were the homes of herdsmen and their families. These
were ringed by low walls of the wooden saddles and bright wool cloths
of riding and pack animals.

Grazing in the water-meadows beside the river were splendid ponies
with long manes and tails. They were all the colours of new-washed
pebbles on a beach, pure white, cream, pale pink, chestnut, grey and
black. When we stopped to rest, men rode over on their beautiful
beasts to pass the time of day and their wives brought the children to
see the bus and look at Roma, who was the first white woman they had
ever seen. They asked our driver, who spoke some Tibetan, from
what part of China she came, for since she wore Chinese winter clothes
she must be Chinese. But they had never before seen a woman with
such light skin and round eyes. He explained that we had travelled
across the world from England. They laughed and nodded and were
satisfied. England was evidently a province beyond Chinghai of which
they hadn't heard. The dark-skinned women with the fine aquiline
features of Romany gypsies, wore long black dresses covering their
ankles. Panels fell over their backs from their shoulders, decorated
with rows of metal, mother of pearl and turquoise discs. On their
heads, tilted rakishly, some wore pearl string caps. At first glance they
appeared to be suffering from a disease which blotched their faces.
This was kutch, a mixture of earth which Tibetans smear on the
skin to protect it from the fierce sun and winds of these high exposed
uplands.

At Yang Pa Ching, where the snow-line ended and the road became
narrower and steeper in its last sixty miles fall into the Lhasa Valley,
the bus wheezed into the yard of a lorry-drivers' camp where two
Russian-made jeeps were waiting to take us on to the city.

My feet felt as if they were shod in deep-sea diving-boots as I
walked slowly to a hut where lunch was served, and my head was a dull
sick throb. Koo She-lone's blood-pressure, which was still abnormal
when we left Sining, had mounted with the ascent to the airfield,
and he sat staring listlessly at a plate of grey, hard strips of dried fish.
There were comforting hot noodles and iron-tough biscuits which we
soaked in tea.

Women from an adjoining room, engaged in making quilts, left
their task to crowd in our doorway and watch us feed, and a swarthy
handsome young man with a tangle of black hair to his shoulders,
wearing a single long turquoise ear-ring, came to the open window

near where our table was set, leaned his arms on the sill and grinned and talked to us of what we knew not.

For the next sixty miles we slithered through fearful gorges, where rocks as big as the jeeps, washed out of the mountainside by the rain, had been smashed up with sledge-hammers by lorry-drivers so that they could squeeze by before the next avalanche came down. The smallest, falling on our roof, would have crushed us to pulp. Now below the last snow, we ran through a wide valley into which the river bursting from the narrow stony banks which compressed it, exploded over the fields which had become a shallow lake. Where it had crossed the road beneath bridges, the water had engulfed them and smashed them so that every few miles we had to turn off into the country and plough through floods which came up to the mudguards, in four-wheel drive. Twice we were impaled on submerged stones and rocked ourselves off by going forward and reversing in quick succession. This part of the route was strewn with big trucks, carrying drums of petrol, which had sunk under their weight in silt and mud, where they had been forced to leave the road. Some had turned over when trying to get round the deep waters by driving at crazy angles on the mountain-side.

Villages built on safe, high ground could be recognized from miles away by forests of tattered prayer-flags hanging over the roofs of mud-walled houses, built like squat towers and protected from the fierce winter winds by groves of trees. The 'flags' appeared to be any old rags of cotton which could be tied to a stick, wedged into an eave or chimney-stack or strung on a line like washing.

Where the river moved away from the road, villages were closer to it. We had left the last yaks grazing behind Yang Pa Ching. In this lower, more sheltered country were herds of small cows, flocks of goats and sheep and very hairy small black pigs shepherded by boys and girls. The children were barefoot and dressed in greasy sheepskin rags, but they were a cheerful sight with their black matted hair tied up in gay coloured braids.

They greeted us with wide grins, displaying rows of even white teeth, and shouts of laughter. One small boy, tending piglets on the verge, was apparently so overcome with astonishment when he saw our pale faces gawping through the canvas curtains of the jeep that he let out a great yell, gesticulated wildly to his friends to make sure they would see us, danced a little jig, then, turning two or three somersaults, collapsed in the road with uncontrollable merriment.

Unlike the children who seemed to regard us as human jokes, the adults stared at us with blank expressions until we smiled and saluted them. Then they nodded their heads eagerly in short sharp bows and smiled back with pleasure, but few put out their tongues in the greeting which we had read was the traditional welcome of Tibet.

Between the airfield and the approaches to the city we had met no armed soldiers. Here and there a few were helping civilians to fill up the biggest holes in the road and squads were repairing bridges. The only men we saw with pistols were a lorry-driver and the driver of our jeep. They told us they carried them for protection against robbers who had been known, though rarely, to attack unescorted travellers.

I found my mind wandering from this superb countryside and sentimentally imagined a future scene in which I sat with my grand-children at a winter fireside where all the best tales are told and begin-ning the story of this journey: 'Once upon a time when your grandmother and I travelled from Peking to Lhasa on the roof of the world . . .'

There was no need of signposts, for dominating the landscape, and seen from every horizon, the Potala Palace, winter home of the Dalai Lamas, towered over the city beneath its colossal walls. But when we reached it we were drained of all emotion and had no energy to sit up and look at the most fascinating building in the world which only a handful of foreign travellers had ever seen. Our bones and muscles a congealed aching mass, we dragged ourselves to our room in the guest house where we collapsed into bed, too weary to hold a cup for longer than it took to swallow a mouthful of tea.

We were wakened in the morning by a pretty, demure girl in short pigtails tied with red ribbons. She wore neat tailored trousers, Mabel Lucy Atwell type buttoned shoes and gay flowered jacket. She an-nounced that the doctor was ready to test our blood-pressures and hearts at our convenience. We told her we would be glad to see him at any time upon which our visitor crossed the threshold, put a plastic satchel on a table and took out a stethoscope and blood-pressure kit which she assembled. She asked, 'Do you feel well after your long journey?' Yes, we felt much better for our long night's sleep. She waved a child's hand towards the pressure gauge standing in its box and said, 'If one of you will hold out your arm we can see how you are.' With brisk precision she manipulated the apparatus, listened to our pulses with her stethoscope and informed us that although our pressures were up a little, this was usual for new arrivals. We offered her a cigarette which she refused. 'I would suggest,' she said, 'that you don't smoke too much,' catching sight of a bottle of brandy on the dressing-table she added primly, 'Alcohol at this altitude isn't advisable.'

I found myself holding my hands over my pipe like a schoolboy caught smoking behind the lavatories and said, 'I am surprised to find a girl so young is a doctor.'

She replied, smiling: 'I am twenty-seven. I was trained in Sian Medical School and volunteered to come to Lhasa where the people need us.'

Suddenly she reminded me of an adorable girl in a Salvation Army bonnet who had sold us *The War Cry* in a Black Country pub thirty years ago and asked us if we were 'saved'. Both were possessed by the same evangelistic fervour.

The doctor warned us to rest and do no work for three or four days until our bodies had become more acclimatized to the thin air at this high altitude. But soon after her departure a cadre came to tell us that the 551st anniversary of the foundation of Drepung, the largest monastery in the world, was to be celebrated next day and we should be the first foreigners to have an opportunity of filming and recording it.

5

FESTIVAL AT DREPUNG

Soon after dawn the roads from the city and villages above the valley were winding ribbons of colour as thousands of pilgrims in gay holiday clothes made their way to the Buddhist town at the foot of a mountain five miles from Lhasa. Tiny points of light gleamed in the hands of travellers as the sun shone on the silver butter lamps which they were taking to burn before the altars.

Before the Chinese Communists came, eleven years earlier, there was no wheeled vehicle of any kind in Tibet, excepting two cars brought from India piecemeal on yak-back for the use of the thirteenth Dalai Lama, who drove them for his own amusement in the Norbulingka (Jewel Park) when he stayed in his summer palace. The only wheels in the country were prayer wheels. Now hundreds of families were jogging their way to the monastery in rubber-tyred carts drawn by ponies, donkeys and mules.

Mothers and daughters, their gleaming black hair newly washed and oiled for the occasion and braided with many-coloured silks, rode in the backs. Tibetan women dress in pinafore-style ankle-length gowns with cross-over bodices and pleats falling from the shoulders at the back which give them graceful fulness. Wide sashes tie them at the waist and underneath vivid blouses of magenta, yellow, peacock, orange, cerise, violet and white are worn. Sleeves hanging inches beyond the finger-tips are flicked back over the wrists with a single graceful effortless motion when they need to use their hands. The costume is completed with hand-woven, horizontally striped multi-coloured aprons, the most splendid having gold-braided pockets.

Fathers and sons rode in front, driving their sleek spirited ponies bedecked with ribbons. Their clothes were more subdued than the women's, but some sported splendid hats with gold and red embroidered crowns and fur-trimmed peaks worn over the right or left ear. Nearly all wore one large turquoise ear-ring.

The grassy slope before the monastery walls was a living Breughel canvas. Thousands of folk jostled amongst the stalls of a fair where happy vendors were doing a brisk trade in bricks of black tea, dried fruits, sweetmeats for the children and hair ribbons. Everyone was buying thick bundles of long incense sticks and the still air was already becoming heavy with their pungent scent as pilgrims lit them before beginning the long climb to the temples.

Shaven-headed, rancid-smelling monks, their brown habits shiny with butter spilt from votive lamps and greasy tea, had joined the crowds and were keenly enjoying bargaining with local peasants for fresh fruit and vegetables. Coming from peasant families themselves, they relished getting something for less than the seller demanded. Some families were sitting out of the heat of the sun in the shade of rocks, eating a bit of breakfast and drinking buttered tea from large vacuum flasks 'made in China'. Men and boys were taking their animals out of their shafts and tying them to walls and trees. Then they fed them before they fed themselves.

A tall lama who had noticed our strange faces in the crowd, offered to guide us through the maze of narrow precipitous lanes to the chanting house, 200 feet above, where the great prayer services of the day were about to begin. We were surrounded and accompanied by men, women and children who discussed us excitedly and pointed out our more surprising features to one another. When we were out of breath and paused to recover, some just stood in front of us and stared intently into our eyes. When it occurred to them that we might think them rude they laughed softly with embarrassment, reassuringly touched us with the tips of their fingers and stepped aside to let us pass. Because the way was too steep and far for small children to walk or be carried, some were on the backs of donkeys and mules stumbling up the rocky ascents almost touching the houses on either side. Many children carried pet puppies in the folds of their gowns and scores of family dogs had come to the festival with their masters and mistresses. These charming, sleek and well-fed creatures resembled Pekingese, but had more pronounced noses and longer, straighter legs. Others were Shih-Tzus, like small miniatures of Old English sheep-dogs.

The principal chanting house on the roof of Drepung overlooked the wide empty sunlit Lhasa valley. Fifty miles away the knife-edged outlines of tall mountains were etched in the crystal air with such clarity that they appeared to be forty miles nearer. Those unaware of any other world might well imagine that these majestic horizons encompassed the physical universe. The beauty and dignity of the buildings in this fair landscape matched the splendour of nature. The whiteness of the wide, perfectly proportioned temple was relieved by gold symbols on the front wall and a deep course of red-painted reeds cut flush with the stonework under the eaves. The main entrance, framed by lacquered pillars and overhung by an embroidered canopy was approached from the terrace by broad shallow steps over which worshippers appeared to float silently into the sombre interior.

No photographic film has been made which could truly reproduce the colour of this scene. No painting can compare with its brilliance, for perhaps nowhere in the world, except in this virgin air, is the human eye so immediately and clearly in contact with physical objects. To a photographer who has experienced this phenomenon, his most accurate exposure will appear as if his camera lens had been obscured by a cataract, however excellent it may seem to others.

When we arrived on the terrace our tongues were parched. A gold and white booted dignitary wearing a gold embroidered tunic under his magenta robes came down to invite us to tea with the Abbot.

Passing through the doors out of the sunlight, we plunged into complete blackness. The high lama conducted us down an aisle between rows of dim forms squatting on the floor. After a few paces they emerged from the gloom and we saw the entire community of Drepung assembled on their carpeted benches waiting to begin the service. Round the walls stood the lay congregation with their lamps and glowing sticks of fragrant incense. As we passed a little girl, a puppy popped his saucy head from her gown and licked our hands. His small owner, overcome with confusion, put her hand over her pet's nose. The lama smiled, but because it was forbidden to bring animals into the chanting house, turned his head and pretended not to see. A grey-haired woman with a fluffy Shih-Tzu in her arms saw the lama before he saw her and with a smile which asked us to ignore her, bent quickly down and put the dog under her wide skirt. Through a narrow door we climbed to another roof by an almost vertical wooden ladder staircase, slippery with butter grease. As I climbed, holding firmly to a stout wooden hand-rail, a hand nudged me in the back and I turned to find a fat monk behind me grinning and gesticulating an assurance that he was there to break my fall if I should slip. My head was beginning to swim after the long struggle from the foot of the mountain, and on the dark narrow stair I felt trapped as in a dark funnel, half choked with the sickly rancid fumes of burning butter which rose from the temple. Then a hand reached down and helped me into the light.

The senior monks' room, where guests were entertained, was furnished with a luxurious carpet and, like the temple itself, with low thickly carpeted benches. The roof was supported by slim columns clothed in finely worked and intricately coloured hangings.

Familiar divinities sat as they had been sitting for centuries in their antique tapestries on the walls impassively regarding the new white spirits who had joined them. Incongruously gazing from a shrine hung with silken scarves were the benign faces of Mao Tse-tung, Chairman of the Communist Party, Liu Shao-chi, Chairman of the Chinese Government, and Chou En-lai, Prime Minister of China.

The Kambu, or Abbot, a quiet portly man was dressed in robes like his monks but with a more richly embroidered undercoat. Hanging below his waist was his badge of office, a large embroidered silk square. In a pouch he carried a vessel of water with which, we gathered, he rinsed his mouth in a ritual of purification. A rosary was looped round his wrist in a thick bracelet. He moved softly across the room to greet us, then lowered his bulk gently to a bench as if invisible hands beneath his armpits were helping him to his seat. He gestured towards us with his fingers and a shabby monk with down-at-heel boots appeared before us silent as a shadow. He placed porcelain bowls on small tables, delicately carved with highly coloured floral motifs and heraldic beasts, and filled them with brown liquid from an enormous earthenware pot. The Abbot raised his own bowl and invited us to drink the first buttered tea we had ever tasted. The appearance of this hot greasy liquid was revolting. As I took a hesitant sip, the Abbot watched me with amused eyes and tilted his head inquiringly to one side. I answered by swallowing the whole contents of my bowl. It was delicious, with a faint tang of salt, replacing some I had sweated out on the ascent to the roof. To the delight of our hosts I drank more bowls straight off, after which I felt completely refreshed. Before we left to go down to the service I consumed three or four more and didn't feel hungry for the rest of the day.

In 1959, eight years after the Chinese armies entered their country, the Tibetans were in rebellion against them. The Dalai Lama fled to India. We quoted to the Abbot his accusation that the Chinese were torturing and killing monks. He shook his head and replied: 'He cannot be speaking of Lhasa. You have seen thousands of people coming to our religious festival today. I cannot think that he believes it.'

We asked how many monks lived at Drepung before the rebellion. The Abbot answered, 'More than 7,000.'

'And now?'

'Only 700 remain.'

'Where have more than 6,000 gone?'

'After the rebellion the Chinese authorities and the Tibetan local government which supported them decreed that monks were free to continue their religious life or renounce it and return to lay life.'

'As in Kumbum?'

'Wherever there were monasteries.'

'Then suddenly, in response to a government decree, more than 6,000 monks who had lived here all their lives decided that they had no vocation for religion?'

'They did not all choose their religious life,' said the Abbot, 'it was chosen for them when they were children.'

We asked a young monk who sat at his side what was his position in the monastery. He pointed to two others, one as young as himself, the other a wrinkled old fellow who said he was sixty but like all ageing Tibetans, looked ten years older.

'We are the representatives of the National Minorities Commission at Drepung,' he answered.

'And what are your duties?'

'To see that the welfare of the community is preserved and to act as representative of Drepung in liaison with the local government.'

'Which consists of those Tibetans who have remained loyal to the Chinese Communist Government?' we asked.

The monk looked at our Chinese companions with an expression which said, 'What kind of a man is asking such questions as this?' But since they, like the Abbot, maintained an indifferent silence he continued.

'The government consists of those who did not take part in the rebellion. You have asked what happened to thousands of monks who left here. It is true that some were glad to abandon their religious life. But unfortunately for Drepung others had violated their Buddhist belief which forbids violence and took up arms against the government. Some were killed in the fighting. Others were taken prisoner. Those who had rebelled willingly were kept in gaol. Others who had been persuaded to join in against their will were released. The lands which we did not need for our support were taken from the monastery and distributed among our serfs. Now we grow as much of our food as we can on the land that is left to us. The older monks who cannot work are supported by small pensions from the government. The "cash" in Drepung in gold and silver was seized as punishment for our part in the revolt, but no religious object of whatever value was touched and there is no interference with the ways of life of those of us who remain.'

'You have not been persuaded to become a Communist?'

Lhasa citizen with outsize prayer wheel on his way to church

Girls of Tibet's first grammar school at playtime

Pupils of a People's Primary School organised by Tibetan parents for their children

The monk gave me an incredulous look. 'I don't think it is possible for a Buddhist to be a materialist,' he said.

Had the Abbot nothing to say?

The head of the monastery unwound his rosary and drew it through his hands. 'We have to admit,' he said, 'that our religious life in Tibet had sometimes departed a long way from the true practice of Buddhism. We grew rich on the labour of our serfs and I am glad they are free. For many, the religious life was not a vocation but an occupation. This was not their fault because having been given to the monasteries as children, no question of choice was involved. I am sorry that Drepung took part in the armed rebellion in 1959 and that so many of our community left us when they were allowed to choose their own mode of life, but I believe that those who have remained are more truly religious. Of course, we were all afraid of the Chinese when they first came because we believed the Communists would kill us and destroy our monasteries, but, as you see, this has not happened.'

As he played with his rosary, did we imagine that in this gesture, the venerable prelate betrayed the nervous unease of a child who isn't being quite truthful and crosses his fingers behind his back to expunge a lie on his lips?

There was no time for more awkward questions for at this moment a servant came to announce that the service was beginning. The Abbot asked to be excused to attend to his duties and we did not see him again.

Down in the temple, now bright with lights for our film cameras, powered by a portable generator brought up by mule cart from the city, low guttural chanting had begun. An old monk saw us looking for a place to put our tape-recorder and motioned us to the bench beside him. We had brought this sensitive delicate instrument 16,000 miles for the moment when we could record these prayers. Every day in Tibet for more than a thousand years this music had been lost with the breath of the singers in the mountain wilderness. Only the fascination of seeing the tape run straight through the reels and the voices coming back through the earphones kept us in our seats. The stench from the body of the monk beside us, saturated with old sweat and dirt, and of all the others, mixed with the hot rancid fumes of burning butter in the huge votive vessels and the sickly sweet and pungent smoke of incense, filled our throats with nausea.

No flesh was visible on our neighbour's bare feet showing through tattered slippers for they were coated with scaly filth which looked as if it were pasted on with a palette knife. The skin of his wrinkled face had the appearance of hide which had been shrunk in water and dried under a grill. Then we noticed that the microphone was in front of his

D

mouth and the deep melodious sounds in our ears were coming from his thin throat which looked like the neck of a strangled fowl.

Apparently chanting was thirsty work for while the service continued, servant monks walked noiselessly down the aisles between the carpeted benches, carrying buttered tea in huge two-handled earthenware pots. When the singers needed a drink they stopped chanting and held out their wooden or pottery bowls, or tins. Whatever size the vessel, it was filled to the brim. Among so many voices, the temporary silence of a score or so was unnoticeable. When one was hungry he took a handful of tsampa (roast barley flour) from a little bag which each carried, mixed it with his tea, rolled it into edible balls and proceeded to eat it. Appetite and thirst appeased, he resumed the chant, which in the absence of a conductor, was intoned in perfect unison with faultless timing. The singing was unaccompanied but for the occasional cadence of sweet-toned little bells. When these sounded, there was a momentary silence and the chant was resumed in another key.

Whatever changes had resulted from monastic reforms, economic equality among the brethren was not one of them. The Abbot and senior monks were sumptuously clothed compared with these poorly clad men who were the only priests left in Drepung to justify its religious life. The Abbot might believe they had remained because they had true vocations but it was also obvious, as at Kumbum, that the majority who had stayed were too old to begin a new life outside. They were too feeble for hard manual work and past the age when they could learn to be useful as teachers or clerks.

The men offering these ancient prayers would soon be seen and heard for the first time in the West by millions of English people sitting before their television screens in a world as remote from this fabulous sanctuary as from the world of Kublai Khan, in which none of these monks would have felt a stranger. They would also be watching the last priests of the last and strangest theocracy in human history singing the Nunc Dimittis of Tibetan Buddhism. In a few years, when they would all be dead, none would come here to take their places. Soon there would be only the treasures of the Drepung Monastery Museum and the gods looking down upon empty benches to be filmed and the voices of guides explaining them to tourists, to be recorded. For the children standing in awed silence, holding glowing incense sticks in their hands, would be at school again next week. There they would learn that the deities whose images sat on these jewelled altars would not protect them from the demons and devils embroidered on banners and marvellously sculptured in wood and stone, because all gods and demons existed only in the imaginations of the monks.

They would learn that they were not born rich or poor, strong or weak, because of their virtues and vices in their previous lives. They would hear in their new science classes that Tibet would not be ravaged by flood and earthquake and that they would not die of small-pox or cancer because their behaviour displeased the heavenly spirits. They would no longer believe that devils would seize the world if they didn't sing and pray to be delivered from them as these old men were singing and praying.

And when the last of these children ceased to believe in them, the last gods and the last demons in Tibet would also be dead.

The people who had come to the anniversary celebration of Dre-pung bore no resemblance in demeanour to Tibetans described by Perceval Landon *The Times* correspondent, who went to Lhasa with the Younghusband expedition in 1904. If some of his reports were reprinted today by the Peking Government, without acknowledgment, they might be mistaken for propaganda of Chinese Communists, seeking to justify their 'liberation' of Tibet fifty years later.

Landon found a country in which Buddhism bore no longer the faintest resemblance to the plain austere creed preached by Gautama Buddha. Tibetan religion was a system of devil worship and the monkish communities spared 'no effort to establish their predomi-nance more firmly every year by fostering the slavish terror which is the whole attitude to religion of the ignorant classes of the land'.[1] Unseen demons inhabited every tree, rock, stream and house and their malevolence could only be placated by the priests. Tibet was peopled with as many bogeys as the most terrified child in England could conjure up in the darkness of his bedroom. But the prayers of the laity could only exorcise evil spirits if they were approved by monks and they were only approved on payment of fees. No feudal lords in the dark ages of Europe exacted their full rights as mercilessly as this narrow sect of self-indulgent priests, wrote Landon.

When they lost their political and economic power after the Chinese put down the 1959 rebellion, the monasteries lost the religious authority which went with it. So it was not surprising that the holiday crowds who had come to this festival showed no sign of subservience to the monks. And if they bore no resemblance to Landon's Tibetans neither did this scene bear any resemblance to the Dalai Lama's des-criptions of his country ravaged by sadistic Chinese barbarians.

1. *Lhasa*, Vol. I, Hurst & Blackett Ltd. (London, 1905).

Lamas had been specially persecuted, he said. The Chinese tried to humiliate them, especially the elder and most respected, by harnessing them to ploughs, riding them like horses, whipping and beating them and torturing them by methods too evil to mention, and while they were slowly putting them to death, they tormented them with their religion, calling on them to perform miracles to save themselves.

But here were more than 30,000 people, nearly all the population of Lhasa, who had come to the shrines of Drepung with their votive butter lamps to burn before the altars. Long before midday the last bundle of incense sticks had been sold at the fair. And now we were photographing a young man wearing on his breast an enamel brooch framing a portrait of the Dalai Lama, for all the world to see.

When the religious service was over we visited the private apartments of the Dalai Lama preserved as they were before he fled from Lhasa. Butter lamps glowed before a photograph of the bland, gentle-faced young man. Two monks in charge of the sacred rooms took heavy gold embroidered silks from a chest and draped them on the Incarnation's small throne so that we could see how it appeared when he was there on ceremonial occasions. They explained that we were specially privileged for members of the public were not allowed to enter this part of the monastery. We asked if they expected to see the Dalai Lama again. They replied that they were sorry he had been persuaded to go away. In the meantime they were behaving as if he might walk through the door at any moment.

Now it was time for the festival play to begin. This antique drama had been performed on every anniversary of Drepung for centuries. The actors were monks who had begun their training when they were children. The stage was an open courtyard protected from the sun by a huge white canopy. The audience sat on the ground and on surrounding flat roofs in tiers. We sat on exotically carpeted benches in the Dalai Lama's private balcony from which, every year, he had watched the performance from behind transparent curtains. He could see the actors and spectators, but to them he was only a vague shadow behind a yellow screen for they were not permitted to gaze on his face.

We looked down on the play over long window-boxes massed with brilliant dahlias. When we raised our eyes over the canopy the Lhasa Valley and the far-distant mountains formed a backcloth of breathtaking splendour.

The cast wore superb costumes of highly coloured and embroidered silks with fantastic hats. There were no intervals and for more than five hours the monks, with the stamina of Olympic athletes, danced and sang and mimed their way through a riot of opera, pantomime, ballet and broad farce in which good spirits warred with devils and demons while mortal heroes and heroines triumphed over human villainy.

From a large photograph on a pole in the centre of the yard, the face of Mao Tse-tung looked down on the scene. Grown-ups who had been coming here every year since they were infants knew every line of the play by heart and greeted popular and unpopular characters as they appeared, with cheers and groans. For those who stayed from beginning to end, there was time for a substantial picnic lunch and a snack or two of tsampa mixed with buttered tea from the large vacuum flasks which every family brought to the theatre.

After twenty scenes or so, we took a walk round the monastery where hundreds of other visitors were exploring the maze of back streets, alleyways and innumerable courts and shrines. In a vast kitchen, monk cooks were brewing a hot mess of barley gruel for their brethren and guests in great copper vats. We ate the food we had brought with us in a long dark room filled with grotesque images in ecstasy or torment. Some were dressed like Victorian dolls in laces and silks with intricately decorated crowns. Some wore cotton, others silver-gilt and silver. We touched the skirt of one and the material fell apart in our fingers.

The heat had gone out of the sky when we joined the last pilgrims going home. The first of them had risen at cockcrow in the mountain villages on the other side of the valley and it would be nearly dawn when they reached home again. Small children tied on their mothers' backs were fast asleep, undisturbed by the shouts of farewell and the bumping and clattering of donkey, horse and mule carts as they lurched down the stony hillside tracks.

Long before we reached Lhasa we were pulling coats round our shoulders for after the burning heat of the afternoon and the stuffy warmth of the monastery, going out into the sweet cool evening air was like walking into a refrigerated room.

Among the crowds we passed two Chinese soldiers hiking back to the city from the festival with a group of Tibetan youths and girls. They laughed and shouted with mock and envious derision as we drove by in our jeep and pretended to thumb a lift. The Chinese privates in their thin cotton khaki uniforms and brown canvas shoes were drab figures beside their gay Tibetan companions, the boys in fur-trimmed hats and the girls in bright striped aprons and colourful long-sleeved blouses beneath their long gowns.

What would the Dalai Lama, with his horrific visions of torture and murder, have made of this encounter—the licentious soldiery of the Communist conquerors walking unarmed on a country road with the sons and daughters or perhaps brothers and sisters of their victims whom they and their comrades had done to death, or humiliated only three years earlier because they wouldn't give up their religion?

6

A LIVING COMMUNIST GOD

Another 'god' has now taken the place of the Thunderbolt, Precious Protector, the Ocean, His Holiness the Dalai Lama, as Acting Chairman of the Tibetan Communist Government. He is the Great Jewel, the Boundless Light, His Serenity the Panchen Lama. Tibetans believe that this portly young man of twenty-five was first born 300 years ago when he achieved perfection in his first human existence. So after his first mortal death, he passed immediately to a state of immortal bliss but out of compassion for his struggling human brothers and sisters repeatedly returned to earth to show them the way to immortality. In 1938 he decided to be reborn for the tenth time, to a peasant woman in the Chinese-ruled province of Chinghai where the Dalai Lama had also elected to reappear in the world for his fourteenth earthly life.

To the Peking Government this high incarnation is a patriot who supports the revolution. To the ecclesiastical and lay lords who fled to India after the failure of their rebellion against the Chinese in 1959, he is a traitor. To the self-exiled Dalai Lama he is a helpless victim of his Chinese upbringing who cannot personally be blamed as an ally of Communism and a true Tibetan who will never abandon his Buddhist faith. Certainly he is the most valuable of all Tibetans to the Peking Government, for while this only equal of the Dalai Lama remains, it can be claimed that Buddhism which believes in gods, and Marxism which denies them, can continue to exist peacefully together.

Whatever his friends and enemies may think of him, the Living Buddha who received us, clothed in richly embroidered gown and boots, with a rosary twined round a very large expensive gold wrist-watch and bracelet, brilliantly fulfilled the hopes of his ecclesiastical guardians who in 1949, when he was eleven years old, quietly recognized the victorious Communists on his behalf. By judging so shrewdly the speed with which the east red wind of change was blowing westwards towards Lhasa, they ensured that their holy charge, whose previous body had died in exile in China, would soon be able to return to Tibet, and that their lands and riches, as well as his own, would be restored.

When the Dalai Lama recently wrote that his only spiritual equal would never embrace materialistic Communism, he of all people should have realised that for a young man who has found no difficulty in adapting himself to life in ten different bodies for three centuries there is no problem implicit in being two different people living in the same body at the same time.

So, completely at ease with two consciences, His Serenity could recite the Sutras—the Buddhist Scriptures—in the Jokhan Temple, and a few days later tell us, without batting an incarnate eyelid, that he was a 'Buddhist Marxist-Leninist revolutionary worker for the people', and without ever having been outside China, Tibet or India he could inform us with equal aplomb that, beyond all doubt, Chinese-Tibetan Communist society was superior to any in the world.

But his unique personal problem requires a unique solution for he is the only 'god' in the world who is a Communist and the only Communist who is permitted to be a 'god'.

He explained that since according to Communist theory the state will eventually wither away, so, according to Buddhist belief, religion will have no purpose when men are perfected. Therefore eventually all governments, together with all theologies, will disappear.

In the meantime a Panchen Lama will be able to make the best of both the spiritual and material worlds by presiding over the secular materialist state and the Buddhist faith at the same time from a splendid new palace which is being built for him in Lhasa when he needs a change from his ancestral home at Tashilumpo Monastery in Shigatse, where some of the most pricelsss religious treasures in the land are to be found.

Motioning us to a comfortable couch and signalling a servant to pour buttered tea into gold and silver-gilt cups, he welcomed us to his country which he assured us had been liberated from the domination of foreign Imperialist aggressors, led by Britain and America.

He was obviously under the impression that Foreign Minister Chen Yi and Premier Chou En-lai could be relied upon not to allow any foreign visitors to Tibet who would not agree with him and his eyes flickered with faint surprise when we reminded him that no British troops had been in his country since 1904 when we unjustifiably invaded Tibet in the mistaken belief that the Russians were threatening our Indian frontier through Lhasa. No American army had ever set foot there.

Roma Gelder and bathing boys at the
foot of the Potala

Gold-crowned symbols like this and the gold-roofed canopies of the Dalai Lamas' tombs on the roof of the Potala can be seen from every Lhasa horizon

The Fourteenth Dalai Lama's private apartments at the Potala summit

The embarrassed silence which followed our unexpected interruption was broken by a low grunt from a man who sat in a corner with a large black peaked cap crammed over his ears. This was Mr. Chiang Tsu-ming, the Chinese Deputy Director of the Tibet Foreign Affairs Bureau, a self-invited guest, glowering with resentment that we should dare to doubt the incarnate political pronouncement of the Panchen.

'Why,' he interrupted, 'do you defend Imperialism? It is well known that Britain is Imperialist. If not, why did Ireland denounce China's actions in Tibet in the United Nations?'

Our youthful host who, from his inquiring look, had never heard of Ireland, leaned forward for our reply. We told him that Mr. Chiang's views on England were unreliable since he didn't know that we hadn't ruled Ireland for forty years. He was also so ignorant of social and economic conditions in Britain that he had assured us a few days earlier that our children still ran about our poverty-stricken cities in bare feet. We suggested that in their propaganda the Panchen Lama and the Chinese Communists sometimes didn't seem quite sure why they had come to Tibet—to free it from British and American Imperialists who weren't there, or to give freedom to hundreds of thousands of Tibetan serfs who were, as the Panchen Lama himself well knew because he had owned some of them.

His Serenity serenely and politely suggested that if we didn't interrupt it would be easier for him to continue. He repeated that Tibet had been dominated by foreign Imperialists, but now, apparently in deference to our feelings, hastened to add that he was referring to American aggressors.

'All the same, he includes the British as well,' growled the irrepressible Mr. Chiang from the corner.

Ignoring him and taking up our cue, the Panchen blandly continued that it had also been necessary to free Tibetans from the shackles of feudal rule and serfdom.

It had clearly been arranged that we should listen to a prepared political discourse, but we hadn't travelled 16,000 miles to Lhasa to hear official pronouncements which we had already read in innumerable pamphlets. We were interested to discover how an incarnation of Buddha could reconcile a belief in a universe of gods and devils with a belief that the only real conflict was between Imperialist capitalists and Communists.

We presumed to intervene once more. When had the Panchen Lama become a Marxist?

With a sigh the young man placed a sheaf of notes which we now suspected had been prepared, and certainly approved, by Mr. Chiang, on the table in front of him and replied:

'I have been studying Marxist-Leninist philosophy for a long time and still pursue my researches. I am following two courses, doing my revolutionary duty to the people and also living the life of a good Buddhist because I have my next incarnation to consider.'

Perhaps the awful thought had occurred to him that if he didn't become a good Communist in this life he might be born an Anti-Marxist tool of foreign Imperialism in his next—which would be an unimaginable embarrassment.

But why did he think he could achieve such a remarkable reconciliation between two diametrically opposed ways of life while the Dalai Lama felt this was impossible?

To our disappointment, this pleasant young person whose situation has been so sympathetically interpreted by the Dalai Lama, answered priggishly—or perhaps he felt this was the role he must play in the presence of a high Chinese Communist official?

'If the Dalai Lama truly repents of his false denunciations of our Chinese comrades, renounces his reactionary friends and is willing to work for the people, he will be welcomed home in Tibet.'

But Mr. Chiang had forgotten his own history and misled his pupil, this time by ignoring official Peking statements that the Dalai Lama was a victim of Tibetan feudal lords and priests who had abducted him to India. If this were true he couldn't be blamed for their actions. According to the Chinese, the same abductors had published statements which they pretended had been made by the Dalai Lama. How then could he repent of something which the Chinese protested he had never said?

When we pointed out this discrepancy, Mr. Chiang pulled his cap further over his ears as if he couldn't bear to hear any more of this outrageous argument which obviously hadn't been his idea of an interview at all.

So we continued to sip buttered tea while the Panchen Lama, who had now abandoned any attempt to amend the prepared narrative in the interest of Anglo-Tibetan-Chinese amity, renewed the assault on Britain and America for the deplorable condition of the Tibetan people which had existed for more than a thousand years before any Englishman stepped over the border. There seemed no point in going over all that again so we asked His Serenity if he would be kind enough to send us his considered views on how Buddhism and Marxism could live together.

With unconcealed relief he assured us that we could still differ and be friends.

But Mr. Chiang couldn't.

As we went down to the garden to film and photograph the Panchen, the Chinese comrade wagged a furious finger under our noses
and exploded, 'You have gone too far in not allowing the Acting
Chairman to say what he wanted,' rushed down the stairs and was
driven off in a cloud of dust, bidding farewell neither to us nor to the
unabashed and courteous divinity.

A few days later a messenger delivered the Panchen Lama's answers
to our questions. They were written on the 'royal' yellow paper used
only by him and the Dalai Lama and bearing his brilliantly coloured
crest.

We do not know if these religious views are in accord with generally
accepted Buddhist belief or whether they are heretical opinions.
Certainly they present intriguing questions for students of Buddhist
theology, for according to Tibetan Buddhist belief they are not only
the answers of a man but of an immortal who is the highest incarnation
of the Buddha himself. And it isn't easy to refute a living Buddha.
The twelfth Dalai Lama was once talking with his theologians when
one reminded him that he had contradicted a pronouncement of the
seventeenth-century incarnation known as the 'Great Fifth'.

His Holiness confounded his audience by asking, 'And who *was*
the Great Fifth?'

There is a legend in Tibet that the fourteenth incarnation of the
Dalai Lama will be the last to reappear on earth. It may well be that the
tenth incarnation of the Panchen in this young man will also be the last
in a world where belief in living gods in human shape is unlikely to
survive belief in demons hiding in stones, trees and rivers. As the
statement of a Buddha who became a Communist, it will intrigue
historians who may visit his country when the great monasteries and
shrines remain only as museums and monuments of one of the most
fantastic and colourful cults in man's religious history.

On 'the auspicious fifth day of the eighth month in the year 936
of the Tibetan Kalaçakran' (3rd October 1962) the Panchen had written:

'From the Buddhist point of view all existence and all material
circumstances are changing every moment and are in gradual process of
disappearance. Even the duration of Buddhism itself is limited and one
day it too will disappear. This has been clearly indicated by our great
all-compassionate and Supreme Teacher, the Sakyamuni Buddha.
Even the teachings of the Sakyamuni Buddha, like any other religious
or political system existing for a certain period in a certain area, under-
go the process of coming into being, existing and finally disappearing.
But the spirit of Buddhism and its good and pure achievements will

exist until the end of the world. Religion is a variety of ideology. It exists because people believe in it.

'You ask in a Communist society can Buddhism exist? Generally speaking all existence is governed by the universal law of disappearance. But Communism cannot directly influence the existence of Buddhism. The Chinese Communist Party is protecting the right of anyone to believe in any religion, or disbelieve. What will the future of religion be in the course of future human development? We cannot say, but in our generation there is no need to worry ourselves about religion being erased from the world.

'It is true that as Communism is materialistic and Buddhism is idealistic they are two contradictory ideologies. Buddhists hold that the good and bad in all existence are produced by good and bad deeds.

'The fruit of happiness is produced by good deeds, the fruit of suffering by bad.

'But the good deeds are of two kinds—those performed collectively by living beings and those performed by individuals; for example, developments of human society, peace and war are produced collectively by people who will all enjoy happiness or endure suffering.

'*The happiness or suffering of an individual is likewise produced by the good or bad deeds he has performed in his previous lives.*[1]

'Whether the future is to be happy or painful will be decided by good or bad deeds performed collectively or individually in the present. There can be no mistake about this. Deeds are performed with a good or bad mind. This is a fundamental view held by all Buddhists. The viewpoint of the Communist however is quite contrary. So it is true, as you say, that there is a great contradiction between Buddhist and Communist views and theories.

'But the Communists are also making every effort to eradicate all social systems in which there is oppression and exploitation of man by man, so there can be one great society in which all people can live an equal and happy life.

'Although the views and theories of Buddhism and Communism are different they are not inconsistent with each other since it is possible for both to strive together to achieve their ideals. We can co-operate politically and do so very well because we have a common basis—the desire for a full and happy life for the Tibetan nationality together with all other nationalities in China under the Socialist system.'

Apparently our suggestion that the Panchen did not seem quite sure from whom the Chinese were liberating Tibetans, foreign Imperialists

1. Authors' italics.

who weren't there or Tibetan serf-owners including the monasteries, had struck home for he now replied:

'Many people believe that Buddhism was responsible for serfdom in Tibet and the oppression and exploitation of the people and that it hindered social progress. I cannot acknowledge that this is the nature of Buddhism. For instance it is said in the Vinaya rules that one should not covet a needle or a piece of thread of others, let alone enjoy the property of others. Far from hurting human beings, one should not even injure or inflict pain on ants or other insects.[1]

'The fundamental spirit of Buddhism is that we should offer all our property and happiness to others and do our best to suppress the causes of unhappiness and pain to others. At the very least we should pray for the increase of happiness and elimination of suffering.

'It is because Buddhism possesses such a fundamental spirit of goodness that it has enjoyed such widespread popularity among Tibetans.

'But in the past there also appeared the darkest and most savage feudal serfdom created by people who were Buddhists only in name. This has now been wiped out by reforms which have ended oppression and exploitation and abolished the privileges of the monasteries.'

We had expressed concern for the welfare of monks who had decided to continue the monastic life.

'Sir,' wrote the Panchen Lama, 'do not worry yourself in this respect. The government provides for the livelihood of all who are devoting their lives to religion and of all old and invalid monks. It calls on all those who are capable of work to take part in productive labour and has provided them with land so that they can maintain themselves with the income as well as with alms offered to them by devotees. If their income should be insufficient the government of which I am Acting Chairman will provide relief funds.

'As a cadre of the Peoples' Republic of China', concluded the Panchen, 'I am performing my duties in accordance with the policies of the Chinese Communist Party and the Central People's Government. There is no question of any misunderstanding between me and them.'

---

1. 'Do not take a needle or a piece of thread from the people' was the slogan of the Chinese Red Army from its beginning. It was this respect for the property and lives of civilians which led to the co-operation of the latter with the Communists against the Kuomintang and ensured their ultimate victory.

7

THE STORY OF APEI

More than a thousand years ago the ancestors of Ngapo Ngawang Jigme were kings in Tibet. In the thirteenth century they survived Kublai Khan's conquest of their country by becoming his vassals. Seven hundred years later Ngapo Ngawang Jigme was a member of the Dalai Lama's lay Cabinet. He owned 4,000 square kilometres of land and 3,500 serfs.

In 1950 this great feudal lord was appointed Commander-in-Chief of the Tibetan Army and Governor-General of Chamdo, where he was sent to defend Tibet from the advancing Chinese. He was taken prisoner according to the Dalai Lama's account of these days. Ngapo (or 'Apei', the shorter Chinese name by which he is more conveniently known) sent two messengers to Lhasa saying he had been defeated by the Chinese who had taken him prisoner. He asked for authority to negotiate an armistice.

Recognising that successful resistance was impossible, the government gave Apei permission to make the best terms he could. When the Dalai Lama sent envoys to Peking to conclude a peace treaty by which the Chinese occupied all of Tibet, Apei was the principal delegate and chief Tibetan signatory of the agreement. In 1956 he became (and remains) first Secretary-General of the 'Preparatory Committee for the Autonomous Region of Tibet'.

This body will govern the country under the general direction of Peking until its regional status and organisation has been decided. The first Chairman was the Dalai Lama and the Chinese insist that he still holds this office which he is prevented from exercising because he has been abducted to India by reactionary courtiers.

Like the Panchen Lama, Apei is regarded by his self-exiled compatriots—excepting the Dalai Lama who speaks no word against them —as a traitor. But if they denounce him as a betrayer of their country, Apei dismisses them contemptuously as men who stood by their country only as long as they could keep the vast riches they owned in it and ran away from the responsibilities to the people when they realised they couldn't.

We met him in his charming Lhasa home overlooking the eastern mountains, with his beautiful wife and the two youngest of their twelve children. The others are at schools and universities in the Chinese interior. Like all the other serfs of Tibet, who formed the overwhelming majority of the population, the 3,500 men, women and children owned by Apei were given their freedom by government decree after the failure of the 1959 uprising. The lands of the lords who rebelled were confiscated. The estates of Apei and others who took no part in the revolt were distributed among the peasants and their owners were compensated. By Tibetan standards, Apei, in his house with metal window-frames imported from England and simple, tasteful but expensive furniture, is still very rich. The Communists paid him handsomely for his lands and properties.

From his replies to our questions it was obvious that his story of the Chinese 'invasion' of Tibet was not going to be the simple straight-forward narrative which has been generally accepted from the Dalai Lama since his flight to India in 1959.

We asked: 'If before 1950 you already believed Tibet to be a part of China why did you fight the battle of Chamdo? If you had won it would you then have recommended to the Dalai Lama that the Chinese should be given your country because it had really belonged to them all the time?'

Apei answered, 'When I was appointed Governor of Chamdo in 1950 I made a proposal to a conference of the former local government that the post should continue to be held by Lalu[1] and that I should be sent to hold peaceful negotiations with the Central Chinese People's Government, by way of Sikang [now incorporated in Szechuan Province].

'After arriving at Chamdo I had not the slightest wish to conduct a war aimed at separating Tibet from the Chinese motherland. I did a great deal of work to make peace. I gave the order to demobilise the local militias and actually went about disbanding them. When the People's Liberation Army started its march on Chamdo there were only clashes of a very short duration with troops stationed at two or three places on the border with the neighbouring province. No heavy fighting took place.'

It could be concluded from this that Apei betrayed his country by

1. The retiring Governor-General of Chamdo who in 1959 was imprisoned for his part in the rebellion against the Chinese.

disobeying the orders of the Dalai Lama's government to resist the Chinese. But it was also possible that he did fight until his army was overwhelmed and that twelve years later, as the Secretary-General of the Chinese-directed Tibetan Government, it was diplomatically necessary to pretend that he had never opposed Peking. Perhaps with his heritage of political experience, Ngapo Ngawang Jigme might also not be embarrassed by making statements, however incredible, if they ensured that his family, which has helped to rule Tibet for a thousand years, would continue to take part in its government. With twelve children there is little danger of his line dying out. It is also arguable that this wealthy aristocrat, who exercised a personal authority over others unattainable by any individual in modern Western society, would not have allied himself and his country with an 'invader' who has stripped him of his feudal rights and power if he did not believe that however onerous and distasteful, the compromise was an obligation which in the face of irresistible fact it was his duty as a Tibetan statesman to accept.

The Dalai Lama and some of his fellow lords had taken the precaution of moving fortunes from Lhasa to the safety of India when the Chinese Army first moved to the borders of Tibet. Before he left for Chamdo in 1950 Apei could have sent his family out of the country with a sufficient fortune to keep it in luxury and he could have followed in 1959 with the Dalai Lama and his party. Certainly it cannot be charged that he was a neglected, frustrated man for whom co-operation with an enemy was his first opportunity of attaining influence and recognition.

The shrewdness which led his ancestors to accept the suzerainty of Kublai Khan when they saw that they could not resist it was the kind of political sensibility which could also have led Apei to recognise that the feudal society in which he owned 3,500 serfs could not survive a revolution in China where two-thirds of the Tibetan race lived.

In the onlooker who has never visited Tibet the self-exiled priests and lords may evoke sympathy as refugees from a happy country in which the people lived under their rule, inspired by a humane religious philosophy.

But this pleasant picture bears no more resemblance to Tibetan reality than the romantic imagery of G. K. Chesterton and Hilaire Belloc bears to feudal Europe. The truth is that this society was—as Landon described it in 1904—a harsh and cruel tyranny in which, because they share the universal instinct for survival, the people made the best of their lot. Serfs of the European Middle Ages did no less. Jews in Hitler's concentration camps did no less. In their hardest days

The Potala from the water meadows on the outskirts of the city

Bedroom of the Fourteenth
Dalai Lama, Potala Palace

Dalai Lama's private promenade, Potala Palace

under English rule, Irish peasants were among the most resilient, humorous, cheerful, courteous and dignified people in the world. Pitiably poor Spanish peasants, whose life they could not endure themselves, are commended by foreign tourists for their fine manners and personal dignity. But the indomitable fortitude and optimism of oppressed human beings in Tibet or anywhere else can only be confused with contentment by those not personally involved in their lives or who profit by such subjection and exploitation. If you do so confuse it in conversation with a Tibetan, he will, as an Irishman might say, spit in your eye behind your back.

It is, after all, possible that Ngapo Ngawang Jigme was not persuaded to accept the Chinese occupation by any desire to salvage what he could of his family's position and continue his life on the most tolerable terms which he could ensure by subjection to the Communists.

Stripped of the superlatives with which Marxists decorate their political language, it is believable that when he says he was persuaded by what he saw in China that only good could come to his people by socialist reforms in Tibet, he is telling the truth and that there is no more to his defection from medieval Buddhism to Socialism than that.

He would not be the first aristocrat to experience revulsion against his own privilege when he saw how it had been won and how, if it were to be maintained, it must be defended.

We spent a few hours with Apei but the background against which he made his decision to renounce his inheritance and tradition is a thousand years old. He cannot be understood unless the social and religious systems which bred him and the history of his people are also appreciated.

Apei replies to charges that he is a Tibetan traitor by saying that his country is an inalienable part of China. This is what one would expect a collaborator with a conqueror to say. But this claim is also made by the Nationalist Government of Chiang Kai-shek in Taiwan, and Britain has acknowledged it in successive treaties with Peking when it has suited her commercial or strategic convenience. She only ignored it when it didn't. When she sought to deny China's rights in Lhasa, Britain was rebuked by the United States.

In 1890 London negotiated a treaty with the Chinese Emperor defining the Sikkim-Tibet frontier and regulations governing trade. No Tibetans were invited to take part in the discussions.

In 1903 Lord Curzon, Viceroy of India, obsessed by fears of Russian expansion towards India—which proved illusory—and affronted by what he considered Tibetan indifference to commercial treaty

E

obligations, was urging his government to authorise a military expedition to Lhasa. He wrote to the Foreign Office:

'We regard the so-called suzerainty of China over Tibet as a constitutional fiction—a political affectation which has only been maintained because of its convenience to both parties.'

When this despatch became known Washington instructed its Ambassador in London to remind Britain that Curzon's denial of China's rights in Tibet could not alter historic facts.

But America's protest did not prevent the British invasion and the first foreigners seen in the streets of Lhasa by Apei's father were the soldiers who had shot their way to the capital from India in 1904.

So it is not surprising that Apei regards British expressions of sympathy for the 'sufferings' of Tibetans at the hands of the Chinese with cynical contempt, for he is well read in the history of our relations with his people.

The story of the massacre of Tibetan peasants armed with ancient muzzle-loading matchlocks and swords by British and Indian troops equipped with mountain artillery, machine-guns and modern rifles, does not have to be exaggerated by Communist propagandists. It was written on the battlefield of Guru by Perceval Landon, correspondent of *The Times*, who described how within a few minutes between 700 and 800 of the Tibetan army of 1,500 were slaughtered without the loss of one British or Indian soldier. 'It was like a man fighting with a child', he reported. That night a young subaltern wrote to his mother in England: 'I hope I shall never have to shoot down men walking away again.' He was so sickened by the killing that he stopped firing his Maxim into the backs of the Tibetans, although the order of Brigadier-General Macdonald, the British Commander, was 'to make as big a bag as possible'.

When the victorious expedition of Francis Younghusband (later knighted for his services) and General Macdonald reached Lhasa they had killed about 1,500 Tibetans for the loss of less than a dozen of their own men.

The Dalai Lama had fled to Outer Mongolia. There were no Russians in the Holy City and no sign that any had ever been there.

Faced with complete fiasco, Prime Minister Arthur Balfour and his Cabinet, with childish petulance, decided that if there was no other way of saving British face the troops had better destroy the walls and gates of Lhasa and seize leading citizens as hostages.

Younghusband found a more decorous and, he hoped, more profitable way of dealing with the situation. He compelled the Tibetans to sign a treaty in the Potala by which an indemnity of £500,000 was to be paid in seventy-five instalments. As security the British would occupy the Chumbi Valley for seventy-five years until the last payment was made. All fortifications between Lhasa and India must be destroyed. Without British consent no part of Tibet must be ceded, leased, sold or mortgaged or occupied by any foreign power. No such power must intervene in Tibetan affairs and no foreign representatives or agents must be admitted to the country.

It might be thought that if Britain had denied China's sovereignty in Tibet the terms of this treaty completely destroyed any pretence of Tibetan independence. But it was altogether too much for the British Government which repudiated Younghusband's insistence that a British trade agent should be stationed in Tibet, reduced the occupation of the Chumbi Valley to a period of three years and the amount of the indemnity by two-thirds. With nice irony the Chinese Government, as the sovereign power in Tibet, insisted on paying the bill and the British Treasury pocketed the money without protest.

Less than two years later, the sovereignty of the Tibetans was a fiction in London. Finding them as indifferent to her interests as they had always been Britain once more recognised China's 'full powers and finding them in good form' signed a new Convention respecting Tibet with the Emperor in Peking without telling Lhasa anything about it.

And in 1907, without telling either the Tibetans or the Chinese, Britain signed another secret treaty with Russia relating to Persia, Afghanistan and Tibet where the interests of the two countries might conflict. By this agreement they both recognized the 'suzerain rights of China' in Tibet.

In 1909 the Chinese Imperial Government restored the Dalai Lama as Vice-Regent bound by the laws of the sovereign state of China and he returned to his capital only to flee to India when the Chinese sent troops to Lhasa to assert their authority.

When he appealed for help the British Government told him it could not 'intervene between the Dalai Lama and his suzerain', and Lord Morley, Secretary of State for India, expressed the opinion that the Chinese return would probably result in a strong Tibetan Government.

In 1911, when the Manchu Dynasty was overthrown by the forces of Dr. Sun Yat-sen, the Dalai Lama from exile declared his country's independence from Peking and in January 1913 returned to the Holy City where in the confusion of revolution Chinese authority had collapsed. It is on this declaration that the fourteenth Dalai Lama has based his claim to the United Nations that the Chinese Communists violated his country's sovereignty in 1951.

Britain's last serious attempt to influence events in Tibet came in 1914 when she summoned a conference at Simla, inviting Tibetans on an equal footing with the Chinese, who were informed that if they did not accept the summons a treaty defining frontiers and making new trade arrangements would be concluded without them.

Russia was not informed of this violation of the St. Petersburg treaty of 1907, but before they could object, they and the British were too busy defending themselves in Europe to argue or quarrel about Tibet. The Chinese denounced the treaty. It was at Simla that the McMahon Line was drawn up. It has never been recognised by China, But ever since many Britishers have regarded this demarcation as if it had been drawn across the Indian-Chinese mountains by the hand of God instead of by the pencil of a British official.

During the Second World War, when the extra-territorial rights of foreign powers in China were an embarrassment to allies fighting for freedom and self-determination, Britain, China and the United States discussed their relations. In an aide-memoire in 1943 the British Embassy in Washington acknowledged 'formal Chinese suzerainty' in Tibet but also hoped to secure for the Lhasa Government 'the full enjoyment of local autonomy', with the right 'to exchange diplomatic representatives with other powers'.

The State Department replied:

'The Government of the United States has borne in mind the fact that the Chinese Government has long claimed suzerainty over Tibet and that the Chinese constitution lists Tibet among areas constituting the territory of the Republic of China. This Government has at no time raised a question regarding either of those claims.'[1]

So the United States officially acquitted Apei of treachery before he was accused of it and China of aggression against an independent sovereign Tibet before she was alleged to have committed it.

1. Edgar Snow: *The Other Side of the River* (Gollancz, London, Random House, New York).

8

THE HOLIEST OF HOLIES

We had done as much work in our first three days in Lhasa as most newly arrived travellers were expected to do in three weeks. Now, after our journey to the Drepung Monastery festival under the fierce sun and our long talks with the Panchen Lama and Apei, we were advised to rest. Like the girl who had examined us after our arrival the doctor who came to check our blood-pressures again looked as though he might be a first-year student. In fact he was twenty-eight and a veteran of the new Tibet medical services. Our rising pressures were being controlled with drugs.

We hadn't felt the need of oxygen kept in huge cylinders in the guest house for emergencies, but after walking about for a few hours our shoes felt as if they were soled with lead. When we climbed the short staircase to our room we went slowly, pausing occasionally, and were glad to sink into armchairs for a few minutes when we got there before exerting ourselves again. If we tried to move quickly over short distances we were as breathless as if we had run a hundred yards. A tot of smooth Chinese brandy helped to tighten our sagging muscles, or we thought it did until the doctor suggested that half a small tot a day would be more than enough. I protested, 'But my doctor at home calls that "old man's milk".'

The young man smiled. 'It's rocket fuel for the heart up here.'

Normally placid people often become irritable when they ascend suddenly to high altitudes. Trivial inconveniences and frustrations provoke the more highly strung into temporarily uncontrollable temper. Perhaps this explained why after being so gently reproved for drinking brandy I was ungracious enough to thank our medical adviser by saying that we didn't wish to be treated as special visitors, taking up the time of overworked medical staff at the Lhasa Hospital.

'You are helping us as much as we are helping you,' he said. 'Every-one coming here for the first time is medically interesting. By checking their reactions we are learning how bodies can be expected to adapt to changed conditions. Because Tibetans didn't know anything about oxygen, they used to think, and some still do, that "mountain sickness" on the high passes was caused by evil spirits who resented humans invading their kingdom.'

When the first Chinese medical units arrived in Tibet they didn't bother to check blood changes carefully enough, especially in pregnant women from the plains, until one after another miscarried because their blood structure was altered. Red corpuscles multiply rapidly at high altitudes to increase absorption of the reduced oxygen in the atmosphere.

'That is why,' said the doctor, 'you will see Tibetans who may not be healthy at all with rosy complexions.'

When it was realized why women were losing their babies those who became pregnant soon after arriving in the country were sent back to the valleys. After living on the high plateau for six months or so they could have children quite safely.

With 8,000 feet of movie film and a thousand still pictures to expose, as well as a comprehensive report to write, we had set ourselves a starting pace which no one could keep up anywhere for five weeks, let alone here where two or three hours' effort was as exhausting as a day's work in England. After only three days we were relieved to take an ordered rest which we had been too excited and impatient to give ourselves.

The natural beauty of Tibet is breath-taking aesthetically as well as physically. Its frontiers enclosed by the highest mountains in the world, its wild grasslands, deserts and broad valleys by smaller but still majestic ranges, it is the most peaceful, secure and restful of countries. Until, as though the gods are suddenly bored by the serenity they have created, the steel-blue sunlit skies are split and shattered by fierce winds and electric storms which explode like the crack of doom. Sometimes demons who, the people believe, live in the dark underground world, join in the empyrean lark and smash the earth above so that villages and their inhabitants are swallowed in vast craters or drowned in the waters of lakes and rivers which engulf the land.

In 1954 large areas of south Tibet were devastated by earthquakes and floods. We were not to be imperilled by such spectacular catastrophe during our journeys. But in this violent world there are more frequent ways of dying than by being knocked on the head by flying rocks.

The most ferocious killer in Tibet is pneumonia and its most common cause exposure to rapidly changing temperatures. Shining through the thin air of the cloudless sky the sun will peel the skin from exposed flesh like a blowlamp. It has been presumed by some travellers that Tibetans don't wash their bodies except on festival occasions because dirt protects them from the ravages of weather. There is also no piped water and unless you live near the banks of a river, stream or lake you won't be encouraged to walk a few miles for a bath after work. Since your family and neighbours smell no sweeter than yourself, they won't be aware of your own condition. Unlike Hindu deities, Tibetan 'gods' don't regard cleanliness as a virtue so there is also no religious compulsion towards bodily hygiene.

But just as the Chinese when they had no knowledge of pathology drank only boiled liquids because they found they often got sick if they didn't, the Tibetans, who knew nothing about the real causes of illness, learned partly to protect themselves from their natural enemies by experience. Hence the standard working dress of the countryman. To labour under the burning sun is intolerable with any clothes on but within a few moments the sun may be hidden by a small bank of cloud and the sudden cold pierces to the bones like a knife. The cloud passes and the sweat pours out again. So you wear a shuba, a voluminous loose-fitting sheepskin jacket. In the sun's glare you throw it off your shoulders and work naked to the waist where it is secured to prevent it falling round your knees. Once more clouds obscure the sun and in an instant you can pull your shuba over your torso again.

If you are careless and cool off for too long, you will get a severe chill. Then, even if you can afford to pay for holy pills containing excreta and urine of a Living Buddha, you will die unless your natural antibodies are more numerous and stronger than the pneumococci waiting for a chance to kill you.

The Chinese doctor warned us, 'Never go out without your coat, however hot it is, and put it on as soon as the sun goes in.' He added (a grim forewarning of near-disaster to overtake Roma forty-eight hours later), 'We have all the antibiotics in Lhasa now but they don't always work quickly enough at this height where the heart can't stand much strain.'

So on our first walk through the city we carried our thick cotton-padded jackets over our arms and strolled back through 800 years into the twelfth-century city. As in a dream, when all sense of waking time is a confusion where we meet and talk with the dead and living in a spaceless, timeless present, we were not surprised. The ragged, dirty, malodorous, sinister, handsome, crippled, sturdy, colourful crowd, jostling amongst the shops and stalls, garnet-habited monks fingering long rosaries, old men and women shuffling along the narrow mudcaked streets twirling their prayer wheels, small distant figures in the shadow of the Jokhan Cathedral; we had met them all before when we were children, in Peter Breughel's paintings, Shakespeare's plays, the *Canterbury Tales* and the pictures in our history books.

A young gallant in a Plantagenet-style fur-trimmed hat walked towards us playing hopscotch over the puddles to keep his fine new knee-length boots clean. A merry-faced white-haired old lady in a long brown gown and shovel hat might have been any housewife shopping in a London street when Crookback was on the English throne.

And then, as one dream scene becomes another, a girl furiously ringing her bell wobbled round a corner on a new bicycle and a white-coated traffic policeman, standing on a pedestal, held out his baton imperiously for her to stop so that we could cross the street. We turned to see if all was clear behind us and were looking at a Humber Super Snipe limousine which was slowing down to let us reach the other side. Sitting in the back an ecclesiastical dignitary in a golden-yellow, red brocaded gown stared with bemusement at our white faces looking at him from above our Chinese clothes. The policeman told our interpreter that he was the Abbot of Sera Monastery.

Now we were engulfed by two or three hundred children who gazed at us as if we were from another planet for we were the first foreigners they had ever seen. Like the crowds at Drepung they discussed us excitedly, touching their noses, stroking their own faces and pointing to ours. But when it occurred to them that they might be embarrassing us, they stood politely aside to let us pass into the cathedral where they didn't follow us.

In the stone-paved forecourt near the shade of two willow trees which legend says grew from a hair of the Buddha, decrepit women, each with her wrists linked by a rosary, prostrated slowly before the massive open doors through which, beyond an open court, the faint lights of votive lamps could be seen burning in the dark windowless temple.

The Potala Palace, which Landon wrote would dwarf London and eclipses Lhasa, is the home of the Dalai Lama and the tombs of his previous incarnations, but, apart from his person, it has no special religious significance for Tibetans. Drepung, the biggest monastery in the world, Sera the second biggest and Gaden, are great ecclesiastical towns where more than 20,000 monks practised their religion. The Lamaserie of Shigatse, home of the Panchen Lamas, is more splendidly furnished and decorated than any of them. But the Jokhan is the Holy of Holies of Tibet.

The Potala is the first building a pilgrim sees when he approaches the Holy City. It is to the Jokhan that he first makes his way to say his prayers. For here is the most sacred treasure of the land. This is the shrine built in A.D. 652 for The Jo, the great Buddha brought by the Princess Wen Cheng from Sian (whose wedding progress we saw marvellously sculptured in butter at Kumbum Monastery) to Lhasa on the occasion of her marriage to King Songsten Gambo.

F. Spencer Chapman, who was a secretary with the British Mission to Lhasa in 1936,[1] described the worshippers at the entrance to the Jokhan, some of whom, for a small fee, were probably doing penitential exercises by proxy for rich sinners who hadn't the time or inclination to attend. He also found a crowd of nearly a hundred beggars, 'some diseased and decrepit, exciting unutterable pity, others able-bodied and clamorous, needing nothing so much as a good whipping'.

The only beggar we saw in Tibet was a monk who appeared to be mentally defective, soliciting alms from pilgrims at the Drepung Monastery festival. Presumably thinking that whipping wasn't a particularly sensible or effective method of dealing with this social nuisance, the new civic authorities, by the time we arrived, had put the healthy to work and told the sick the way to the new hospital.

The main gate was guarded by an elderly monk smelling as if he hadn't been washed since he was born. He sat on a huge hassock wrapped in a voluminous cloak of yellow padded silk, shining with butter grease.

Immediately beyond, in a gloomy lobby, low whispered mutterings of 'Om mani padme hum' (Hail to the jewel in the Lotus), the Hail Mary of Tibetan Buddhism which is on the lips of the devout in every waking hour, rose from the walls by which more worshippers prostrated.

We approached the first shrine through an ancient galleried courtyard. Landon had observed that the 'paintings on the wall were barely distinguishable through a heavy coat of dirt and grease and it was difficult to imagine the colours with which the capitals of the pillars and the raftered roof [of the verandah] overhead had originally been painted'.

Now the buildings blazed with colour. The pillars glowed with fresh red lacquer and the intricate carvings of animals, birds and

1. *Lhasa. The Holy City* (Chatto & Windus).

flowers on the capitals of the pillars supporting the roof were gay
with new blue, red, green, gold, yellow, turquoise and white paint.

In the '59 rebellion monks and lay rebels locked themselves in the
Jokhan armed with rifles and old machine-guns. There have been lurid
descriptions of heavy damage done to this and other temples by
Chinese troops. But in a report on the fighting Captain Yang King-
hwei, who was in charge of an infantry detachment, has stated that he
with other Chinese commanding officers was ordered not to hit the
Potala, the Summer Palace of the Dalai Lama in the Norbulingka nor
the Jokhan. Certainly any major new repair to this ancient structure
would have stood out from its background like a livid scar and there
was none to be seen. The touch of a flame in the antique, bone-dry
timbers would have set all the building alight. In a second court, immediately before the temple, was a garden, lit by the bright colours which
seem more vivid in Lhasa than anywhere else in the world, of asters,
dahlias, hollyhocks, snapdragons and stocks.

We passed into the first chapel through a rancid haze which hung
in the still air over the threshold like a transparent curtain. Inside, with
our first breath, our lungs were choked with the now familiar, thick,
sickly sweet fumes of yak butter, burning in enormous bronze vessels,
and incense glowing before holy images.

The congregation of monks was at service, sitting in two rows,
facing one another. A colossal golden Buddha gazed down on them
from a tall canopied throne. A cantor sitting at a table before a small
altar containing scores of smaller images and pious decorations, led his
brethren in their sung prayers, conducting the ritual by ringing a little
silver bell.

I sat myself between them with the tape-machine recording the
chant. Soothed by the soft rhythmic monotony of the music I felt my
body becoming weightless, as though in a dream it was suspended
between the stone-paved floor and the ceiling. A hand touched my
shoulder and I came to with my head between my knees as I was
passing into unconsciousness through a cloud of incense and butter
fumes.

Overwhelmed with nausea, my companions had fled to the courtyard for fresh air. An old monk whose face was a parchment mask
which cracked into a thousand lines when he smiled, helped me to my
feet and led me out. My throat retched until it was cleansed of the
noxious mixture and we plunged back into the pungent darkness.

Now we were guided through the principal sanctuary into narrow
fusty corridors. From recessed shelves in the walls hundreds of small
divinities, some dressed in frills and laces, watched our stumbling

progress with laughing, lascivious, impassive, maniac, malevolent, sardonic, benign expressions. In the deepening gloom, dim outlines of ragged figures appeared to rush towards us like agonised apparitions in a nightmare and then to float silently by. Looking back we saw they were the shapes of men and women hurrying along a line of huge brass prayer wheels in the form of drums which lined the corridor. As they turned each one, it clicked like a turnstile. They believed that by this mechanical gesture they were moving on their tortuous journey towards Nirvana.

Now stooping to avoid bumping our heads on low lintels we followed monks through curtains of iron rings linked with bars wrought and shaped like horses' bits, hanging over the entrances of small chapels in the thick walls. We breathed the smoky grease-drenched air as if through sodden blankets.

Each shrine contained a bronze urn of butter burning before a crowned image whose bulk almost filled the chamber and a number of lesser Buddhas sitting before innumerable smaller lamps. These corridors and chapels form the innermost sacred circle of Lhasa.

We shuffled our way from one to another until an old woman with a rosary clasped in her raised imploring hands stood in our way. We looked up and found we were at the feet of The Jo.

Before this priceless and most precious image of the Tibetan faith were rows of large, beautifully fashioned and proportioned butter lamps of solid gold, shaped in the form of Christian chalices. In the reflection of their soft light, jewels decorating the god and his altar glittered in the darkness like clusters of stars.

Upon a throne flanked by pillars of solid silver and beneath a canopy supported by two superbly fashioned silver dragons, the face of the Buddha looked down on us with a timeless expressionless calm.

On his head he wore a thick banded golden coronet decorated with turquoise and leaves in each of which sat a small golden Buddha. Beneath the centre leaf was a turquoise said to be the biggest and most perfect in the world. Tradition tells that this diadem was a gift of the great fifteenth-century reformer, Tsong Kapa, the St. Benedict of Tibetan monasticism. The breast of the statue was richly adorned with necklaces of gold, pearls, turquoise and coral.

It is a Tibetan belief that The Jo, whose body is made of gold mixed with iron, silver, copper and zinc, symbolizing the construction of the earth, was not the work of a human artist but of Visvakarma, creative spirit of the universe.

From this serene presence we called on the hideous guardian goddess of the Holy City, Palden Lhamo, whom some Tibetans believe was reincarnated in Queen Victoria. The widow of Windsor would not have been amused. The repulsive three-eyed woman of the Jokhan rides a mule as she eats human brains from a skull. But the Tibetans made a good prophetic guess when they said that while Victoria lived, her subjects would not invade their land. Three years after her death British Imperial troops marched into Lhasa.

When previous travellers came to this shrine they found it overrun with small 'holy' brown mice which were so tame they could be stroked. When they died they were ground to powder as an ingredient for medicines. But we saw none. Perhaps they feared that the Communists might chop off their tails with a carving knife.

Fourteen thousand pounds of butter are still burned at the Jokhan every week. Since the community is no longer permitted to levy religious taxes on the people and it owns no land or serfs to produce an income, it depends on the alms of the devout who freely give what money and butter they can afford. As at Drepung and other monasteries which took part in the '59 rebellion, the cash has been confiscated. But the government pays a subsidy for the maintenance of old and infirm priests and for the upkeep of the fabric.

A senior lama described how lay rebels, helped by monks, fired from the roofs into the streets, killing and wounding some citizens. There were marks of bullets on walls but the most inconvenient damage was to the well in the courtyard which rebels filled with rubbish, excreta and the putrefying bodies of dogs before they surrendered. They had defecated and urinated in rooms of the temple. The army cleaned out the well and restored a clean water supply.

There are 2,000 images and statuettes in the Jokhan, some of precious metals and lavishly bejewelled. None has been disturbed by the Chinese nor has any object of devotion or piece of furniture been removed by them.

We asked, 'How do the Communist authorities, who don't sympathise with your religion, treat you personally?'

The lama replied: 'They don't believe in our religion but they treat us courteously. No one is permitted to make public remarks which are offensive to us. A daily newspaper is published in Lhasa. You will not find anything in it which is contemptuous of Buddhism, but of course, it sometimes criticises the old social system.'

'Do as many worshippers come to your ceremonies as formerly?'

'Yes,' said the lama. 'Also in the shops you can buy incense, prayer wheels and sheets of prayers. If the authorities were suppressing our religion they wouldn't be there, and if people weren't still religious, they wouldn't ask for them.'

In ancient, bare wood-floored rooms beneath the roof some of the elder brethren who could no longer climb the steep ladders between the floors and were unable to attend services in the temples below, were musing away their days on low carpeted benches which were also their beds. Their gowns were heavy with grease which covered every inhabitant and every foot of the Jokhan with a thin, slippery film. This part of the building was lit by small windows covered with yellow paper but it was still too dark for reading. I put down a camera on a bench near a venerable monk and our Tibetan interpreter quickly picked it up. I made to sit down beside the old Religious and my companion caught my elbow with a firm gentle grasp to keep me on my feet, whispering a warning that the room and its occupant were certainly verminous.

We went out of the musty cells into the cool sweet air blowing over Lhasa from the snow mountains which encircled us, to photograph the roofs splendidly gilded, painted and decorated with monstrous dragons and little bells.

Light flashed in the sun from the gold pinnacles of the Potala at the other end of the city. Here, above the cloying stench of grease, butter, smoke, incense and old sweat, was a scene of natural beauty and unsurpassed human creation. It had been a world in which most human beings, enslaved by fear and ignorance, found life endurable only through the hope of a happier incarnation after death.

The benevolent monks who showed us the Jokhan had formerly lived on the enforced offerings of the people who did not dare, or even did not wish, to refuse their demands for fear of a more unfortunate lot in their next existence if they incurred the displeasure of their pastors. The Tibetan priest could exercise a total tyranny over the laity because only he could speak on their behalf directly to the gods. If the layman was refused this service because he did not pay what was asked of him, then he was totally abandoned.

By quoting the precepts of Buddhism the Tibetan theologian could deny that a man's salvation was dependent upon such a correct human relationship, but the precepts of Buddhism had no more to do with its practice in Tibet than had the precepts of Jesus to do with the burning of Christian heretics at the stake.

Some English travellers who preceded us to Tibet regarded this primitive society with contempt. (In 1904 the working people at home were often referred to as 'the lower orders'.) It was contemptible enough but like us, as children, some of these writers had probably sung with thoughtless, cheerful assurance, the Christian hymn:

'All things bright and beautiful,
All creatures great and small
All things wise and wonderful,
The Lord God made them all.
The rich man in his castle,
The poor man at his gate,
God made them high and lowly
And ordered their estate'

which almost precisely echoes Tibetan Buddhist sentiments.

It was also a chastening thought that fifty years before we were
born children of eight worked eighteen hours a day in English mills
owned by good Christian industrialists and were whipped awake with
leather straps by their church and chapel-going foremen when they
fell into exhausted sleep over the machines.

These Tibetan priests who had been sent by their parents to the
monasteries as child novices between the ages of eight and eleven were
not being held responsible by the Chinese and Tibetan Communists
for their adult behaviour. They were not regarded with contempt for
the ignorance which was none of their fault. They and their congrega-
tions could render to Buddha that which was Buddha's but they no
longer had power to extort from the people what belonged to them,
which was perhaps why we found the same relaxed atmosphere at the
Jokhan as at Drepung.

The same penitents were still performing their devotional exercises
in the dark corridors and entrance lobby and in the yard before the
great gates when we left the 'cathedral'. We noticed here and elsewhere that no young people were among them.

A large crowd had gathered around us, and a little boy, eager to
get a closer view of our strange faces, ran in front of one of the worshippers as she rose from the ground and accidentally stepped on her
skirt. With a yell of rage she cuffed him smartly round the head with
her rosary wound round her wrists like handcuffs. The ragged urchin
made a derisive gesture and fled from her furious hands into the crowd
of onlookers which appreciated and applauded the comedy with
shouts of laughter.

9

DEATH OF THE DOGS

From roof-tops or from distant mountain peaks the setting of Lhasa is incomparable. But, apart from views of the majestic Potala, at ground level it is a comfortless collection of mean streets flanked by flat grey stone and brown mud buildings completely bereft of charm. Their monotony is relieved only by gay windows which in summer and autumn are massed with brilliant flowers planted in any empty old can the inhabitants can find. The elevations of the buildings, peculiar to all Tibetan construction, also help to break the sharp angles of the flat-roofed houses and shops. Walls slope inwards from the foot, narrowing at the top. Doors and windows follow the same line so that they too are narrower at the top than at the bottom. This gives them the appearance of being recessed and the effect is heightened by black bands painted on the sides of window and door-frames.

The overwhelming impression is still of dirt and squalor. There is no domestic drainage system and no arrangement for the disposal of sewage. Even with new medical facilities, probably only the climate can save a large part of the population, formerly kept low by venereal and other diseases and a numerous celibate clergy, from being frequently devastated by epidemics. Some years ago, 7,000 people in the capital died of smallpox, one of the most dreaded illnesses in Tibet. A stone tablet near the Jokhan put up by the Chinese in the eighteenth century advising precautions against it was the first (and last) public health notice in the country until the organisation of the present services began in 1952.

Eleven years before we came, the streets, cleaned only once a year, were choked with heaps of putrid rubbish in which dead animals as well as household refuse were left to rot. Citizens squatted wherever they happened to be, to defecate and urinate. Otherwise they used the yards of their houses (as they still do) as lavatories. The city was infested with fierce wild dogs which killed and consumed one another when they were unable to scavenge enough food. Some, driven mad by hunger, attacked humans if they caught them alone. Because theoretically Tibetans as Buddhists must not take life, none of these wretched creatures, however diseased or injured, could be destroyed. There was not one to be seen in the city when we were there. We inquired what had happened to them. It was explained that the new medical authorities couldn't tolerate such a menace to health but neither could they offend religious sentiment by killing animals. So they were rounded up and placed in compounds where they were left to starve and eat one another. The last survivor died of hunger. The Tibetans, relieved of the sin of causing death, were content with this macabre solution.

There are still hundreds of charming pet dogs in the city. We came upon a delightful scene by the ford at the back of the Potala where there is an ancient chorten.[1] A grey-haired old lady was walking round it clockwise—the prescribed ritual—twirling her beautiful, small silver prayer wheel and murmuring prayers as she went. A tiny, fluffy, white puppy trotted close at her heels. When he was tired he sat down, faced the other way and waited for his mistress to come round again. When he got his breath back, he joined in her devotions once more.

From past accounts we had expected Lhasa to be far more unpleasant than it was. Undoubtedly it was duller for no longer did Lords and their Ladies and high ecclesiastical and government officials in splendid exotic clothes ride through the streets on richly dressed horses, followed by retinues whose numbers denoted the ranks of their masters and mistresses. But it is a cleaner place to live in than our predecessors found it. There is no rubbish in the streets which are almost free of human excreta which once fouled them. Occasionally we stumbled over people who suddenly and unselfconsciously squatted in our path to perform their natural functions, but children and adults are being taught to relieve themselves more discreetly in out-of-the-way places and here and there latrines had been built behind low mud walls at the sides of the roads. Some Tibetans seem to enjoy using them for they can be about their private business and, since the walls are only breast high, watch their neighbours go by on the other side at the same time.

The city is poorer in some of the smaller luxuries which were formerly imported from India and Europe. A few years ago the wealthy could buy Swiss watches, German cameras, Scotch whisky, London gin and French brandy and perfumes. There are none left. A

1. A memorial containing holy relics.

Evening shadows over the Lhasa Valley from the tomb of the Thirteenth Dalai Lama. The pieces of rag hanging on the line are prayer flags

A lady of Lhasa

Mongolian worshippers at Kumbum Monastery, Chinghai, of which Thubten Jigme Norbu, brother of the Fourteenth Dalai Lama, was Abbot

street dealer offered us some of his last stock of Indian matches at
2s. 6d. per box. Another had a few tins of Cherry Blossom shoe-polish
at 5s. a tin. When the batteries of my electric razor gave out, a Nepalese
trader produced a Gillette for £4. But there were reasonably priced
silks and cottons from Shanghai and Peking and, perhaps the most
welcome benefit of all, the large cheap Chinese vacuum flask. As in
China, clothing materials are strictly rationed because everyone can
now afford to buy some of them and there are not enough, even with
increased production, to meet demands.

Jewellery was prohibitively expensive and there was none worth
buying. A small crudely made turquoise pendant of poor quality on
a brass wire ring and chain was £7. Better and cheaper rings could be
found in an English seaside junk shop. But since nearly all the citizens
seemed to possess some small personal ornament, an ear-ring, necklace
or bracelet, perhaps there had been a run on stocks of the more attractive pieces when serfs first became free to earn money, and only the
unsaleable was left.

Much of Lhasa's commerce is conducted in the streets where, in
fine weather, merchants, taking advantage of the fresh air, set up stalls
in front of their small unventilated shops. Groups of cobblers sit
making the thick-soled highly decorated boots worn by lamas and
the better off who can afford them on festive occasions. Some of these
craftsmen have been persuaded by Communist cadres to pool their
skill and resources and work as mutual aid teams, sharing the cost of
their raw materials and profits. Some have already done well enough
to buy new sewing machines from China and more than double their
old rate of production.

The dark airless rooms, reminiscent of pictures of the first home
workshops in the English industrial revolution, are the beginnings of
mechanised factories which will have to be established as living
standards rise.

Greengrocers' stalls were piled with fruit and vegetables which at
this altitude can grow to fantastic size in the ultra-violet light of the
thin air so that everything looks as if it has been produced in super
hot-houses. Cabbages were so big that we could only just put our
arms round them and carrots and radishes were two feet long and as
thick as a man's arm.

Buddhists are forbidden to eat flesh. Tibetan Buddhists eat as much
of it as they can get when they can afford it. The gods must look the
other way at dinner time or the sinners would surely be poisoned by
the yak beef exposed in huge hunks on filthy stalls and crawling with
enormous bloated bluebottles. When we asked monks, who cook

F

large quantities for themselves, how they reconciled its consumption with the rule forbidding it, they replied blandly that unfortunately in the long bitterly cold winters it was essential for the preservation of health, but when we arrived, the city sweltered in a heat-wave.

Casuistry is a theological science in Tibet. If stray dogs are left to starve and eat one another, those who leave them to suffer are absolved from sin because their own hands have not done the killing. There was theoretically no capital punishment in Tibet. Criminals, political or religious enemies, or serfs who were occasionally murdered by their owners, were not officially executed or murdered. They were tortured and mutilated, but if death from their injuries occurred later and not immediately from the hands of those who inflicted them, no sin was committed. A more refined way of killing was to throw a victim from a high place. It was the ground below which caused his death. From time to time, the roofs of the Potala, 400 feet above the rocks, have been found most convenient for the disposal of the unwanted.

It is perhaps unfair for Christians to criticise Tibetan Buddhists without recalling that for the same reason and by the same reasoning, Christian priests have also washed their hands of the blood of heretics condemned to be hanged and burned by the secular arm.

The principal shopping centre, where butchers have their stalls, is also the Parkor, Lhasa's second sacred circle which runs outside the Jokhan. Merit can be gained by walking round either of the first two and if you choose the Parkor you can make a few purchases at the same time. For those with little time or energy to spare, these short strolls are acceptable to the gods. If you wish to earn their highest favours you must do it the hard way by going round the Lingkor which in five miles completely encircles the Holy City. It is good to walk round twirling your prayer wheel which with each turn sends invocations flying off to heaven. It used to be better at the same time to give alms to the beggars who lined the route to help the pilgrims as well as themselves, but now these pious parasites have been diverted to more immediately useful occupations.

It is most meritorious to proceed all the way by prostration. To do this, you equip yourself with flat wooden or leather palm-protectors which are strapped to the hands. Then you begin the journey by stretching yourself face downward at full length on the ground with arms outstretched. You rise, walk to the place your finger-tips have reached, stretch full length again and repeat the process. When you have completed the circuit you will have prostrated more than 5,000 times. Some have been known to collapse with heart failure on the way. In the eyes of Tibetans they were specially blessed for it is believed that all the sins of anyone dying on the Lingkor are immediately forgiven. As in the European Middle Ages, when the rich hired substitutes to perform their more arduous physical penances for them, it was not unknown for sinners to engage others to stand in for them on the Lingkor circuit. Apparently automatic absolution for dying on the holy way is also available for those of any other faith or of no faith at all, but being still unacclimatised we were in no condition to risk it.

It is recommended that all Lhasa citizens as well as visiting pilgrims should make this sacred journey every day, but when we walked over part of it, we saw only one man prostrating his way along.

A manufacturer of photographic light-meters would starve to death in Tibet, for when the rainy season is over skies are perpetually blue on most days but it is also the most difficult country in the world for a westerner to photograph. As soon as we produced a camera in a town, we were followed by hundreds of adults and children who wanted to be in the pictures. They crowded around us so that we could hardly move our arms. Then we would shout in Tibetan, 'Go away.' Yelling with pleasure at our discomfiture and with comical gestures of feigned fear, they scattered and instantly flocked back. They reeked of dirt and sweat. Most of the children had running colds and since, like toilet paper, handkerchiefs are unknown, they wiped their noses on their sleeves and then pushed against us to get a closer view of us and our equipment. After a few days in Lhasa when we were familiar figures our audiences got the hang of what we were trying to do, so whenever we asked an interesting looking character to stand apart from the throng to take a close-up portrait, the rest obligingly stepped aside.

But they also delighted in embarrassing our subjects by telling them to wipe their noses, put their hats on straight and stand up smartly. Overcome with confusion, some of them stared into the lens with squint-eyed idiotic expressions or exploded into giggles just as the button was pressed. Once, an old man picked up a roll of film which had fallen from my pocket and held it out to me in filthy greasy fingers. Then, thinking he might have offended me by touching it, he quickly put out his tongue in the traditional form of respectful greeting. To his astonishment, I stuck out my own tongue in response. The crowd roared with laughter and two little boys slapped each other on the back, threw themselves on the ground and kicked the dust with glee. These were exhausting, hilarious expeditions.

We went to look for the strangest community in the city, the Ragyaba, scavenger-beggar-butcher-undertaker 'caste'. Corpses are not buried in Tibet. Like the Parsees of Bombay, who put out their dead on towers of silence to be consumed by vultures, Tibetan Buddhists wish no trace of their old bodies, which their souls have discarded, to remain. Formerly those of the nobility and high ecclesiastics were burned. The most usual method of disposing of bodies was to hack them to pieces and leave them for wild dogs, pigs and vultures to eat. In the country this service for the dead might be performed by male relatives or friends. Those of the poorest who could not afford the services of an undertaker were put into rivers and sometimes suspended in waterfalls.

In Lhasa the grim work of dismemberment was done by the Ragyabas, outcast scavengers who lived in hamlets of hovels outside the city. The Chinese are now treating their odious trade as a problem of social hygiene and as a separate sect they are disappearing.

10

MEDICINE—OLD AND NEW

Tibet, naturally one of the most enchanting countries in the world is still one of the dirtiest and most hazardous. Any illness which in itself might be of small account at lower altitudes can be mortally dangerous in the oxygen-starved atmosphere.

On the night following our first walk in Lhasa, Roma, who had a slight cold, collapsed with the symptoms of typhoid fever. Her temperature rose to over 105 degrees and she became delirious. She was racked with pain and violent sickness and within a few hours was only half conscious and completely helpless. Two doctors from the hospital brought a dainty little Chinese nurse from a city clinic to take charge and another girl with plaits, who announced herself as a pathologist, to take blood and other samples with which she hurried back to the laboratory on her bicycle. In between attacks of vomiting the nurse gave oxygen and antibiotics to Roma without which her over-strained heart might not hold out. The laboratory report came back within an hour. It was not typhoid. There was no explanation for the sudden collapse but a severe chill which had set up enteric complications. It was difficult to believe that a mere cold could reduce a healthy person to such a desperate condition in a few hours. Next morning the temperature was still 105 degrees and in the evening an alternative antibiotic was tried. Unknown to me, but to relieve my anxiety, the two young doctors had sent a radio message to the senior Chinese surgeon in Tibet who was seventy miles away.

In the middle of the following night a tall grey-haired man of sixty-two, who had jeeped for six hours in darkness through precipitous mountain tracks and flooded valleys, reached us. He confirmed the diagnosis of his junior colleagues. The new medicine was slowly reducing the fever but the strain on the heart was still serious. Roma was bathed in alcohol and the retching having abated, she was able to breathe oxygen continuously. Now she fell asleep, but wakened several times to ask anxiously why the Chinese Communists and the Tibetans, who could hardly afford to do anything once, did everything twice. This was the last of the delirium but it wasn't the last shock.

Koo She-lone, who had come to interpret the senior surgeon's instructions, suddenly broke down in the middle of a sentence and wandered through the door with a vague expression on his face. I followed him into the corridor and caught him in my arms as he was sliding down the wall on which he was leaning. We lifted him into bed and one of the young doctors examined him and took his blood-pressure. It had fallen dangerously low.

The nurse fanned Roma with a newspaper and applied cold compresses to her head. When I wakened in the chair where I had fallen asleep in my clothes, our patient was peacefully sleeping, breathing easily for the first time in three days and the nurse was dozing with the paper fan dangling in her fingers. I got up and collided noisily with a pedestal. Roma opened her eyes from which the heat had gone, said, 'I'm better,' and fell asleep again. Defying doctor's orders, I poured myself the stiffest brandy I had ever drunk and then another.

After forty-eight hours' rest and medication Koo She-lone recovered.

The doctors came twice every day until Roma was on her feet. They didn't wish to talk about themselves but we learned that like all other Chinese medical staff they had volunteered to serve in Lhasa or anywhere else in the country for as long as they were needed. They went to their homes for a three-month holiday every three years, but had no thought of returning there permanently since they couldn't imagine a time when they wouldn't be required here. They were reconciled to staying in Tibet for the rest of their lives.

For young people brought up in the great Chinese cities—Peking, Shanghai, Sian, Chengtu, where they had qualified—a more comfortless place couldn't be imagined. Plays and concerts were given in the new theatre. There were occasional dances and weekly film shows, and there was always, inescapably, the Potala, which after a few weeks was a great weight in the eyes. But apart from these diversions there was little interest in the city to stimulate a lively mind and the only other towns within visiting distance were duller and more primitive.

The landscape of the lush green Lhasa Valley and the splendid snow mountains which enclose it are lovely, but as an Italian restaurateur friend in the delightful town of Orta San Giulio replied when we envied his surroundings, 'You can't *live* on a panorama.'

These young people weren't to be judged by the standards of those who wish to get on in their profession and enjoy a rich and

interesting life. They were missionaries inspired by zeal to do good for
the sake of doing it although they would have been embarrassed by
such an appraisal of their motives. They were not encouraged by hope
of reward in Heaven in which they didn't believe. They must, of
course, have heard of accusations by the Dalai Lama and those who
went with him to India that their comrades were exterminating the
Tibetan race by torture and murder and that they themselves as doctors
(who were in Lhasa when the atrocities were said to have begun) were
contributing to the crime by sterilising Tibetan men.

We would have invited their comments on these charges but in
the face of their devotion to thousands of sick people, which we were
to see for ourselves, it would have been an indecency to repeat them.

Instead we went to see the only form of medical treatment which
would have been available to us if we had lived in Tibet before they
came. At the 'traditional' hospital, Mr. Liang Hung, Director of the
Public Health Bureau, introduced us to its former principal, the
High Lama Chinrob Nobo, Tibet's most famous doctor. This eighty-
year-old monk was the Dalai Lama's personal physician. Now infirm
and nearly blind, he lives in semi-retirement on a government pension
in a luxurious apartment.

Here he is surrounded by his household and religious treasures
appropriate to his high ecclesiastical rank—rows of gold and silver
images in finely carved and painted cases, holy water vessels and other
rare antique objects of Buddhist devotion. Bearing a striking resemblance to Pope John, the gentle old man received us on a couch
which was also his bed, covered with beautiful carpets and heavily
embroidered cushions. The canopy and walls of his alcove were richly
decorated with paintings of Buddhas, birds and animals. He was
dressed in a gown of fine russet silk with wide yellow sleeves.

Nowadays, when he feels well enough, he sees one or two patients
a day, personal friends and cases which have baffled his younger colleagues. During our visit he treated a lama and the baby of a young
woman by laying on of hands and words of advice.

Before the Chinese came in 1951, only monks could become medical
students and, like all the other 500 Tibetan doctors in the country,
Chinrob Nobo was trained at the school of medicine on the top of
Iron Hill, the highest building in the city, overlooking the Potala,
which was established 500 years ago. There they were taught a system
of healing comprising old Chinese medicine including acupuncture
and moxibustion, astrology and religious magic therapy.

These practitioners ministered only to the higher ranks of lamas,
the nobility and officers of the Army. Poor monks and laity were

entirely dependent on prayer and such simple home remedies as were
known to them. In fact they were probably no worse off than those who
could afford 'qualified' doctors and some may have lived longer because
they escaped the attentions of 'holy science'. If they could afford it they
might purchase pills containing excreta of living Buddhas or draughts
containing their urine which were considered sovereign ingredients
of prescriptions.

With terrifying confidence—terrifying, that is, to any patient aware
of its implications—Dr. Chinrob and his professional colleagues were
able in their sublime innocent ignorance of scientific medicine to
believe that a patient could die only through a doctor's negligence. The
Buddha was infallible and therefore if a physician was thoroughly
conversant with the Scriptures he must be able to cure any condition.
If he failed, then he hadn't read them conscientiously or had forgotten
the relevant passages.

It took a Tibetan monk-medical student much longer to qualify
than a student of modern medicine. Nine years of the Lhasa curriculum
were required to memorise the four standard textbooks, the first of
which was published 2,000 years ago and was reckoned to be still up to
date in 1962 because the first author was an inspired high incarnation
who could not have been allowed to err. It was revised by a Living
Buddha who lived to 125.

Before a student passed his finals he must be able to recite all the
textbooks or any part of them from memory. But since the memories
of even the holiest lamas sometimes failed, they couldn't be blamed for
occasionally forgetting to apply the right remedies and allowing their
patients to die accidentally. There was no need of post-mortem exami-
nations, which were forbidden by religion anyway. The cause of death
could always be discovered by reference to the textbooks which would
show the doctor where he went wrong.

The venerable 'Dean' was already weary after examining his two
patients. His failing eyes could barely see us and he was so deaf that he
found difficulty in hearing our questions. We left him snoozing among
his cushions and went to discuss the medical revolution with his
successors.

The traditional medical school is now part of the new traditional
hospital near the city centre. This is a pleasant two-storey house
enclosing a large courtyard filled with flowers round which the ground-
floor clinics for out-patients are situated. In an upper room, hung with
silk banners and old religious paintings, the senior members of the
Faculty were waiting for us on the usual carpeted benches. They wore
white doctors' coats over their monks' gowns and white caps. A thin

Detail of canopy of Thirteenth Dalai Lama's tomb which contains 300,000 ounces of gold

Holy water bowls and cases of divinities of the Buddhist Pantheon forming a wall of the Fourteenth Dalai Lama's sitting-room

OPPOSITE

above: Fourteenth Dalai Lama's throne in his private reception hall, Potala Palace

below: Couch and table of Fourteenth Dalai Lama's private sitting-room, Potala Palace

Chortens festooned with prayer flags

old gentleman with a wisp of white beard and a pair of twinkling eyes behind thick-lensed spectacles announced himself as Ah Wang Chu Tza and introduced his colleagues who were specialists in their various departments.

He courteously explained the basic concepts of Tibetan medicine according to which, he said, all human beings, animals and plants were composed of metal, wood, water, fire and earth. Good health was maintained when these elements were kept in balance. For example, if anyone was deficient in metal, he would be weakened. His bones would not develop in infancy and growth would be permanently retarded so that he would be stunted or deformed. Balance could be restored by increasing or decreasing the basic elements. For example, the fire of life burned low in old people. This could be brightened by the external application of heat or by administration of medicine prepared from plants which thrived in the hot sun. So far this was familiar therapy. We had swallowed pints of iron tonics as children and sulphur tablets to cool our hot spring blood. Wood was a puzzler until we remembered the taste of charcoal biscuits, and while cortisone is prescribed in extreme cases, most of the old folk we know who are plagued by rheumatism still seek relief with a hot water bottle and rum which certainly comes from the sunny side of the world. But the mystics of diagnosis were more complicated.

Tibetan Buddhism forbade the making of a hole in the body although this didn't prevent the exposure of holes already there by the gouging out of eyes of criminals and religious and political opponents. What is most remarkable about Tibetan traditional medicine is the practitioners' ignorance of anatomy. A corpse was so little reverenced in the absence of its departed spirit that it could be hacked in pieces for pigs and carrion to eat.[1] But no 'doctor' in Tibet ever cut up a body for scientific reasons to discover how it was made and how it might work.

So the walls of the medical school which Ah Wang Chu Tza took us to see were draped with charts of the human frame, some designed a thousand years ago, showing the circulation of the blood beginning in the right arm. The heart of a man was drawn on the left side of the body and that of a woman on the right. The pelvis, in male and female, was depicted in such a way that walking would have been impossible.

Ah Wang Chu Tza said that in the ancient classics there were references to insects causing disease but this had not led to the study of bacteriology of which he had never heard until Chinese doctors came to

1. The corpses of Dalai Lamas were embalmed, encased in gold and entombed in the sitting posture of the Buddha.

Lhasa. Perhaps it was just as well for if this good man had been encouraged to experiment in a country where the killing of a fly was a
sin, he would certainly have been denounced as an heretic. Some ancient
charts showed scalpels and other recognisable surgical instruments of
Chinese origin which it had been forbidden to use in Tibet so they
had only pictures of them.

Only one operation—amputation of a limb—was permissible but
it was rarely performed in the absence of skilled surgeons and suitable
instruments. However, if it was considered desirable, unconsciousness
could be induced by means of an anaesthetic, of which there was an
unlimited supply, prepared from the roots of a Tatura tree.

A Western physician would have been fascinated to hear the monk
doctor explaining that a Tibetan anaesthetist would calculate the
amount of anaesthetic in exactly the same way as himself—by the size,
weight and general health of the patient. But he would also have found
it difficult to discover the three pulses which Ah Wang Chu Tza
assured us were in each human wrist.

Mercury has long been known in Tibet as a treatment for syphilis.
When its obvious symptom, the chancre, dried and fell off, it was
believed to be permanently cured. The secondary and tertiary stages
were regarded as new and more severe infections. Apparently it was
suffered by women undetected.

From simple herbal remedies and prescriptions which might not
seem strange in any English village and which are sometimes recommended today by the most up-to-date practitioners, Tibetan medicine
departs into a world of legend and superstition where all contact
with exact knowledge is lost.

A key specialist is the calendar man. At the Lhasa traditional hospital
he is a young monk named Tsu Cheng Chu Tza who is in charge of
the dispensary containing a stock of thousands of herbs. It is his responsibility to see that these and all water used in medicines are collected
according to strictly prescribed rules.

The stars are grouped in twenty-eight constellations and the day
divided into sixty divisions, thirty for the day and thirty for the hours
of darkness. The constellations are studied to decide when the most
suitable weather will occur for the gathering of plants and digging up
of roots and during which division of the day or night it will be most
auspicious to do this work, which must always be performed by monks.
When we were in Lhasa half the members of the Faculty were out in
the mountains and valleys collecting the harvest for the coming winter.

But once more, without these physicians, chemists and pathologists
being consciously aware of it, they were students of empirical medicine.

Their forefathers had devised an elaborate magical religious system which governed every human activity and included all rational and useful experience together with superstition in a witch-doctor's cloak of irrational mysticism. So, according to the Tibetan medical calendar, January, February and March were inauspicious months for the collection of water, not for the good reason that it was not running so freely then and more likely to be fouled but because the gods had so ordained it. And, as in China, long before the existence of harmful bacteria was known, water was boiled by the Tibetan doctors before it was used in medicine because they had learned that people sometimes became sick if it was not.

At the same time they prescribed pills containing excreta of the Dalai Lama and other Living Buddhas, and used their sacred urine in draughts. We had read accounts of this practice by other visitors but had been inclined to regard it as the kind of invention with which some travellers from strange lands like to shock their friends at home. When we mentioned it to Ah Wang Chu Tza the old man was overcome with embarrassment. He looked at his colleagues with a silent appeal to help him out and then at the Director of the Public Health Bureau in whose presence he obviously didn't wish to confess such a medical outrage before foreigners. 'No,' he said softly, 'we don't use such methods.'

'Then those who wrote of such things were not telling the truth?'

Ah Wang Chu Tza struggled silently with his conscience for a few moments and answered, 'Well, I have heard of such treatment.'

'But wasn't the use of such medicines also highly valued by lama doctors and patients because it was supposed to contain something of the holy and therefore healing properties of the living Buddha from which it came?'

Ah Wang Chu Tza was now sixty-three years old and had been a practitioner all his adult life. Hadn't he prescribed it too because he had also been taught to believe in its powers? We weren't suggesting he had committed some kind of professional misconduct. After all, as in all other countries, medical students could only learn what they were taught. The old man smiled with relief that the situation was now understood and we were not seeking to humiliate him and his lama colleagues.

'Yes,' he said, 'I did believe in it and occasionally recommended it to patients, but the doctors from the medical schools in Peking and other Chinese cities have convinced me that it can do no good and may be harmful.'

Then he added, surprisingly: 'It wasn't only the urine and excreta of Living Buddhas which was looked on as vauable for medicines. For example, the urine of any eight-year-old boy was considered to be highly efficacious.'

'Why was that?'

Ah Wang Chu Tza looked at his fellow doctors, who made no comment.

'I don't know,' he said. 'I'm not sure that anyone knows. It was just believed and everyone accepted it.'

He explained that such examples of religious therapy were an exception to the general rules of treatment which were based on more scientific principles. It was true that pathology as practised by modern doctors was unknown in Tibet. They were ignorant of chemical analysis but this didn't mean they couldn't diagnose illnesses from symptoms which they could see, smell and feel. Modern doctors might sometimes call them by other names but they were the same illnesses. For example, the rate of a pulse or the heat of a body indicated a state of health or sickness. Diagnosis of a patient's condition could be helped by observing the colour and density of urine. Wasn't that true? It could not be denied. When abnormalities were detected medicines which had been tried for centuries could be successfully applied. Modern doctors didn't always know how the drugs they used were made? No, they didn't. Ah Wang Chu Tza was now back in his stride.

'And all sick people in the world didn't die before modern medicine was practised?' he said.

If he had known about it he might also have pointed out to Western sceptics that none of the five or six thousand drugs in his Tibetan hospital had so far produced deformed and limbless babies as Thalidomide has done.

So we didn't ask him why he thought powdered rhinoceros horn could cure lung infections.

We could suppose that he and his companions, who believed that the earth was flat and shaped like a shoulder of mutton, had also some good reason for the conviction that the most auspicious time for taking a pulse was on a Monday morning and that medicines should be prepared when the moon was waxing for then their ingredients were at full strength. But since they were all now so courteous in their acknowledgment of the superiority of some forms of modern medicine, it would have been ill-mannered to continue drawing attention to their less convincing techniques.

Ah Wang Chu Tza was enthusiastically in favour of co-operation between the old Tibetan methods and the new brought from China. He and his colleagues now realised that some patients who might otherwise die could be treated by surgery at the modern hospital and they referred such cases for operation. They had been convinced by demonstration that new drugs could quickly and permanently cure diseases if they were treated in their early stages. They had been shown how in the laboratory doctors could diagnose some complaints immediately by using their special equipment so that patients could be treated effectively.

With modest pride Ah Wang Chu Tza added that they were now happy to welcome the doctors from the new hospital and teach them something about the ancient Tibetan arts of healing.

We walked through the clinics where two or three hundred men, women and children and a dozen or more monks were being treated. Ah Wang Chu Tza said that the average attendance was 300 a day and sometimes more than 400 came.

We asked, 'Does the Bureau of Public Health insist that surgical cases which you can't or won't handle must be sent to the surgeons at the new hospital?'

'No,' said Ah Wang Chu Tza. 'Such decisions are left to those who are treating patients.'

'But supposing,' we said, 'that you diagnosed a case of appendicitis which didn't yield to medical treatment and quickly developed to the stage where without surgery the patient might die of peritonitis, delay in surgery might kill him.'

'Of course,' said Ah Wang Chu Tza, 'we know now that this could happen and although I couldn't personally recall such events, it is reasonable to suppose that some people did die in the past because we couldn't operate. It would be wrong and unnecessary to permit that to happen today. If we are in doubt we can telephone at once to the new hospital.'

As we were leaving this endearing old monk and his fellow doctors, we asked him, 'Then you now think it might not be sinful for surgeons to make holes in the bodies of patients if they can save lives and that modern scientific medicine is good?'

Ah Wang Chu Tza reflected for a moment and looked at us with anxious eyes. 'Yes,' he said. 'There is no denying that there is much good in science.'

Then he added wistfully, 'But I am still sometimes worried about the evil spirits.'

When we had travelled 5,000 miles through China in 1960 we had found old and modern medicine being practised everywhere. At the great Tung Ren Municipal Hospital in Peking, with its twelve operating theatres and all the latest facilities for treatment, there was also an acupuncture and moxibustion department where in addition to these traditional methods of surgery thousands of sick people are treated with herbal remedies and techniques which have been known for thousands of years.

To our surprise, as well as claiming cures for functional disorders, the traditional doctors had no doubts of their ability to treat organic conditions such as appendicitis, and even poliomyelitis, successfully. We had assumed that the government was playing politics (and for time) with medicine and justifying such out-of-date methods because it couldn't provide enough modern doctors and facilities. It was an English friend, Dr. Joshua Horn, a Fellow of the Royal College of Surgeons, now a senior consultant at one of China's greatest hospitals, who suggested that before taking such a superficial view (not to say a politically prejudiced one) we might ask ourselves why the government which had so vastly improved modern scientific medical services should practise such expensive and time-wasting self-deception.[1]

Mr. Liang Hung said that in Tibet, apart from the study of traditional medicine, which it would be foolish as well as unscientific to ignore, there was a more immediate compelling reason for encouraging it and treating its practitioners with respect and sympathy.

'In this country,' he said, 'it isn't just a question of studying medical folklore which, as elsewhere, contains the useful practical experience of centuries. We have to understand that in the minds of the lama doctors and their patients their medicines, which will undoubtedly relieve many illnesses and cure some, are mixed with magical practices and superstitious rituals. For example, you wouldn't be impressed if your doctor wrote a prayer on a piece of paper burned it to ash and told you to swallow it instead of sending you to a dispensary for medicine, but you wouldn't convince a lama doctor or his patient that this method wouldn't affect disease one way or another just by telling them so. You would simply offend them, hurt their feelings and get nowhere.

'But in the past ten years we have persuaded about half the people in Lhasa and other areas in need of treatment to come to our modern hospitals and clinics. We have persuaded the lama doctors that we have their interests at heart by providing better buildings for them to work in. We give them wages so that they needn't ask patients for money or gifts in kind which they can ill afford. And we encourage them to learn a little about modern medicine such as simple hygiene by taking

1. In 1963 two physicians at a London hospital reported that acupuncture had been practised with success on patients whose condition had not responded to other treatment.

an interest in their methods and showing we also want to learn from them. This creates mutual confidence and respect.'

Mr. Liang Hung described the early experiences of the doctors who came from China to start the new hospital. For some weeks no Tibetan patients came and then one morning a sick lama appeared. The records department now wish they had asked him how he found his way there because this turned out to be an historic visit. His complaint was apparently relieved to his satisfaction for within the next week more than twenty other monks came. They were impressed by their medical treatment but even more by the fact that they were not asked to pay anything. Then followed the triumphant morning when the first lay patients arrived. If it was all right for lamas it must also be permissible for them.

But, said Mr. Liang Hung, some came with all sorts of unexpected recommendations. A serf suffering from stomach ulcers was asked how long he had been ill. He said he had been going to a sooth-sayer on the Lingkor for two or three years. He paid him a small fee each time, received a prayer on a bit of paper and was told to repeat invocations. On his last visit he had told the soothsayer he wasn't any better. The latter demanded his usual fee but instead of prescribing, told him that the gods wished him to go to a certain building. He had followed directions—and found himself at the hospital. The sooth-sayer told him to return next day when he would receive fresh instructions about future treatment. He paid another fee and was referred to the hospital again. So the shrewd quacks continued to get their money and passed on their patients to the doctors. But since these early days many had gone out of business because their clients, who soon found they could be cured for nothing, ceased to patronise them.

For a long time, Ah Wang Chu Tza and his colleagues were busier than their modern counterparts. Surgery was a sin and without the magical blessings of priests prescriptions were offensive to the gods. In warning people against the new hospital there was the important, and perhaps overriding consideration that once the doctors began to cure those who had been incurable, because in their wisdom the gods wished to punish them with continuing illness, the lamas' monopoly of medicine would be broken for ever, quite apart from the fact that valuable revenue, in the form of fees for prayers and rituals for the sick, would be lost.

The authority of the priests in the theocratic state was complete. Anything which threatened it was to be resisted, until some lamas themselves could no longer resist the pain they were suffering from their own physical afflictions. Perhaps it also became known that one of the hospital doctors had been called by the Dalai Lama to the Potala to examine him and that a sister of His Holiness had been seen by a hospital gynaecologist.

Soon after the first monk came a small special ward in the new hospital was set aside for monastic patients and success was assured when a priest, who would have died without it, consented to his life being saved by surgery. Within a year the medical staff had to be increased. Then the first Tibetan student went to Peking where after some preliminary education he entered medical school. Two days after our meeting with Ah Wang Chu Tza we filmed this native modern surgeon performing an operation for acute appendicitis on a young peasant from a village fifty miles up the Lhasa Valley.

The new hospital was opened in 1952. It now has 250 beds and a medical staff of 210. Among sixty doctors there are four Tibetans, trained in Peking and Sian. Among the nurses are forty Tibetan women who are also qualified midwives.

Chinese men and women, who according to their accusers had stood by unprotestingly while children were forced to shoot their parents and defenceless people were cruelly done to death in the streets, were so solicitous of their patients' feelings that they were careful not to kill the vermin with which they were infested lest they should offend religious beliefs.

There is more to running a modern hospital in Tibet than knowing about medicine and surgery. Apparently, to gain the confidence of the sick it is necessary to combine the qualities of a surgeon or physician with those of a psychologist and possess the patience and sympathy of a Father Damien at the same time.

It is essential that a hospital and everything and everyone in it should be clean. Tibetans are usually dirty and often lousy. The Medical Superintendent, who came to Lhasa across the mountains on horseback eleven years ago, told us that before they saw their first patient the Chinese nurses and doctors, who were all volunteers, were taught how to treat them as human beings.

Tibetans who weren't used to washing would regard an enforced bath as a personal affront or assault on dignity. So, if a part of a patient's body must be cleaned it must be done with the most tactful courtesy. If he were verminous a doctor or nurse must ignore it. But if it was essential to remove a louse then it must be removed discreetly and put safely elsewhere, preferably in a dish. If it was killed the patient would consider he had been made a party to an unforgivable crime and more likely than not would leave the hospital and never return. Even more importantly, if a louse moved from a patient to a nurse or

Detail of golden canopy of Thirteenth Dalai Lama's tomb which rises through three storeys of the Potala

Detail of great chanting house façade at Drepung, largest monastery in the world

Buddha of Sera Monastery

Monk at service, Johkan Cathedral

a doctor they must pretend not to notice but when it was convenient
to do so without ostentation they could pick it up and put it out of
harm's way.

The Superintendent said this behaviour became so much a part of
normal procedure that in the first few months, doctors and nurses
didn't depart from it even when a patient was unconscious. 'I was
assisting a surgeon at one of our first operations,' he said, 'when I saw
a louse which had crawled from the patient to his forearm. He flicked
his wrist to shake if off but it stuck. So I picked it up and was looking
for a dish to put it in when the humour of the situation struck me. There
was the patient on the table, blissfully unconscious under deep anaes-
thesia and there I was worrying about his louse. So I killed it. But there
were no Tibetan nurses present—we hadn't trained any yet for theatre
work—or I wouldn't have dared. After that we deloused unconscious
patients in the preparation room, making sure that no Tibetan assistant
was in sight.'

For the first year or two there were only Chinese nurses. But then,
from the new schools, where they had learnt a little science, came the
first few Tibetan volunteers. It was a long time before the first went
into the operating theatre. Later she and others told the Superintendent
that they always went to the temple to ask forgiveness for committing
sin in helping at surgery. Now they didn't worry any more because
it seemed to them that the gods couldn't be offended when they
helped to save the lives of dying people or relieved them of suffering.

The pleasant scent of disinfectant and continual scrubbing with
soap and water could not remove the pungent smell of stale sweat and
unwashed clothes from this hospital. This could only be dispersed if
every patient were soaked in a hot bath as soon as he arrived and everything he wore was burned. And then it would come back with the
relatives who usually lodged with the sick in their rooms and wards
until they were better.

We found old women helping to look after their husbands who
would have refused to come without them. Children seemed never to
be without their mothers. The doctor we should have liked to have
been with us here was Sir James Spence. Many years ago some babies
in English hospitals died inexplicably. Those were the days when some
doctors were so concerned with the dangers of infection that, according
to the latest theories, infants were isolated in glass-walled cubicles. Some
of them died all the same, from no identifiable germs. It occurred to
Dr. Spence that perhaps they had been killed by loneliness. At any rate
he would have none of the glass-cubicle technique in his Newcastle
hospital. When we went to see him he had persuaded the authorities

G

to buy a few houses which he transformed into medical and surgical nurseries where small patients were nursed by their mothers who prepared their food and lived with them as if they were at home, until they were well. When infants had operations, the first people they saw when they wakened were not strange doctors or nurses but their own mothers. They didn't die mysteriously or from infections brought by their parents.

Because some patients would not have stayed without them, the doctors in Lhasa also encouraged mothers and relatives to come with the sick and injured. According to the textbooks the hospital should have been devastated by infections—we saw a mother with filthy, greasy hands adjusting a clean bandage over a new abdominal wound to make her son more comfortable—but the Superintendent said there had been no disasters.

Perhaps the Tibetans, by constant exposure, had acquired immunity to germs which would kill us. Certainly, he said, some would enjoy immunity but like everyone else all over the world Tibetans died if they didn't receive medical attention when it was imperative. Smallpox had killed countless numbers in the past. No one would ever know how many had died of pneumonia and such conditions as peritonitis and strangulated hernia, let alone venereal diseases, which were prevalent everywhere. The idea that Tibetans like other people who lived in primitive conditions were tougher than those who enjoyed more civilised amenities was a myth, usually fostered by those who mistook endurance for strength.

We told the Superintendent about the theory of Sir Charles Bell, the British diplomat in Tibet who deplored the barbaric punishments inflicted on Tibetans, but concluded that they weren't as horrible as they might seem to foreign observers because the victims didn't feel pain like Europeans. 'If you like to risk what he might do to you in return,' he said, 'you can easily test that sort of nonsense by sticking a pin into the next Tibetan you see.'

The success of the Lhasa hospital will be measured not by an increase but by a decrease in the numbers of patients. After the first lamas came for treatment and made it respectable there was a flood of people with every kind of ailment, from sores to tumours. The majority were cured in a few visits. When we came to the city the average number was about 330 a day, including a large number of women coming for ante- and post-natal examination, and babies at the child-guidance clinic.

A tenth of the male population, with a few promiscuous exceptions, living celibate lives in monasteries was one of the reasons for a low birth-rate. Another was the custom of polyandry, by which one woman married a family of brothers and polygyny by which one man married a family of sisters. But venereal diseases were a cause of sterility and there was a high rate of maternal and infant mortality, although the extent of this will never be known. The return to lay life of thousands of monks who are now marrying and producing families and the decrease of polygyny and polyandry in a more prosperous society will rapidly increase the population. But the most important immediate factor is that the new medical services are reducing the incidence of sterility by treating venereal diseases and maternal and infant mortality by ante and post-natal care.

The most dramatic work is done in the hospitals, but 170 medical units are working all over the Tibetan countryside where the emphasis is on preventive medicine.

The most popular department in Lhasa seems to be the eye-clinic where we found short-sighted folk who hadn't been able to see to the end of the street in a crystal-clear atmosphere where a mountain ten miles away seems almost near enough to throw a stone on to it, looking with expressions of delighted astonishment through new spectacles.

The happiest scene in the hospital was a room where a teenage girl lay in a bed festooned with ropes and pulleys to which her legs were attached. A Tibetan house physician said she came from a mountain village in the north-west. She had fallen from a rock and landed thirty feet below with both limbs smashed. She had undergone four operations during the past year. Her recovery would be slow but the orthopaedic surgeon was now sure she would walk normally again. Before surgery came to Tibet she would have been hopelessly crippled. A grey-haired peasant woman sitting by her bed was looking intently at the page of a book over which the girl was slowly moving a finger, and repeating letters after her. This was the patient's mother and her daughter was teaching her to read.

THE LITTLE WORLD OF DA CHUEN

For three weeks we travelled in the countryside. Choose one of a hundred villages in the Lhasa Valley to describe the lives of the peasants eleven years after the Chinese Communists came and you have described them all. We could visit any we liked for we had insisted that there should be no arranged journeys. We had a jeep, a driver and a Tibetan interpreter and each day we decided where we should go. We would drive off down a road or track not knowing where we might arrive until we saw a place which looked interesting. Then we went to it. This was how we found Tsai Gon Tang, which lies among fields of barley on the way to Chengtu in Szechuan nearly 1,500 miles away. Mountains crowned with perpetual snow look down on the roofs of squat mud-walled houses like those in which our Saxon for-bears lived.

We walked through a grove of trees (such as surround all Tibetan villages) and came to a beautiful ancient shrine in the shade of which a girl was playing with her baby. She introduced herself as Da Chuen, the wife of a local farmer. An older woman—she later told us she was fifty-one but like all middle-aged Tibetans looked ten years older—announced herself as Losang Wa Mo. A small boy and girl who were chasing a piglet round a pond were her grandchildren. We sat on a grassy bank out of the glare of the sun while they told us how they lived before the Han (Chinese) people came and how conditions had changed during the past three years since the Tibetan revolt and the flight of the Dalai Lama from Lhasa.

'Three years ago,' said Da Chuen, 'everyone here was a serf owned by the lord Guo Sang Tze. He lived in the city but I don't remember seeing him. His business was done by a bailiff. We had pieces of land. We didn't pay rent in cash, because we hadn't any to pay with, but gave up half or more of the crops to our owner. With what was left over we fed ourselves. If there wasn't enough the landlord didn't take less for himself but lent us the food we needed and we paid him interest by doing extra work for him. We were always in debt.'

But the Chinese had come to Tibet eleven years ago. Had they brought no changes? No, said Da Chuen, she and her neighbours hadn't noticed any, apart from the road from China to Lhasa which passed by Tsai Gon Tang. As far as they were concerned they continued to live as usual. Chinese soldiers came to put up telephone wires but they couldn't speak with them because they didn't talk the same language. They heard rumours that the Chinese had come to Tibet to liberate them from foreigners but they didn't know what foreigners were because they had never seen any so they didn't understand what this talk was about.

If they received no wages from the landlord, how could they clothe themselves?

Losang Wa Mo explained that most of the villagers had a few sheep which they bought with cash earned by collecting and selling firewood. They spun the wool for their own clothes. As long as they paid Guo Sang Tze's bailiff what he demanded they could do what they liked with the land excepting that he told them what crops they should grow and what animals they must raise.

Besides the accusations of the Dalai Lama against the Chinese, we had read Communist charges that before the serfs were freed after the 1959 rebellion, feudal lords had often treated them atrociously for not paying debts on time or being insufficiently subservient. Sometimes they were tortured and even killed. Had any inhabitants of Tsai Gon Tang suffered such punishments? Losang Wa Mo and Da Chuen had not heard of them.

They were poor, but so was everyone else. It was true they couldn't leave the land without the serf-owner's permission but they hadn't heard of anyone in the village who wanted to do so. Where would they go anyway? It was also true that they couldn't get married without his consent, and when they did their children were serfs who also belonged to the landlord. But it had always been like that in Tibet. No one had ever known any other kind of existence.

The Dalai Lama had written that before the Chinese Communists came, his people lived contentedly in their Buddhist faith without envy of others. We asked Da Chuen and Losang Wa Mo if they had envied the rich and those who weren't serfs. At first they didn't understand the question but when it was repeated laughed incredulously. Obviously we were joking. Losang Wa Mo snorted: 'Who wouldn't envy someone better off than himself? That's human nature. But a lord was a lord and a serf was a serf. That was how arrangements were made.'

Until 1959. What happened then?

Then, said Losang Wa Mo, the world turned upside down. There was fighting in Lhasa between some Tibetans and the Han people but they only heard about it later. Then Guo Sang Tze's bailiff wasn't seen in the village any more. Instead Chinese officials and soldiers came and told the people they were no longer serfs and that the land of the landlord belonged to them. All debts were abolished and the old land deeds were burnt.

After a while more officials came and there were meetings with the elders of the village. The land was split up, so much for this family and so much for another, according to how many mouths there were to feed.

So life was better since 1959? Now Losang Wa Mo was sure we were pulling her leg. The Chinese had told her they were Communists, but as far as she was concerned this meant that she was better off than she had been before. She could neither read nor write her own language so that Chinese pamphlets printed in Tibetan were no more than pieces of paper useful for lighting her stove fire until someone read them to her.

But what she could understand, and explained with a housewife's attention to practical detail, was that where before she and her husband had owned nothing they now possessed two yaks, one for milking and the other for work. Her family also kept more than two-thirds of the crops from the land which now belonged to them, although it was cultivated collectively by all the villagers, like all the rest. What they didn't need for themselves they sold to the government and so for the first time in their lives she and her husband had been able to provide small luxuries for their cottage, which had been given to them and for which they paid no rent. They and their two sons who were still at home had more to eat and better clothes to wear. This year, because of the worst rains for fifty years, the crops were poorer than usual but the local government had already explained that there would be an adjustment in the proportion to be given up as tax so that the peasants would receive as much for themselves as in 1961.

What kind of small luxuries were they now able to afford? Da Chuen took us to her home in a muddy courtyard where small ragged boys, dodging among the walls, pretended to shoot us with bows and arrows made with rough sticks. There were no windows in the tiny dark space which was kitchen, living-room and bedroom. A wood-fired stove was the only furniture on the earth floor excepting a wooden platform fixed to a wall which was the family bed. Cooking utensils hung on a wall but Da Chuen's pride and joy was a new butter-tea churn. She explained that when they were serfs most people couldn't make the tea properly. They would put a small lump of yak butter in a cup and stir it in. Now it could be properly mixed as it should be and the first article every family bought when they were able to earn enough money was such a churn. Carpenters had worked overtime to make them. During the past year they had also bought a Chinese vacuum flask so that her husband could take hot buttered tea to his work in the fields.

Da Chuen was twenty-two years old and if she had washed all over twenty-two times in her life she had been exceptionally fastidious. Her last bath certainly hadn't been this year, although the river flowed less than a quarter of a mile from her front door. If there were sharply defined distinctions between the social status of peasants and high lamas, it would require extra-sensory perception to distinguish the smell of one from another.

But if we were no longer astonished by the odours we were surprised to find people like Da Chuen and Losang Wa Mo bearing no resemblance to those described by Landon, who wrote of 'the slavish terror which is the whole attitude towards religion of the ignorant classes of the land'.

The villagers of Tsai Gon Tang seemed indifferent to the fate of a decaying temple, whose priest had gone off to get married. Perhaps they were relieved not to have to keep him. It was now occupied by a group of young Chinese and Tibetan agriculturists who were making a study of crop conditions in this part of the valley. But Da Chuen and her husband still put prayer flags over their house to ward off evil spirits. We felt this was more the precautionary equivalent of touching wood (or of some English Christians attending church at Easter and Christmas) than a conviction that if they didn't the roof would fall in. It won't occur to Losang Wa Mo's eldest grandchild, seven-year-old Gnu Zhu Wa Mo, who goes to the first elementary school the valley has ever known, that a piece of cotton possesses magical powers.

We had expected to find hospitals and schools in Tibet but now Da Chuen took us to see a new social service, the first old folks' home and orphanage in the country. Like others in the village, the cottages were dark, windowless, mud-walled, earth-floored rooms. An English farmer would be prosecuted for keeping a tuberculin-tested cow in one of them, but the aspect from their narrow front doors was delightful, for they were built round an old courtyard which had been transformed by the farmers into a garden filled with flowers. Incongruously, the ancient inhabitants, the oldest ninety-two, were dressed in rich colourful clothes of fine silk and costly brocade which the matron, a lively Tibetan peasant woman, told us were taken from the homes of the nobility who had joined the rebellion. It was rough justice, but still justice, she said, that those who had worked to provide the nobles with this splendid apparel should now be wearing it themselves.

The home, like the village school, was maintained by a fund provided by the sale of surplus farm produce. These services worked out at a few pence per head of the village population a month. A former lama who had left one of the smaller monasteries was the teacher. He was paid a small wage in cash but received his food and lodging for nothing. The matron, a widow with grown-up children able to fend for themselves, was employed on similar terms.

The Dalai Lama had written that before the Chinese came there was plenty of food for all and shortage was unknown, but since their arrival because vast quantities were requisitioned for the Army and the economy was disrupted, there had been famine for the first time. In the evening we discussed the situation with the local farmers. Losang Wa Mo's husband, who, like his father and grandfather before him, was born here, said it was true there was more than enough for everyone to eat before the Chinese came but the landlords and nobles, who with the monasteries owned all the land and those who worked it for them, got most of it. What was left for the peasants when they had paid taxes in the form of the produce they grew was not more than sufficient to keep a man fit for his job. The staple diet was tsampa which was good and nourishing but if he and his family got a piece or two of meat on festive occasions they counted themselves fortunate.

The Chinese Army, he said, had not taken an ear of barley from their fields. Far from it—they grew as much of their own food as they could on land which was allocated to them and obtained the rest from the surplus which was collected as tax. But since they were rice eaters and Tibet wasn't a rice-growing land they brought this from Szechuan and he had seen lorry loads of it coming up the new road from Chengtu.

When they were in a hurry to gather the harvest, as now, because so much had been ruined by rain and they were afraid of losing the rest, Chinese soldiers came to help the villagers and if we had gone into the surrounding fields earlier in the day we should have seen some of them reaping. If we returned tomorrow we should find some still there. There was no need for us to do so because during our talk, Chuang Wei, our assistant movie cameraman, who had gone off into the country to get some pastoral film shots, came to say he had taken scenes of the army helping the peasants to gather the barley. During the next few weeks we saw them wherever we went, harvesting for their own granaries and helping the civilian population wherever they needed extra labour.

But it was the condition of the army horses and mules which provided the most striking confirmation of the story we heard in Tsai Gon Tang. They were nearly all thin and underfed while those of the Tibetans, like the ponies we saw in the grasslands, were fat and sleek. We were so indignant at what we thought was neglect of these poor beasts that when we met the head of the Agriculture Department we complained that the Chinese should be ashamed of showing such indifference to the welfare of animals for which the Tibetans had high regard. The Director apologised and explained that the Army, which had some difficulty in feeding itself, was short of fodder for the horses and mules and since there was an order strictly forbidding them to take any from the inhabitants, they didn't get as much to eat as they should.

Apparently even Chinese Communist bureaucracy, which we had found was usually run with common-sense sympathy when dealing with human beings, could be stupid when it was concerned with animals. And this was all the more extraordinary in a country where religion forbade ill-treatment of a fly and where otherwise the Chinese had been overcautious in ensuring that they did not offend Buddhists by breaches of etiquette. For example we had been briefed on how to behave not only in temples but in the streets so that we shouldn't walk round a holy memorial in an anti-clockwise direction. In fact we walked everywhere without regard for conventions and no one paid the slightest attention. The Director solemnly promised to bring our complaint to the notice of the proper authorities. It struck us as comical that we had come 1,500 miles to see if human beings were being tortured to death and found the only complaint we could make was of the ill-treatment of Chinese Army horses and mules.

12

FACTS ABOUT FOOD

When the American Secretary of State, John Foster Dulles, announced to the world that the Communists had broken up Chinese families by imprisoning them in commune barracks where husbands and wives slept in separate dormitories and children were segregated in state nurseries, apparently it didn't occur to newspapers which reported him that it couldn't be true. For if it was the Chinese Government had succeeded in re-housing more than 600 million people in less than two years, which was something the American building industry—or, for that matter, the entire resources of all the building organisations in Europe as well—couldn't achieve. But perhaps unconsciously, like a person whose brain listens to a record while he is asleep, Mr. Dulles had learned from Dr. Goebbels, who organised the Nazi propaganda machine on the assumption that if you wish to convince people of untruth it must be so outrageous that it will stun hearers into a condition where they are incapable of questioning it.

After the Cuban crisis a United States Minister surprised the Press by stating that mis-statements of fact had been issued by the government. He insisted that the publication of what he described as 'managed' (or untrue) news was justified when it was in the interest of the State to lie.

Soon after the Chinese Communist troops entered Tibet the same newspapers were reporting that millions of Chinese civilians were streaming after them from starving China, their only luggage being empty rice bowls and chopsticks. It was not long before readers were told that Chinese refugees were eating Tibetans out of house and home and as a result there was famine in the land. As in the case of the commune barracks story, it didn't apparently occur to those who printed this new nonsense that it couldn't be true either. They had also forgotten that they had printed articles which proved it was impossible.[1]

The stories of starving Chinese peasants invading Tibet like locusts were printed at the same time as the news that after the crop failures of 1958, 1959 and 1960, hundreds of thousands of peasants who had gone to work in Chinese factories during the great 'industrial leap forward' were being sent back to the land to produce more food. This was true and the Peking Government made no secret of it. On the contrary it announced that in this emergency the industrial programme must be cut back and it was now urgently necessary for hundreds of thousands of farm workers to return from the towns to the land. It couldn't at the same time be true that millions of peasants who were desperately needed to grow more food in China were being sent into Tibet to search for rice, which didn't grow there anyway. But the journalists, who couldn't remember, or apparently didn't care, how they contradicted themselves from one day to another, also displayed remarkable ignorance of Chinese and Tibetan geography and elementary facts about populations.

There has been no reliable census but for administrative purposes the Chinese estimate the number of people in Tibet to be about a million and a quarter. The Tibetans, who have lived for generations in the provinces of Sinkiang, Kansu, Chinghai, Szechuan and Yünnan number about two million. So again, if it is true that millions of Chinese are emigrating from China proper, their behaviour is inexplicable for while they wander hundreds of miles over the bleak inhospitable Chinghai plateau into the eastern marches of Tibet where nothing grows but grass for yaks and sheep, they are leaving hundreds of thousands of Tibetans behind them in Sinkiang, Kansu and the farming areas of lower Chinghai to eat the food that is growing there.

The only other way into Tibet is by the road running from Chengtu, the capital city of Szechuan, which is so rich in varied crops yielding two harvests a year, that it is known as the heavenly country. Apart from the fact that, like other farming areas of China, Szechuan now needs all the hands it can get to increase its already abundant production for export to more needy areas, it makes no sense to suppose that those who are fortunate enough to live in this fertile country would find any reason for walking a thousand miles over

1. Most of the journalists who were knocked silly by Mr. Dulles' propaganda hammer are presumably still unconscious for in May 1963 Mr. Mervyn Jones, who visited China as a tourist and reported his impressions in the *Observer* found it necessary to inform his readers that as far as he could discover the story of commune barracks wasn't true.

15,000-foot mountain passes into Tibet where there is nowhere to live and no food for them to eat.

We saw no signs of a mass invasion of the country by civilian Chinese. Lhasa is a garrison town and, apart from the western frontiers with India, the greatest concentration of troops is in this district. We saw more soldiers working as farmers than drilling and marching.

Mr. Wang Yuen-hsiang, Director of the Tibetan State Bureau of Agriculture and Animal Husbandry, impressed us as an administrator who would have been capable of high responsibility in the civil service of any country. As the senior official responsible for the organisation of food production, it was necessary for him to know how many mouths there were to feed. He told us that the total number of Chinese civilians in Tibet including women and children was about 40,000. It was not expected that this would increase very much because a great many were technical experts of all kinds, administrators, teachers, medical people and others whose skill and knowledge were also badly needed in China proper.

Mr. Wang didn't pretend that he had an easy task and was candid in confessing that some attempts to increase food production in the country had already failed because even with the most persuasive propaganda it had been impossible to induce peasants, bound by centuries of traditional farming in which, as serfs, they had not been encouraged to exercise initiative, to accept improved methods of cultivation.

This season had been the rainiest for fifty years. When we questioned the accuracy of this estimate, because obviously there had been no meteorological service in Tibet to keep rainfall records, Mr. Wang smiled appreciatively. 'You are quite right but I hope you don't think I'm starting by making political excuses for an unsatisfactory harvest. We only know this because the older inhabitants tell us so and farmers have reliable memories about weather.

'As a result of the rain there will be a food shortage this winter and we have already arranged to distribute twenty million catties of grain to the people. Some of this will come from the interior and the rest from stores confiscated from the granaries of landlords who took part in the rebellion, which have been kept as reserve.

'This was available because before the liberation of the land and serfs, the landlords took as much as five-sixths of the crops as rent. So in normal years peasants lived on a bare subsistence level. In 1961 we harvested 450 million catties of barley, which is the staple diet, and this year hoped for a 5 per cent increase. The weather has frustrated us and we shall not get it. But with the stocks in the landlords' granaries and a subsidy from the interior to make up the balance, no one will receive less food than last year and there will be no necessity for general rationing. The only people on rations now are Chinese and Tibetan cadres. Army horses and mules (as you have seen for yourself) are also rationed but the animals of Tibetans are not.

'We have no reliable statistics of agricultural production before 1959 because we didn't control farming but there has been a steady increase since then. Barley crops in 1959 totalled 350 million catties and in 1960 420 million.

'Tibetans are poor but the country is potentially immensely rich. Production was low because serf labour is inefficient and the methods of cultivation were antique. As you have seen, the wooden ploughs still in general use and the loose-headed wooden flails for threshing are the same as those employed in the European Middle Ages. When the feudal land system was abolished in 1959 we distributed more than a thousand improved deeper-cutting ploughs to peasants but they aren't used to them and haven't taken to them. Twice we have started agricultural training classes but have had to suspend them because the great majority of the peasants who attended them couldn't read. Now we rely more on practical demonstrations but we are short of skilled instructors and progress is slow.'

Seventy per cent of the area in Tibet which can be farmed is grassland. Only 25 per cent is devoted to grain and vegetable crops. The rest is mountains. But now that food can be more equally distri- buted the protein diet of the people can be increased. Yak beef can be of excellent quality and as palatable as Aberdeen Angus steak when it is properly cooked. There is also no shortage of mutton. In 1959 there were ten million head of sheep and yak and a million and a half more in 1961. It was hoped that there might be a 5 per cent increase in 1962, but the grass was poorer than in previous years and this was now un- likely to be realised. As with grain and meat, there had been no accurate statistics of butter production but it was estimated that twenty million catties had been made in 1961. As far as could be ascertained this was less that in 1960 and 1959, the reason for the reduction being that after livestock was distributed to the peasants, they concentrated on breeding to increase their own herds instead of producing milk which had formerly been taken by their landlords.

Again, it wasn't known exactly how much edible butter had been used as religious offerings but from estimates made in monasteries all over Tibet it was probable that at least a third of the national pro- duction had been burned every year and certainly a quarter of this nutritious food supply was still going up in flames before Buddhist

altars. Since this was the custom of the country and the peasants were
now under no sort of compulsion to give it but offered it freely, the
government had not interfered. But as head of the agricultural services
it obviously pained the atheist Mr. Wang to think of all those needed
calories flickering away in thousands of shrines.

As in the rest of China, there is an acute shortage of tractors and
other powered implements in Tibet. There are none on peasant holdings
and only a score or so on experimental state farms which have been
established to study crop production and animal breeding. Unlike the
interior of China where there is little animal manure and in the
absence of an adequate artificial fertilizer industry the farmer must
rely on human excreta to feed his fields, there is no shortage in Tibet.
Here, also, between 60 and 70 per cent of arable areas can be irrigated
by river water. The temperatures in the valleys are not extreme and
the sunlight at high altitudes promotes abundant growth. When there
is no prolonged drought or excessive flooding it is good farming
country. Tibet was backward only because the social system before
1959 made progress impossible and, from the feudal lords' point of
view, undesirable.

Seven hundred thousand of the estimated population of a million
and a quarter were serfs. More than one man in every four was a monk.
There were perhaps 10,000 'middle-class' families of merchants, shop-
keepers, small traders, pedlars and the like, and artisans. The remainder
were beggars.

Theoretically all the land was owned by the state. In fact it was
owned by about 200 noble families, the monasteries and the local
governments of the Dalai and Panchen Lamas. A small minority
of people were slaves. They had no rights and owned nothing. They
were usually household servants. Their descendants were born into
slavery, from which there was no escape.

Serfs were permitted to cultivate the land of their feudal owners,
in return for *Ula* which was labour and services. In addition, they had
to give service for their lords without payment. They could be called
on to provide fuel and water, to repair or build houses or barns, etc.
They must also furnish transport—animals and men to look after
them—for their lords and for anyone holding a government order
entitling him to this free privilege.

Since Buddhism forbade the ill-treatment of any living creature it
was theoretically forbidden to inflict physical punishment on human
beings. In fact, the feudal lords, including the rulers of the monasteries,
made their own laws to suit their convenience. They could, and sometimes did, inflict atrocious punishments on runaway serfs who fled

from manors because they couldn't pay interest on debts, or because of ill-treatment by a brutal or particularly rapacious bailiff. In some cases they were killed or died of their injuries.

While the landlords contributed to the maintenance of the government by taxes, they saw to it that they did not suffer any decrease in their own standards of living, however heavy the demands which might be made on them. Tribute from serfs was fixed according to landlords' needs and unless there was a disastrous harvest due to natural calamity it remained as constant as they cared to make it. Whatever the crop yield the serf must pay his dues. If he was unable to give up the demanded proportion of food without starving himself and his family, then he had to borrow back what he needed at interest which might amount to 50 per cent. He might also have to borrow seed for next season's crop.

As in former days in China, where peasant families, even in such a rich province as Szechuan, were never out of debt to their landlords and passed this burden on to their children and grandchildren, many Tibetan serfs were likewise permanently enslaved.

13

THE STORY OF
TSEREH WANG TUEI

If a serf was injured or ill, or for any other reason could not farm his land, it was distributed for other serf families to work. If he ran away from his lord's estate he became 'duichun', a masterless or 'black' man. He was an outlaw and anyone harbouring him could be severely punished.

The cruelty and rapacity of some landlords may have been exaggerated by the Chinese Communists. Obviously there were many who, while they saw no evil in a system which was in itself cruel and unjust, were not personally malicious and had pity on the condition of their people so that they would not treat them with the brutality which propaganda sometimes ascribes to all serf-owners. Nor, horrible as they were, could some of the punishments be seen out of the context of the society in which, until a few years ago, all Tibetans lived.

We are now revolted by descriptions of medieval, and much later tortures suffered by civilised Europeans, although apparently only by the thought that men could be found to inflict them with their bare hands. Our bowels of compassion are not so physically moved by the thought of Japanese children flayed by atomic fire lit by pressing a button in the sky. The highly cultivated St. Thomas More was prepared to die for a religious principle but as a judge he made no complaint against the savage punishments and tortures of his day.

It is futile to deny that some Tibetan customs were barbarous and that the treatment of serfs (apart from their subjection to a system which kept them in needless poverty and humiliation) and others who offended against the 'law', was frequently abominable. To pretend, as the Dalai Lama and other self-exiled ecclesiastical and lay lords pretend,

Travelling lama

We met this old woman walking round a chorten in a country road, saying her devotions with her prayer wheel and with her pet puppy trotting at her heels

Tibetan schoolgirls wearing Pioneer—Communist youth movement— scarves

that before the Chinese came Tibet was an ideal society in which the people lived content with their religion and their lot is to defend a serf system as an ideal state just because this also happened to be a religious one. Chesterton and Belloc romanticised feudal Europe on the ground that as long as serfs were sure that God was in his heaven they were content to leave it to their temporal and ecclesiastical lords to arrange their lives for them on earth, as it suited their convenience. No serious historian, Catholic or otherwise, believes this.

All the colourful religious trappings of medieval Europe still exist in Tibet—the great churches with their splendid gold and jewelled shrines and gorgeous draperies. Only the great lords and their ladies, who when they appeared with their retinues of servants must have given Lhasa the appearance of a pageant, have departed. But the inheritance of poverty and ignorance remains. It requires no Communist propaganda, only a talk with a former serf, to convince one that serfdom isn't a desirable condition in a religious or any other kind of state. If we had asked to meet a dozen Tibetans who had been mutilated by their masters we should have been confronted with a dozen. But one was enough.

Tsereh Wang Tuei had the tall lithe body of an athlete but where his eyes should have been were two sore holes and one hand was a twisted claw. Without emotion he told us that he was born a serf of Drepung in the village of Peichang, on the edge of the grasslands where we met him. He became a herdsman, looking after sheep and yaks. When he was twenty years old he stole two sheep belonging to a petty official of the monastery, named Gambo. For this crime he was taken before the monastic magistrate who ordered that both his eyes should be put out.

Tsereh Wang Tuei drew his hand across his face as he described how one was gouged with a knife and the other sucked from its socket with a half-hollowed ball. Then adding a little private punishment of his own, Gambo instructed the 'executioner' to tie up Tsereh's left hand with rope and twist and pull it until parts of two fingers came off. To complete the torture, the bleeding hand was wrapped in salted yak hide. When the leather had shrunk it was permitted to be removed. What was left was a useless piece of flesh and crushed bone.

We asked Tsereh Wang Tuei, 'Are you a Buddhist?'

'I was,' he said.

'But not now?'

'No,' he replied. 'When a holy lama told them to blind me I thought there was no good in religion.'

H

When he was twenty-nine he married a widow and they now have two sons and a daughter. When the serfs of Drepung were freed, Tsereh Wang Tuei was given three yaks and a cow. He now works softening hides which he can do at home and his wife helps him and looks after their animals, which include some chickens and pigs. He also receives a disabled man's pension of a few shillings a month from the new local government.

There was an amusing sequel to this sad meeting when we went to the court of the Chief Justice. We expected to find an elderly gentleman surrounded by functionaries of the law. Instead we were greeted by a grave-faced young man of thirty-five wearing a plain grey suit, sitting in a small plainly furnished whitewashed office.

We didn't tell him we had met Tsereh Wang Tuei but I asked him, 'What punishment would you order me if you found me guilty of stealing two sheep?'

Taken aback by this unusual introduction, or perhaps imagining that my brain had been affected by the altitude, he decided to humour me and asked quietly, 'When did you steal two sheep?'

'I haven't stolen any,' I said, 'but I want to know my punishment if I do.'

'I can't tell you that,' said the Chief Justice, 'unless you tell me why you steal sheep. I can't make a judgment without knowing the facts and before I sentenced you—if you were a thief—I should have to know why you did such a thing. Were you in your right mind for example?' He looked at me with amused solemnity. 'Or perhaps you were hungry and took them on the spur of the moment without really thinking what you were doing. Or were these the first sheep you stole? Had you made a habit of stealing? You would have to explain these things to me.'

'But supposing,' I retorted, 'that I didn't want to tell you why I had done it. After all, some criminals won't say why they have committed offences. Let us suppose I plead guilty. I have a right to know what my sentence is. There must be a sentence for stealing two sheep.'

'No, there isn't,' replied the Chief Justice. 'As I have told you it would all depend on the circumstances. For example, if you were an old thief, then some way would have to be found to try to reform you. If you stole because you were hungry then I should want to know why you hadn't enough to eat. If you did it on impulse and it was your first offence and you said you were sorry I might not sentence you to anything.'

'You mean to say,' I protested, 'that you haven't a simple way of punishing people for such simple offences. Have you no legal code?'

'If you put it like that,' said the Chief Justice, 'we haven't.'

'Not even for murder?' I asked.

'We haven't had a murder since I became Chief Justice,' he answered.

'All right,' I gave in. 'I took the sheep because I was hungry and on an impulse and I'm sorry.'

'Then,' said the Judge, 'I shall not give you any punishment but order an inquiry as to why you haven't enough to eat. Unless you are lazy someone must be responsible.'

'Now,' I said, 'supposing I have stolen before and am quite unrepentant. In other words I'm a bad lot.'

The Chief Justice thought for a moment. 'In that case,' he said, 'I might consider sentencing you to work for six months on the land for the people as retribution.' Then he added hastily, as though afraid that he might have given the first foreigner he had met too harsh an impression of new Tibetan justice: 'After all you did say you weren't sorry. But there might be mitigating circumstances. You might be stubborn through bad temper and be really sorry despite your protests that you weren't. That could make a difference. You are hurrying me now to make a judgment about a theoretical case without hearing any evidence. But in an actual case of course I shouldn't permit myself to be hurried.' He looked at me with an inquisitive smile. 'May I ask why you choose two theoretical sheep to steal?'

Then I told him the story of Tsereh Wang Tuei. 'I just wanted to find out,' I said, 'the difference between being judged by a religious Tibetan magistrate and an unreligious one.'

The Chief Justice had a sense of humour. 'Well,' he said, 'you are forgetting one difference. The sheep in the case of Tsereh Wang Tuei were owned by the monastery and so the magistrate had a personal interest in the judgment. I don't own the animals you propose to steal.'

Then what crimes worried him and his fellow judges?

'I suppose,' he replied, 'that you may think I am introducing politics into the discussion, but usually when people don't need to commit crime they don't do so unless there are some peculiar personal reasons. The most common offences here used to be pocket-picking and then there was some bicycle stealing when bicycles were first imported. Perhaps those who took them just thought they would like a bicycle. But seriously, Tibetans have usually been law-abiding people. There were those who stole cattle. This was a popular custom amongst some nomads and there was some robbing of travellers in the wild countryside. But generally speaking there wasn't much of what you might call private crime. So the punishment of serfs had nothing to do with what you might call ordinary justice. Their owners could decide when they had offended against their interests and treat them according to their whims. In fact the nobles on their own estates and the monasteries were laws unto themselves. There were no state courts or judiciary as we understand them.'

The Chief Justice explained that a new legal code and administrative system was being worked out for Tibet. Bearing no relation to actual conditions, feudal justice could no longer be successfully applied in a country which had ceased to be feudal.

Generally speaking, feudalism ended with the liberation of the serfs when their owners also forfeited their rights and lands. Monastic courts had been abolished. But although social and economic feudalism had disappeared, feudal customs remained. So it was also practically impossible to apply in Tibet the legal code which guided judges and magistrates in all the rest of China.

For example, only monogamous marriage was permitted in the interior but in Tibet, polyandry and polygyny had been practised for generations. It would be undesirable, as well as unjust, to break up families which had been created according to ancient usage. Their members had committed no offence. The proper way to deal with this situation said the Chief Justice was to introduce new laws which would not affect the condition of those living according to old custom but make it an offence for it to be followed in future. But it might also be unnecessary to deal with the matter by law at all.

The basis of polyandry and polygyny was economic. A brother married with several sisters or a woman married with several brothers in order to keep land held under a landlord within a family. With an entirely different system of land ownership, the necessity for this kind of arrangement had ceased to exist and the custom could disappear within a generation without government interference. It wasn't a serious problem and it didn't matter if it took a long time to consider how best to deal with it. So, the new marriage laws introduced into China by the Communists, and designed to protect the family, safeguard the welfare of children and give equality to women, haven't yet reached Lhasa.

There are urgent problems in China, some of them created by mistakes in government policy which require urgent government intervention. This brings inevitable discomfort, inconvenience and some suffering to those whose lives have been disarranged.

This was to be seen at Lanchow railway station, where, in the middle of the night, we had found peasants being returned to the land from the factories after the industrial programme had been set back by the necessity to grow more food. It is true that the peasants had contributed to their own misfortune by exaggerating, in their enthusiasm, the bumper harvest of 1958. But local Communist cadres had undoubtedly encouraged them to do so. The government was responsible for accepting the figures of grain production too readily, even after allowances (which proved to be inadequate) for exaggerations had been made.

The government was also entirely to blame for acting on the incredible assumption that good farming weather would continue in future years and pushing forward the 'great leap forward' in industry which depended on a succession of bumper harvests. But however great this blunder, it was not followed by another which would have been far worse—the exploitation of food shortages and the creation of black markets. Whatever the failures, inflation had not been one of them, let alone the catastrophic collapses of the currency which brought ruin and hunger to millions in the last days of Chiang Kai-shek.

Here in Tibet, wherever the situation permitted unhurried solutions of problems, the government, perhaps having learned from mistakes elsewhere, preferred them. The introduction of new laws and the administration of justice was an example.

We asked the Chief Justice if he was a 'qualified' lawyer. As soon as we asked the question, we realised it was a stupid one. For as a Tibetan, if he had been trained in the law which was no longer applicable, his experience would have been useless. No, he told us, he had studied law in a Chinese university to give him a background to the administration and dispensation of justice. He was now gaining practical experience with his brother judges and magistrates in dealing with cases which came before them. With the reorganisation of the economic system there were none of the complicated civil suits dealing with property and land settlements which formerly occupied the Tibetan courts. Simple crime could be dealt with on a common-sense basis as could matrimonial problems. The Chinese legal code is being applied in Tibet wherever it is practicable. Except in cases of treason, capital punishment has been abolished—in fact, not just in Buddhist theory. Mutilations, such as blinding and the crippling of limbs, are forbidden. Monks can no longer be physically punished for disobeying monastic or religious rules, or offending their superiors.

The Chinese have trained a Tibetan force of civilian police who control traffic and generally do the work of a constabulary in England. They are under the control of city and local councils. Lhasa is a garrison town but the Army is not directly concerned with civil affairs.

14

THE DIVINE INVENTION

God-kings in Tibet are a comparatively new invention.

Buddhism did not appear in Lhasa until the seventh century when Songsten Gambo—'I, the barbarous King of Tibet'—married two Buddhist women—a Princess of Nepal and the Princess Wen Cheng of China.

It was not until the thirteenth century that the Emperor Kublai Khan created the first Grand Lama the 'pope' of Tibet. But the people had to wait another 300 years before his successor decided that he was also a god.

In 1622 the Abbot of Gaden installed a seven-year-old boy, Nag-wan Lo-zan of Drepung Monastery, as Grand Lama. When he was twenty-five, this ambitious young man invited the Mongol Prince Gusri Khan, from Kokonor in Chinghai, to invade Tibet and make a present of it to him. With this gift Nag-wan Lo-zan accepted the title of Dalai (The Ocean) Lama and in 1650 the Emperor of China confirmed his title. He has become known as the 'Great Fifth'. In fact he was the first of the Dalai Lamas.

But to be the temporal ruler of Tibet by consent of the Chinese Emperor was still to be a man and human authority could be disputed and overthrown. Nag-wan Lo-zan therefore thought it expedient to announce that he was the first incarnation of the Buddhist deity Avalokita (known to Tibetans as Chenrezi), and on the red hill above the city of Lhasa he built the Potala Palace, naming it after the legendary home of Avalokita in India. He seized monasteries which did not belong to his own sect—the Ge-lug-pa—and compelled them to accept its disciplines. He is believed to have destroyed Buddhist writings which conflicted with his claim to divinity. Before Nag-wan Lo-zan invented his own celestial origin, there was no record of any Grand Lama claiming to be a god. But it was not long before he created another and established the divine succession in the Buddhist Church.

Now this Living Buddha, 'Precious Protector', 'The Presence', the 'Inmost One', who according to his religion had achieved perfection in his previous life, removed all those whom he feared might threaten his omnipotence. He was described by John Grueber, an Austrian Jesuit who visited Lhasa during his reign and is believed to have been the first European to visit Tibet, as the 'devilish god the father who puts to death such as refuse to adore him'.

None dare deny him for as both god and temporal king he could not only reward or punish his subjects in this world but influence their treatment after death.

Forty years after Nag-wan Lo-zan's accession, the Abbot who installed him at Drepung died and the Dalai Lama, who had regarded himself as the old monk's spiritual son, announced that he had been reborn. The child in whose body he was said to have reappeared on earth was declared to be an incarnation of Amitabha (to Tibetans, Opame) the Buddha of Boundless Light who was the spiritual father of Avalokita (or Chenrezi). This child was the first Panchen Lama.

His creation has caused embarrassment ever since when there has been disagreement between these two divine incarnations and never more so than in 1959 when the fourteenth Dalai Lama fled to India and the tenth Panchen remained, on this occasion to take his place as Acting Chairman of the Provisional Government. For while Dalai Lamas have usually, but not always, exercised the greater temporal power, it has also been claimed for them that they are the senior spiritual rulers of the Church. But in his anxiety to honour his old mentor—and incidentally strengthen the Lamaist hierarchy—the 'Great Fifth' presumably did not foresee the disputes which might arise over his pre-eminence in his future incarnations. As the divine Avalokita, he had acknowledged that the Panchen Lama he had himself created was Amitabha, his spiritual father who, it could now be argued, was a higher incarnation than himself, since a father is senior to a son.

Theologically, however, this has not worried the doctors of the Tibetan Church who regard both incarnations as an indistinguishable duality—two in one and one in two, who are essentially the same but different manifestations of eternal truth.

Their politically conflicting interests have been exploited by the British, who sought to favour one or the other when it suited their interests, as well as by Chinese rulers who have been concerned to maintain a balance of power between the leaders of the Tibetan Church so that their authority in the country would not be impaired by the political ascendancy of either. From time to time, both Dalai and Panchen Lamas have popped in and out of the country like jacks-in-

Tibetan shopkeeper with his family. The bundles in the can on the left are incense sticks which customers buy to burn before temple gods. On the wall and on the right are prayer sheets for sale

Tibetan hat fashion—Plantagenet style

OPPOSITE

above: Herdsmen from the grasslands

below: Yaks in Lhasa market place

Ngapo Ngawang Jigme, former member of Fourteenth Dalai Lama's Cabinet, Commander-in-Chief of the Tibetan Army; now Secretary-General of the Provisional Government of Tibet, with his wife and the youngest of their twelve children

boxes when one has threatened the other through his supporting factions.

So, when we discussed the flight of the fourteenth Incarnation with lamas of the great monasteries and one of the most eminent theologians in the country, they expressed regret that he had been persuaded, or persuaded himself, to leave Tibet but did not speak of his departure as an astonishing or outrageous event. They were used to this kind of thing.

There are some who in attempts to discredit the Panchen since the flight of the Dalai Lama argue that he can only be true to his nature if he devotes himself entirely to spiritual affairs and eschews all concern for the material world. If he interferes in material matters, i.e. approves of reforms introduced by the materialistic Communists, the validity of his incarnation as a god may be questioned. On the other hand the Dalai Lama is being true to his godlike nature when he is also occupied with material problems.

This is not only comical Tibetan Buddhist theology but pre-posterous history. It would be difficult to imagine a more ludicrous spectacle than rationalists seeking to prove that a myth is a reality as long as he is on their side and that he is an illusion if he is on the other.

It should have occurred to such political historians to ask themselves why if the Panchen Lama has now forfeited his 'divinity' because he is engaged in material pursuits, his previous bodies did not forfeit it long ago, since he has been a land- and serf-owner, ruling as a temporal lord over vast estates, for more than 300 years.

It has been possible to present the 'invasion' of Tibet by the Chinese, not only as a political outrage and brutal suppression of one sovereign state by another but as a sacriligious act because a god has been de-throned. And now, it is said, his spiritual kingdom is being destroyed by the desecration of temples and the torture and murder of its priests and people. It is assumed that if the fourteenth Dalai Lama had not fled from Lhasa when he did, the Chinese would have imprisoned or killed him.

But he did not have to wait for the Chinese to come to be done to death. He has been murdered time and again in his previous bodies by Tibetan priest-statesmen who owed him worship and strangled or poisoned him, sometimes when he was a child, sometimes when he was a man, but always when he stood in their way to power.

According to legend there had been four Dalai Lamas before the 'Great Fifth', but in fact he was the first created by himself and the 'god' who is now regarded as his sixth incarnation was, in fact, his second. The present incarnation according to this succession is not the four-

teenth appearance of Avalokita (or Chenrezi) on earth but the tenth.
However, since they derive from the invention of Nag-wan Lo-zan,
the numbering of the reigns is of no importance excepting for those
who are concerned to sustain a myth.

The Dalai Lama loved by the Tibetans for his personal attractions
was the sixth (in fact the second) who was also the first believed to
have been murdered by his own priests. He rebelled against the discipline of celibacy and scandalised the 'establishment' by his dissolute
life. He had many mistresses and stole from the Potala in disguise to
make merry with convivial friends. He also brought them to the palace
where the presence of women in the sacred apartments was forbidden.
He wrote erotic poetry which is still read with delight. If he had to be
an incarnate god, he preferred to be a Tibetan Pan rather than an
Indian ascetic. But since a god couldn't be allowed to be a human
being without destroying the illusion on which Tibetan society was
built, it was necessary to destroy him. He was imprisoned and no more
was heard of him. Since another incarnation could not logically appear
while his predecessor was alive, it is presumed that he was killed. But
then, apparently, it occurred to those who deposed him that mortal
men could not destroy an immortal deity so they were compelled to
pretend that he had not really been a genuine god at all.

The Tartar King, Ginkir Khan, appointed a lama, Ngwan Yeshe
Gya-mtso, to take his place and the sorcerers and oracles announced
that only the breath, but not the soul, of the dead god-king had passed
into his body. Then it appears they had second thoughts. Perhaps the
faithful wouldn't be convinced by such a specious explanation. At
any rate before long it was proclaimed that the soul of the licentious poet had been reborn in the child of a monk of Drepung
Monastery.

However the god-makers still hadn't reckoned with the Chinese
Emperor who had approved the Dalai Lama chosen by the Tartar King
and now imprisoned the little son of the Drepung monk. Then he
changed his mind, released him and put him in the Potala. But eight
years later, in 1728, he was deposed again on suspicion of being an
accomplice to the murder of the King of Tibet, although as a minor,
he could hardly have played a responsible part in palace politics. Now
another Lama was put in his place. He didn't last long either and the
deposed boy was restored. In 1749 the Chinese put to death his Regent,
who ruled during his minority, and the Tibetans rose and massacred
his killers.

The first Dalai Lama to be seen by an Englishman was the ninth.
Thomas Manning who went to Lhasa in 1811 described him as 'poeti-

cally and affectingly beautiful'. A few years later this boy was also murdered, it is believed, by his Regent. In his next incarnation he was once more assassinated, probably again by the Regent, who was arrested on suspicion, deposed and banished by the Chinese.

The god-king fared no better in his next reappearance in the world. His lama Regent killed him before he was eighteen years old.

In the middle of the nineteenth century surveyors were sent into Tibet by the British Indian Government, posing as travellers. One of them saw the new incarnation (the eighth or twelfth by whichever reckoning one cares to choose) of the Dalai Lama and described him as a 'fair handsome boy' of twelve or thirteen. This meeting took place in 1866. Eight years later, when the god was twenty-four he died. It was believed that he was poisoned by his former Regent.

So within 170 years five Dalai Lamas had been put to death. It is perhaps not surprising that those who apparently persuaded the fourteenth Incarnation that his life was in danger in 1959, feared that the Chinese Communists who did not believe in human divinities would not hesitate to kill one who politically opposed them. The murder of gods was a well-established political tradition in the great lamaseries.

It is also understandable that those who see in Tibetan Buddhism a gentle philosophy of tolerance and Dalai Lamas as a succession of Tibetan Albert Schweitzers dedicated to 'reverence for life', should find tragedy in the despoliation of this ideal by Communists dedicated to materialism. But this imagined religion had nothing to do with that which was preached on the roof of the world.

If sometimes life was not as depressing as the Communists say it was and all feudal lords were not barbarous oppressors of their serfs, Tibet did not convey the impression of contentment (which the fourteenth Dalai Lama would have us believe was enjoyed by all his people) to those who visited the country before the first Chinese who was to become a Communist was out of school. Dr. A. L. Waddell, Chief Medical Officer with the Younghusband Expedition and author of the classic[1], who would almost certainly have abhorred Marxism, looked forward to the day when the people would be freed from the 'intolerable tyranny of monks' and the devils they had invented to terrorise the people.

Perceval Landon who went with the doctor to Lhasa in 1904 described the Lamaism he found to be 'an engine of oppression', 'a barrier to all human improvement', 'a living type of all that we in the

1. *The Buddhism of Tibet or Lamaism* (W. Heffer & Sons, Cambridge).

West have fought against and at last overcome, of bigotry, cruelty and slavery'.

Captain W. F. T. O'Connor, secretary and interpreter of the Younghusband Expedition, like Landon, was a member of a society in which the sharp distinctions in Britain between the higher and lower orders were then only slowly becoming blurred. So while he was offended by the deplorable condition of the common people of Tibet, he could compare their situation favourably with the poverty of Irish peasants, without expressing any contrition for England's responsibility in Ireland. At the same time, blithely disregarding events which had brought him and his companions to Lhasa, he found the most deplorable aspect of Tibetans' ignorance was their folly in declaring war 'upon the greatest power of the modern world with no better means of manufacturing arms than a hand-power wheel and a forge for an arsenal under the superintendence of one Mohammedan blacksmith'. He found the stubborn resistance of the poor peasants to the British invasion 'almost pathetic'.

He concluded that, on the whole, the country was well governed and the people well treated, although, he added, 'they are not, it is true, allowed to take any liberties or to infringe the orders of their superiors, but as long as they confine themselves to their legitimate sphere of action (*as serfs*)[1] and, above all, abstain from political offences (*from protesting against their serfdom*)[1] their lives are lived happily and simply enough in a patriarchal sort of way'.

He found no contradiction with this opinion in his discovery that Tibet was governed by two classes, 'the great landowners and the priests, which exercise each in their own dominion a despotic power from which there is no appeal'. Nor in the 'extraordinary spectacle of a simple agricultural people, superstitious indeed to the last degree, but devoid of any deep-rooted religious convictions or heart searchings, oppressed by the most monstrous growth of monasticism and priestcraft the world has ever seen'.

These rulers, said O'Connor, like some of those in the European Middle Ages had 'forged innumerable weapons of servitude, invented degrading legends and stimulated a spirit of superstition'.

More than 100,000 monks—'a host of ignorant pretentious sluggards' —were maintained in idleness by their serfs who farmed their monastic estates.

But besides what O'Connor indulgently described as this more legitimate source of livelihood, 'the monks obtain yearly large sums

1. Authors' italics.

both in cash and kind in return for their religious offices at births, deaths, marriages and festivals. The extent of these squeezes is only limited by the degree of the priestly rapacity and the poverty of the victim.'

To comprehend the extent to which the monasteries bled the country, he continued, it was only necessary to enter one of the larger lamaseries and to mark the extraordinary contrast at once presented by its huge solid buildings and rich trappings as compared with the houses of even well-to-do people in the neighbourhood.

Dr. Waddell's account of Tibetan Buddhism was published in 1895. Landon and O'Connor wrote the story of their journey to Lhasa in 1905. The life and conditions they described remained the same until 1951 when the Chinese Communists came to Tibet. There were no radical changes until 1959, when the fourteenth Dalai Lama and those who had taken part in the rebellion fled to exile. The Chinese, with those Tibetan ecclesiastical and lay lords who supported them, had up to that time brought about some reforms by persuasion. For example, interest rates were reduced, hospitals and schools were built and roads were made so that for the first time it was possible to bring motor transport into the country. But there was no social, economic or religious revolution until after 1959. By 1962, when we arrived, progress was gathering speed but we found a country which bore all the marks of a society which had stood still for centuries.

Apart from the fact that monks have no longer any secular authority over the people and their numbers in monasteries have been greatly reduced since they have been free to stay or leave, the Buddhist religion remains as it was.

Thirty-two years after Landon, Waddell and O'Connor described their experiences, Spencer Chapman wrote:

'The Lamaist monk does not spend his time in ministering to the people or educating them, nor do laymen take part in or even attend the monastery services. The beggar beside the road is nothing to the monk. Knowledge is the jealously guarded prerogative of the monasteries and is used to increase their influence and wealth.'

This traveller discovered a social system 'rife with bribery' and so ingrained that it was an inseparable part of it. Lamaism, he wrote, had 'in many ways reverted to an earlier form in which half the population lived parasitically on the working laymen who had little hope of salvation'.

Mr. Chapman described monks from Drepung as 'unwashed insolent parasites', adding, 'never have I seen a more evil-looking crowd'. Occasionally, he said, a monk gazed at him with 'sullen malevolence, perhaps realising that we [the British Mission] represent progress and that progress spells the end of the unquestioned and unquestioning power of Lamaism'.

The people are no longer victims of priestly rapacity but those willing to listen are still told that there are twenty-eight heavens of varying sorts which are situated some 168,000 miles above the realms of the ungodly spirits who are in eternal conflict with the gods. There are also 136 hot hells ranged in tiers. The topmost is at a depth of 11,900 miles below the earth's surface. The one at the bottom is 40,000 miles down.

Dr. Waddell pointed out that the more philosophical lamas believed that the atrocious torments suffered by the damned were morbid creations of people's imaginations, but the majority and the laity were convinced that they were actual material places to which they might be condemned.

Not unnaturally perhaps, the most severe punishment is reserved for those who have reviled the Buddha, harmed or attempted to harm Lamaism or shed the blood of a lama or holy man. They are confined in perpetual flame but their bodies are never consumed. Heretics who question the religion defined by lamas are cooked in cauldrons of molten iron.

But if you don't catch it hot you catch it cold, for there are also eight hells in which victims are permanently immersed in ice-cold water. If a sinner escapes these horrors he can hardly miss one of 84,000 other hells where there are varying degrees of suffering. If he isn't good enough to go to a heaven or bad enough for a hell he may become a ghost. He will then suffer eternal hunger and thirst.

There is a special state of suffering for those who are miserly, covetous, uncharitable or gluttonous in their earthly lives. The mouths of these wretched spirits are said to be as small as the eye of a needle and their gullets are no wider than a hair. Food changes in their stomachs to sharp knives and saws which pierce the bowels, making hideous wounds.

A Tibetan doesn't have to go to a hell or become a tormented ghost if by his virtues he can sufficiently please the gods to earn a place in a heaven. But the snag is that he cannot approach the gods at all except through the good offices of a priest. So, if he has any sense he will please the priest first to make sure his case is being put sympathetic-ally to the temperamental deities. In these circumstances it is hardly surprising if the laity concealed a dislike of their earthly condition, for if they expressed it they could be sure they would forfeit a recom-mendation to paradise and be a lot worse off after they were dead.

And when they were reborn on earth they might not return as human beings at all but as flies, lice or mad dogs. On reflection it might not be so bad being one of these since it was considered a religious crime to hurt them.

The present fourteenth Dalai Lama offers another explanation for the uncomplaining submission of his people to a system in which the majority were serfs and the remainder privileged priests, officials and landlords who lived on their backs.

According to him, life for many Tibetans was hard but they were not victims of desire and in their simplicity and poverty perhaps they enjoyed more peace of mind than people enjoyed in most cities in the world. 'A poor Tibetan', he has written, 'was less inclined to envy or resent his Tibetan landlord because he knew that each of them was reaping the seed he had sown in his previous life.'

These are the words of a man who is said to have a modern outlook and whom Mr. Spencer Chapman describes as 'enlightened'. They express the basic philosophy and myth of Tibetan Buddhism.

Whether or not all sophisticated Tibetans believed in this supernatural hocus pocus, it was an ingeniously contrived system which ensured the preservation of an ecclesiastical and secular aristocracy whose power was self-perpetuating.

Great squirearchies were created by the ennoblement of the Dalai Lama's relatives who were given large estates which were inherited by their heirs. The priests, being officially celibate, could not legitimately reproduce themselves naturally. They went one better by nominating some of themselves as Living Buddhas. So, the all powerful monasteries were not only ruled by men but by incarnations who had returned to earth with indisputable authority to express the heavenly will. The religious aristocracy ensured its own succession by the simple expedient of maintaining a supply of 'gods' to take the places of those who, in the ordinary course of nature, died. Just as there was no Dalai Lama who was a god before the 'Great Fifth' created himself, so there is no record of Living Buddhas before his reign. Dr. Waddell concluded that they were also an invention of this astute politician who 'is known to have taken the greatest liberties with the traditions and legends of Tibet, twisting them to fit in with his divine pretensions, and to have shaped the Lamaist hierarchy on the lines on which it now exists'.

The selection of Dalai and Panchen Lamas was however the most carefully contrived. The highest of incarnations were always chosen from poor peasant families for good political reasons. For either of these to appear in the world as the son of a nobleman or rich landlord would confer intolerable privilege on the family and set up dangerous tensions amongst the aristocratic factions of the laity. Recently they were also found as far away from Lhasa as possible, in territory directly governed by the Chinese.

No two accounts of these discoveries are identical. There were frequent occasions when the names of candidates were placed in a golden urn, presented for the purpose by the Chinese Emperor. The Dalai Lama was the infant whose ballot paper bore the appropriate sign. One of the stories of the finding of the fourteenth Incarnation says that the High Lama entrusted with the search for the new body of the thirteenth, saw the house of his parents in the Chinghai village of Tengster reflected in a lake. But it is also related that another boy who was interviewed ran away from the delegation.

Apart from the fairy-tales told about these miraculous events it is certain that the approval of Chinese emperors was necessary before Dalai Lamas could be enthroned. When they were selected by ballot, it was an Imperial representative from Peking who drew the names from the urn and who presided at the 'coronation'.

For their own convenience the British and Russians might latterly have preferred to describe Chinese sovereignty in Tibet as 'nominal suzerainty' but it was a peculiarly powerful kind of suzerainty which was recognized by Tibetans as having the authority to supervise the selection of their religious king who was also a Buddha.

While being compelled to acknowledge the superstitions of a religion which brought atrocious injustice to the people, some speak of its profound wisdom. No one, and certainly no Chinese or Tibetan Communist we met, would wish to deny that, apart from its theories of incarnations and reincarnations and the supernatural mumbo-jumbo which enveloped Tibet in a cocoon of ignorance and poverty, the simple precepts of Buddhism—to be kind and just to others, etc.—are good.

It is also doubtless true that some monks, as well as laymen, endeavoured to live by high principles which set the welfare of others above self-interest. And no one can visit Tibet without observing amongst the poorest people a personal dignity and courtesy which has endeared them to all foreigners who have come in contact with them. They have all the humour and charm of the people of Galway, of whom they reminded us because they are also amongst the most handsome people in the world. Certainly the religious precepts which they accepted and which their religious and secular rulers exploited, helped to form their uncomplaining and submissive dispositions. But they could hardly have endured life at all if they had not been able to hope

Pilgrims going to service in great chanting house at 551st anniversary of Drepung Monastery

The old lama medical college on Iron Hill and the road to the Norbulingka (Jewel Park) from the private promenade of the Dalai Lama, Potala Palace

that they might, by their patient and uncomplaining acceptance of their present conditions, earn the right to a happier existence when they were born again.

The rich spiritual inheritance which, according to some who fear Communism more than they understand Tibetan Buddhism, is being destroyed by the Chinese, was in fact not there to be destroyed. It existed only in the imaginations of those who mistook the mechanical observance of ritual and religious custom for spiritual experience.

Dr. Waddell was too practical a medical scientist to be taken in by the claims of Tibetan lamas and holy men to special powers. But there have been others, hardly less credulous than the most superstitious peasants, who have suggested that by mystical exercises and secret formulae known only in the lamaseries on the roof of the world, holy men could levitate so that they could rise in the air at will and sit an inch or two over a pile of rice without disturbing a grain. Other more experienced practitioners could defy physical laws by appearing in the same body at several places in Tibet—or anywhere they chose in the world for that matter—at the same time. Naturally our Chinese friends were privately scornful of such bizarre activities, though they were careful to conceal their amusement within sight or earshot of Tibetans. But as materialists they were hardly reliable informants on mystical matters. So we decided to consult one of Tibet's most learned and distinguished theologians.

I

15

THEOLOGY THRIVES

We wished we knew the secrets of levitation when we visited the Lama Tu-Teng Ka Tsung. The home of this venerable doctor of the church stood at the end of one of Lhasa's more squalid and evil smelling streets. For all that it was one of the better addresses in town. The only way to his apartment was by a series of dark, narrow, almost vertical ladders which passed through a human beehive of innumerable flats and rooms. We knew that we had come to the right place by a series of religious signs and symbols which decorated the entrance and walls. As we stepped on the wooden stair treads we slithered about as if we had walked on to an ice-rink. They were worn smooth as glass by years of use and highly polished by spilt butter. We gripped the stout guide rails and pulled ourselves up by our arms a foot or two at a time, using our feet to rest and push us off on the next short flight. With every straining breath our lungs were filled with the reek of stale incense. This must be a very pious place indeed. Suddenly a little hole of blue sky at the stair top, which was our only light, was blacked out as though someone had put a lid over us. We hung on for our lives. Then we were pulled by firm hands through the darkness which was the black trilby hat of a young man who helped us on to a flat roof. When we had pulled our Tibetan interpreter after us, our rescuer was able to introduce himself as the holy man's disciple. Looking at us with expressionless eyes, which appeared as if they were seeing straight through us and studying an object behind our backs, he bowed until his nose was in line with his navel and held out his hands with upturned palms as though offering us a gift on an invisible dish. And then we saw he was directing our attention to a short bald-headed little man in a monk's gown and gold embroidered undercoat which glittered in the sun, standing in a small carved doorway, his face crinkled in a broad welcoming smile. This was his master who waved us into his sitting-room.

The floor was covered with a multi-coloured carpet decorated with improbable birds and beasts and natural flowers of the country. One wall was an intricately carved and painted case filled with scores of Buddhas of silver gilt, silver and brass. On a long shelf before its glass-panelled doors stood a row of silver bowls, some of which contained holy water. On tables and chests sat other smaller gods clothed like dolls. Some of them wore little crowns made of gilt wire which had slipped over their ears or noses. Regarding us with bright glassy stares, they looked for all the world like dwarf demons from a tapestry over the glass case, who had come out for an all night party and been taken unawares before they could recover from their hangovers and get back to their places in the picture.

On another wall hung several splendid hats. Our host explained that as a dignitary of the church he had worn these on ceremonial occasions. One of them, surfaced with gold lacquer, resembled a shallow-crowned wide-brimmed bowler. With the nostalgic air of an old retired fox-hunter pointing out his favourite topper in the hall, the theologian said he had used this remarkable object when riding his horse in very special processions. As his eyes fondled it they seemed to add—'in the good old days'.

The disciple who had disappeared through a curtain when we entered, now reappeared with a large brown pot of buttered tea and plates of biscuits and dried fruits. His master invited us to rest on soft carpeted benches and settled himself on a broad seat supported by a large silk-covered bolster and cushions which resembled a small informal throne specially made for sitting-rooms.

Tibetans are generous to guests but we had been warned before we arrived that they were sensitive about their hospitality and to refuse anything which was offered might cause grave personal offence. Now, as the theologian leaned forward and poked around a plate with grubby greasy fingers for the tastiest biscuits which he handed to us, we were reminded of a story told to us the day before by one of the hospital doctors.

He and three other graduates of Peking Medical School who had volunteered to come to Lhasa were being warned by colleagues returned from Tibet on leave of the conditions they would face. It was explained that the people weren't used to washing and were usually lousy.

Never by so much as the flicker of an eyelash must a doctor betray revulsion in the presence of a patient stinking like a garbage heap. If they visited sick Tibetans in their homes they would almost certainly be offered tea, even if it was the last in the house and they might have to share a bowl with the host. However repulsively dirty it might be they must accept it politely.

At question time, one of the volunteers asked nervously, 'What do you do if a Tibetan offers you a drink from his bowl and he has a syphilitic sore on his mouth?'

With a roar of laughter, the doctors from Lhasa shouted in unison, 'You drink it just the same.'

Now we noticed an angry sore as big as half a crown in the middle of the theologian's bald pate. After we had taken biscuits from him he began to feel for it, picking off flakes of dried scab with his right thumb and middle finger and flicking them on to the floor. With fascinated horror we watched them floating down, missing our tea bowls by inches. Since he probably washed only once every month or two and only then if he was unusually fastidious, and Tibetans don't use toilet paper, we might have tried distracting his attention by pointing out objects in the room and slipped the food into our pockets when he wasn't looking. But there was no chance. The disciple watched us with hawk-sharp eyes and as soon as we had swallowed one biscuit, he darted forward, seized a dish and bending low so that his outstretched arms were above the level of his head, held it towards us until we took another. The moment we had drunk a quarter of an inch of tea he snatched up the big brown pot, filled out bowls to the brim again and with the same gesture held them under our noses until we had taken another sip. Only our vigorous noddings and shaking of heads, and broad smiles indicating that we were more than well satisfied with his attentions restrained his ceaseless ardour so that after five or six minutes of these preliminaries, conversation with his master became possible.

If we had already eaten typhoid or dysentery nothing could save us now, but we were spared further peril by an offering of dried fruits. Only Tibetans and perhaps yaks could masticate these iron-hard sweetmeats and for the remainder of our visit we kept the disciple at bay by taking a suck at one from time to time. We made no impression on them and until we had finished them it would presumably have been ill-mannered of him to press us to take more. But it was clear that we were expected to finish the big pot and when we left buttered tea was almost running out of our ears.

Tu-Teng Ka Tsung, who looked ten years older, told us he was fifty-nine. He was admitted to Sera Monastery as a novice when he was seven. He showed exceptional aptitude for religious study and as a young man was made Abbot of Chuba Lamasery. He took no part in the 1959 revolt against the Chinese, for he didn't believe in violent action and since the Communists had not discriminated against religion he saw no reason for attempting to destroy them.

The holiness of the theologian, or shrewd and timely political judgment, had served him well, for he was now better off financially than at any time in his life. He explained that because he held a distinguished position in the hierarchy, the new Lhasa local government had provided him with his present house and a salary of £21 a month. So it was not surprising that he could regard the disestablishment of the Church without personal rancour or anxiety. Our host, like the Abbot of Drepung, said he regretted the decline in the number of monks, but since the majority had no true vocations religion was better served by those who remained, and were genuinely devoted to it. The fact that Tu-Teng Ka Tsung might think expediency demanded this admission now, didn't make it any less true. Of course, his words could sound like Communist propaganda when he declared that monks should not have owned vast estates and serfs but should have lived in poverty as recommended by Buddha. Obviously he had no intention of following this precept and abandoning the security of his government salary but we could hardly suggest he was a Communist-trained parrot because he expressed the view that serfdom and exploitation of the poor was undesirable and inconsistent with the faith which he continued to profess.

The theologian had never read a word outside a Tibetan religious book. He was unaware of any other country for he had never seen a map and he was learned only in the preposterous metaphysical system peculiar to his faith. But, like others we met, he was not entirely lost in the dream world where people sometimes behaved, outwardly at any rate, as if gods, ghosts and demons were as tangible as their next-door neighbours.

His facility for living in reality and imagination at the same time reminded us of our infant daughter Alison who would rush to a chair when we were about to sit on it and breathlessly warn us that it was already occupied by 'Tatha Whelan'. This spirit child whose parents, we were told, lived in Chicago, a thousand miles away, came to spend every weekend in New York for a year or so. The illusion of his presence, in which naturally we were expected to share, occasionally became so vivid that if we observed Alison in silent conversation with her invisible companion we were scrupulously careful not to interrupt. When one day we politely inquired if he would be arriving on Friday or Saturday we were told without emotion that he would not be coming at all because he had died suddenly. A week or two later he was replaced by a horse who shared the house with us for a winter until one morning he walked out into the spring meadows never to return.

So although with part of his mind Tu-Teng Ka Tsung could not rationally justify the exploitation of serfs by Lamas, he could remain convinced by another that a man's condition in this life was a direct consequence of his actions in a previous incarnation. Presumably he did not allow himself to ask why, if this were true, men and women who could be seen to have led blameless lives since they were children were condemned to poverty and servitude by those whose sins on their own religious reckoning should have kept them indefinitely in one of the more uncomfortable hells after their previous earthly lives had ended. Like a child living in fantasy and reality at the same time, he didn't find this self-deception intellectually confusing because it was necessary to practise it unless the entire fabric of the illusory Buddhist universe was to fall to pieces and the social system which derived from it was to collapse into chaos.

All Tibetan monasteries have employed wizards and sorcerers who exorcised evil spirits and sought guidance from the heavenly spirits with whom they conversed in real or simulated trances. When the Chinese came to Tibet, the state oracle was instructed to ask the gods whether the Dalai Lama should stay in Lhasa or leave the country. They replied that he should go and he fled to the border from which he could quickly move to India. The messages of the gods through the raving mouths of oracles were unintelligible excepting to monks who were trained to interpret them.

We risked giving offence to our host by suggesting that such words supposed to be spoken by spirits were meaningless to any human being and that the employment of oracles was a political device. The government and rulers of monasteries having decided what they were going to do sanctified their decisions with heavenly authority which could not be disputed. In fact the oracle interpreters wrote down the answers which had already been given to them by their superiors.

He answered by reaching for a dish and smilingly offering us more biscuits. Like all other High Lamas we met, he made no attempt to explain or justify the magical paraphernalia of his religion. He presented himself as one of the more intelligent and respectable ecclesiastics described by Dr. Waddell who 'despised such gross exhibitions as an unholy pandering to the vulgar taste for the marvellous'. He said he had read that by intensive meditation some holy men were capable of making their bodies lighter than air, rising above the earth, flying long distances and even being in several places at once but he had never met one nor heard of anyone who had. He lifted his eyes in respectful surprise when we told him that the thirteenth Dalai Lama had com-

plained that one such levitating monk whom he didn't wish to see had
appeared in his presence when it was known he was in an entirely
different part of Tibet. It was perhaps too much to expect that he would
doubt the word of His Holiness and he made no comment on this
episode.

To any Christian who accepts the supernatural phenomena of the
incarnation and resurrection, this lama appeared as reasonable as
the Abbot of Downside or the Archbishop of Canterbury when he
spoke of prayer as being a preparation for heavenly life. We had no
means of discovering whether he was privately as superstitious as the
most ignorant monk or layman but there was now no need for him to
acknowledge it publicly if he was. Neither he nor any other Religious
depends any longer for his livelihood on the pretence that he is a
magician as well as a priest. It is futile to try to persuade people living
in the new society that their welfare depends on priestly influence with
heaven when quite obviously it is dependent on their own efforts and
the decisions of human politicians. And plainly when there is no
profit in the pretence, there is no purpose in it either.

However, if the Dalai Lama believed that the gods had warned
him to escape from the Chinese, wasn't there perhaps some reason for
accepting the words of oracles? The theologian was not to be trapped.
He raised his hand and the watchful disciple was at our side with the
teapot in an instant. While he filled our bowls again, our host thoughtfully picked at his scab. Then he answered: 'The government consulted
the gods when the Dalai Lama left Tibet on the first occasion. I have
not heard that they did so on the second. It is my private opinion that
he was persuaded to leave by his earthly advisers and I cannot help
thinking that since I and many others who have held important positions in our religion, have not suffered any injury, it is unthinkable
that he would have come to any harm.' We told him that some foreigners were saying that since the Panchen Lama had stayed in the country
and was working with the Communists as acting chairman of the
government, he was not the true incarnation of his previous body. For
the first time the old man laughed—'They will never persuade the
Dalia Lama to believe it,' he said.

16

A TIBETAN CRITIC

If it was difficult to credit that the theologian was as privately enlightened as he publicly appeared, it was also difficult to believe that the Communists were always as reasonable in their treatment of Tibetans as Peking propaganda said they were. They might not be suppressing religion nor torturing and slaughtering the inhabitants but if we had been under his jurisdiction we should have preferred to avoid the ill-tempered intolerance of Mr. Chiang, the Deputy Director of the Foreign Affairs Bureau. If we could see for ourselves that stories of physical cruelty were ridiculous, we had also seen that some Chinese claims for the improvements they had brought were ludicrous even if they were harmless. During one journey in the countryside we had remarked on the trees surrounding villages which added such charm to the landscape. 'Oh yes,' said an enthusiastic young cadre who had come to Lhasa ten years before, 'they have been planted since the liberation.' They had obviously been there since the villages were first built, perhaps fifty years ago.

Cha Teh is a nobleman who was formerly the Mayor of Lhasa and a brother-in-law of Ngapo Ngawang Jigme (Apei) the Secretary General of the government. As an adviser on Tibetan affairs in the local administration, he is also one of the most outspoken men in the country. He is not a Communist and has remained a Buddhist.

There were many lords with great wealth. Cha Teh was not one of them. He was an aristocrat, but although his house is a sumptuous mansion compared with the hovels in which most Tibetans live, no English housewife in a modern council house would care to live in it. The living-room in which he received us was furnished with shabby divans and covered with well-worn carpets. The kitchen-style table at which we sat was covered with American cloth. The garden was filled with lovely blooms but indoors there were artificial flowers in cheap vases, probably imported from India. Crude prints of the Summer

Palace in Peking and the Potala hanging among a collection of family photographs were the only wall decorations. The general effect was entirely tasteless and the whole establishment needed a coat of paint.

The servant girl who brought us buttered tea and a dish of sweets could also have done with a good wash and brush up. Cha Teh himself was hardly more spruce. But apart from official occasions when they covered themselves with rich clothes, most upper-class Tibetans had presented a pretty scruffy appearance. In fact they probably lived much like most noblemen of the European Middle Ages. They appear romantic in tapestries but compared with them a modern English working man enjoys fabulous comforts. He told us that before they were freed he had three household serfs. The maid now waiting on us was paid a wage and worked for eight hours a day.

The former Mayor was a civil official in the capital when the Chinese came and remained in Lhasa all through the rebellion.

'It has to be admitted,' he said, 'that the feudal system of Tibet was the most backward in the world. The Dalai Lama knew it and when he now says he wished to introduce reforms he is speaking the truth. But he was frustrated by those who surrounded him, except Apei of whom he thought highly.

'The agreement signed by the Peking and Lhasa Governments stipulated that reforms must be carried out. It was obviously impossible for two million Tibetans to be free outside Tibet and for the rest to remain serfs here.

'In 1954 the Dalai and Panchen Lamas went to Peking to discuss the future of our country and in 1956 the Foreign Minister Chen Yi came here to see conditions for himself. He told us that reforms could only be introduced if they had general support, not only of the serfs but of the upper classes. The lamaseries were to be left to deal with religious abuses. At that time many noblemen, landowners and monks were in favour of improvements, but it was also apparent that some of the leading ecclesiastics and members of the government were not enthusiastic about reducing their own power. So instead of enforcing progress, Chen Yi recommended that time should be given for more conservative Tibetans to adjust themselves to change and the Central Government agreed to postpone reforms for six years.

'There are some who will say that the Peking authorities were then too preoccupied with internal problems to take firm action here but the same people now charge them with provoking popular revolt three years later when China was faced with famine after disastrous harvests. This makes no sense to Tibetans like myself who observed these events from beginning to end.

'After their initial relief that the Communists did not regard them as enemies who must immediately be deprived of their wealth and authority, some of the ecclesiastical and lay lords who had most to lose by reforms began to hope that they might delay them indefinitely. This should cause no surprise. The rich and powerful wherever they might live have never been anxious to give up their privileges voluntarily and the leaders of our ecclesiastical and lay aristocracy were the most privileged in the world.

'But why anyone should imagine that the serfs and the poor, who were the majority of the population, should rebel against reforms by which they had everything to gain is beyond all reasoning.'

Cha Teh took a long drink of buttered tea and, looking at us over the rim of his bowl with a sardonic smile, said:

'It is true most of our people were very poor and ignorant but foreigners should not imagine they were also stupid.

'However, when critics of the Chinese say that the 1959 rebellion was not a sudden outburst but grew slowly into an explosion they are quite right, but they assume the wrong reason. If some members of the Tibetan Government and their supporters had hopes of preserving their authority, Chen Yi and the Central Government unwittingly dashed them when it was announced that reforms would be postponed until 1962. Instead of accepting this as a breathing space in which they could work out social and economic changes, they received it as an ultimatum that in six years their power would come to an end. This was when they began to plan their vain and hopeless scheme to overthrow the Chinese which ended in their complete defeat and caused the deaths of many innocent Tibetans. They were also irresponsibly encouraged by people abroad who ought to have had the sense to see that although some of them might be temporarily deceived, there was no hope in the long run of encouraging serfs and poor men to fight a war for those who wished to keep them in poverty and servitude against those who had promised to free them from it. And since it was impossible to imagine foreign forces invading Tibet to liberate the people from Communists however much they might fear or hate them, it was incredible that the rebellious lords should be so stupid as to believe they could expect help from abroad. But they did. Some American arms, probably parachuted by Chiang Kai-shek's Air Force, were found in the country but they could and did make no difference.

'The preparations for the rebellion were no secret here. The Peking Government was well aware of them and to my knowledge time and again warned the Lhasa authorities to put an end to them. The Dalai Lama himself realised that any such revolt would end in disaster but he was unable to control those who were determined to go through with it.'

This was an entirely favourable picture of Chinese actions, but was Cha Teh asking us to believe that the Tibetans had no reasons for resentment? The Peking Government itself had often condemned the unsympathetic arrogance of some of its own officials to those who criticised Communist politics.

'Of course,' he answered, 'the Central Government had many shortcomings. For example, they sent us enthusiastic cadres who had no knowledge of Tibet and no understanding of the Tibetan outlook on life. They could only antagonise the people. I was particularly concerned about the treatment of religion. There was no persecution and the Hans didn't speak against it or the lamas, but some of the young Tibetan cadres did. Perhaps they had good reason to resent the abuse of power by monks but it would have been better if they had been more firmly discouraged from expressing their opinions because they could, and undoubtedly did, give the impression that when reforms were introduced, religion would be suppressed. I was myself anxious that, although reforms in the monasteries must be faced, lamas and monks should not be antagonised. But however foolish some of these young people were—and those of us with any authority who were in favour of reforms did everything we could to restrain them—they did nothing to justify armed rebellion. This had nothing to do with Tibetan patriotism. It was a revolt by the rich and privileged against the poor and underprivileged. It was not a struggle by one country against another. It was a civil war in which some Tibetans and Hans were on one side and some Tibetans were on the other.'

While he discounted horrific stories of tortures and murders by the Chinese Army, Cha Teh was more critical of the government's actions after the suppression of the revolt than before it began.

We had asked him how many of those who took part in it were still in prison.

'In my opinion,' he said, 'there are too many. After the rebellion was over many Tibetan people lost their heads and demanded that all those who had taken part in it should be killed or imprisoned. Of course the government didn't agree to such furious reprisals but it still does not discriminate sufficiently between the rebels who plotted the revolt and took an actual part in the fighting and those who showed sympathy, probably because they were frightened into it.

'My information is that after it was all over 10,000 people in Lhasa were arrested and gaoled. This was a quarter of the population. Most of these were called in for questioning and the majority were released. But while I am sure that most of those who remain in gaol are guilty of taking life and encouraging others to do so, I know that some, personally known to me, are what I would call "middle of the roaders" who were and are innocent of any desire to overthrow the government.

'In the heat of those early days, they might have resented some actions of cadres and expressed sympathy with the resentments of those who rebelled but they could now be released without harm to anyone. I am most concerned because some of them have not been formally accused, let alone tried. I know that efforts are being made to speed up investigations and bring those who are thought to be guilty to trial but I am not convinced that enough is being done quickly enough to set free the innocent. I know that the situation was critical and presented the government with a problem it didn't create. All the same there is a danger of continuing injustice.'

At any rate, in a country where any opposition was said to be ruthlessly and instantly crushed, here was an important Tibetan member of the local government who was not afraid of speaking his mind.

Cha Teh was also severely critical of the arrangement by which although old and infirm lamas and monks were given small pensions by the state, the younger ones were compelled to work for their food. While disapproving the abuses of the monastic system by which priests exploited the superstitions of the peasants, as a Buddhist he was concerned that they should not be so occupied with material cares that they were compelled to neglect their religious functions. He had not heard of Cistercian contemplatives who combine farming and the spiritual life with conspicuous success.

He was also anxious about Tibetan cadres who, despite the law forbidding them to do so, still spoke disrespectfully of religion and scandalised the faithful.

Did he think that Buddhism could survive in a world whose future would be shaped by a materialist philosophy?

Yes, he said, he was sure it would for it was impossible to suppress religion which was a spiritual phenomenon and an intangible which the material could not touch. Its outward forms might change in Tibet and it was necessary that its secular power should be diminished but while Socialism or any political arrangement might alter a man's condition and should do so when it was unsatisfactory, it could not affect or destroy the nature of man himself.

This was an unconscious rebuke to ourselves for after our visits to Kumbum and Drepung, we had identified the outward forms of

Lamaism with the spiritual convictions of Buddhism, so that we had assumed they would disappear together.

When we discussed our experiences with Chen Yi on our return to Peking, we found that Cha Teh had an unexpected ally in the Communist Foreign Minister who was himself an atheist. For when we told him that although we had seen no sign of repression, we expected that Buddhism would die within one or two generations of modern scientific education, he replied: 'You are mistaken. This belief is so deep a part of Tibetan culture that it is as much a part of the people as their arms and legs. We couldn't eradicate it if we tried and we don't propose to try. We are concerned with man's material condition. His soul is his own personal affair. If people cease to believe in religion it will be because they feel no need of it. As long as they do, belief will continue. The trouble in Tibet was that religion was more materialist than our materialism.'

When we saw Cha Teh again he was anxious we should not assume from our first talk that he was accusing the government of deliberate injustice to innocent citizens who had been imprisoned after the rebellion and were still awaiting trial. He was sure that responsible officials were doing their best. We had related our conversation with him to some Chinese who, instead of welcoming his opinions as proof of free speech, complained that Cha Teh was still a class-conscious nobleman who was mistakenly sympathetic to rebels. This seemed to us such a grotesque distortion of his attitude that we arranged a second meeting with him to reassure ourselves that we had properly understood him. He was now certainly more concerned to excuse inconsiderate Chinese behaviour than on the previous occasion but it was impossible to believe that he was not an honest man who refused to be diverted from the truth for fear of falling into official disfavour. His Chinese critics should have been grateful for a man whose denials of the atrocities they were accused of committing were more convincing than their own because he also didn't fear to protest against their lesser, but still objectionable, failings. Not for the first time during our long journeys through China and Tibet in the past three years we felt that sometimes the Peking authorities had more to fear from the obtuseness of some of their own people at home than from their critics abroad.

17

INTERLUDE

After the rains ceased we travelled hundreds of miles under a burning sun, visiting villages, religious houses, schools and farms. When we first came, it had been our intention to return to China by the highest road in the world which was built by the Chinese Army and runs for 1,413 miles from the city at an average height of 13,000 feet over twelve rivers and fourteen mountain ranges to Ya-an and then on to Chengtu, the capital of Szechuan Province. The local government was ready to provide jeeps and expert drivers and arrange accommodation in hostels used by lorry crews en route. But this journey would be a strain for people in first-class physical condition and after working almost non-stop for twelve or fifteen hours a day since our arrival we were suffering from the effects of the high altitudes. Roma had made a remarkable recovery from her short, severe illness, but if she was attacked by another infection in the wastes of eastern Tibet, far from any hospital and with no supplies of oxygen, she could be in serious danger. Besides, if we covered 100 miles a day, which would be good going, and weren't held up by landslides or floods where rain was still falling, it would take us two weeks to cover the distance. There would be little time and less energy for filming, photography and interviewing. After exposing less than half our movie and still film, tape-recording hundreds of feet of sound and writing thousands of words of notes, sustained concentration became more tiring and there were many places and people still to see in the Lhasa area.

The Chinese were anxious for us to go to Szechuan overland because they wanted us to see for ourselves that stories of continuing rebellion by Khamba tribesmen and the people in the Kham area were untrue. They cabled Peking to ask if a helicopter could be brought in over the Sining road route to take us part of the way. When the reply came that this was impossible they sought to reassure us that although the jeeps would be uncomfortable, they could be packed with eider-downs and we could take a case of medical supplies with us.

It was ironic after our insistence on freedom to travel wherever we pleased that we should have to place this restriction on ourselves. But Koo She-lone had also worked himself to near exhaustion and his blood-pressure was kept under control only by constant medication. Chuang Wei was just recovering from a badly poisoned hand which he had ripped in opening one of our air-tight metal film cases, and was still under hospital treatment.

We now had to make up our minds whether to do as thorough a job as we could by spending the rest of our time in the Lhasa area or hurrying through the rest of the country and getting a sketchy impression just for the sake of being able to say we had been there. Apart from the fact that we had set our hearts on travelling over the spectacular road to Chengtu, there was no purpose in making a journey to find a situation which didn't exist. The Chinese would hardly have been anxious for us to see Tibetans fighting against them, and they were disappointed when we decided not to go. But with this decision we had given ourselves two extra weeks to work where we were and for the first time since we arrived we could afford to relax.

The guest hostel was comfortable but its sanitary arrangements were primitive. Revolution is always hard on someone but the Chinese Communists have sometimes contrived to make it harder than it need have been. Everything which Tibet doesn't produce, which is almost everything but meat, wool, barley and butter, has to be brought from the interior by lorry over the Sining and Szechuan-Lhasa highways. After a 100 miles, with 1,300 still to go over the high passes, the drivers must feel as though they are riding a giant dipper in a fair ground. After a few hours we felt as if we had been tumbled around in a washing machine. But with the vital cargoes, they had also brought massive stuffed arm-chairs and settees for the guest house. Apparently this design is the standard for new official furniture. They appear as if they have all come from the same factory where the workers are giants who measure them by their own bulk. China is desperately short of transport and oil. The space these monstrous suites have occupied in trains and trucks taking them all over the vast continent must have been enough to contain a small town.

Piping would have been more useful in Lhasa. There was no running water. Washing supplies were stored in vacuum containers. There was no W.C. but a room had been thoughtfully set aside for us. This was divided by a blue curtain on either side of which was a wooden bucket. After we had begged a bottle of disinfectant from the hospital it was a tolerable arrangement. But in the absence of flushing closets, we thought the Tibetan custom of using any piece of spare ground as a lavatory was more pleasant and probably more hygienic since the refuse was burnt in the fierce sun or washed straight into the ground by rain storms.

After hot, sweaty, dusty days, we longed to soak out the dirt and soften our aching muscles in a hot tub. Then we discovered Chinese and a few Tibetans queueing up outside a communal bath house. Our companions hadn't mentioned it because they had supposed we should prefer squeezing water over ourselves from our private basins.

We stepped over the threshold into Arabian Nights luxury. A small dressing room was equipped with two divans covered with thick snow-white towelling. Incense was burning in small metal holders. A large porcelain tea-pot and two bowls stood on a side table. From a portable radio came music of a Peking opera. Leading off this room were two cubicles, each containing a standard bath. On the doors hung soft towel robes.

We undressed and put on the robes. Immediately, an immensely tall Chinese, wearing long blue trousers, a sleeveless singlet, white surgeon's mask and blue-peaked cap, appeared with a kettle of boiling water and made tea in the porcelain pot. He handed us cigarettes, offered a light and went to fill the baths. He returned with two pairs of wooden sandals, indicated to Roma the room which he had chosen for her and announced me to mine.

I climbed into the water and began to soak in the soporific heat made fragrant by a stick of incense stuck behind a tap. I was lying in a blissful doze when I felt two powerful hands in my armpits and looked up into the eyes of the bath master staring at me over his mask. He lifted me firmly to a sitting position and soaped my head. This operation completed, he seized me under the arms again and with encouraging sounds sat me on the edge of the bath. Now he took my hands and placed them on the opposite edge so that with my arms outstretched my body formed an arch over the water.

With long firm strokes of his right hand, which he had wrapped in a piece of hot towelling, he began to massage out the dirt. With it came all the ache in my backbone. This blessed rhythm was continued for five minutes or so until I was almost soothed asleep again. And then once more I was lifted to my feet and lowered into the water. To my disappointment the master pulled out the plug and the water ran away. Thinking this was the end I sat up, but he placed a restraining hand on my shoulder, wiped round the bath until no trace of my scum remained,

A Tibetan herdswoman

Lama houses, Sera Monastery

replaced the plug and ran water in again, adding cold until the heat was just bearable.

Now he soaked a spotless cloth under a basin tap, squeezed it out and sprinkled a scented lotion on to it. Folding it into a pad he gently wiped my face with it and laid it over my forehead. I was left alone until he returned with a cigarette and a bowl of jasmine tea. All the weariness was flowing out of me, together with the stink of butter and the unwashed holiness of temples and lamas, which had soaked into my flesh so that smoking two ounces of strong black flake tobacco every day hadn't been able to smother it. The master stood by until the cigarette was burning near my fingers when he removed it with the empty tea bowl.

Now he took the scented cloth from my head, re-soaked it with hot water, poured the heavenly essence into it again and replaced it on my brow. With smiling eyes he once more helped me to my feet and, as if by sleight of hand, produced two wooden boards. He placed the shorter of them across the bath behind me and covered it with a thick towel folded to make a pillow. He passed the longer piece between my legs, fixing one end to the head board and the other to the bath between the taps. Supporting my back with his left hand he drew both my legs on to the long board and lowered me to the pillow until I was stretched flat like a man on a rack. I sensed that only now was the really serious business of the bath to begin.

Wrapping his right hand in a towel cloth again, he seized my right leg, lifted it over my other and placed my foot on the wall. With long sweeps he scrubbed the dirt out of the leg. This done to his satisfaction he repeated the process with the other. Only chest, stomach and arms remained to be cleaned. Bracing my muscles for the assault, I watched myself turning to cooked salmon-pink while my insides filled with a warm glow as though I was slowly swallowing old brandy which seeped down through my intestines and legs into my toes. When the massage was finished all my visible surfaces were soaped, the boards were removed and I was lowered into the water which was drained away again. For the third time the bath was filled and now I felt so light that I had the illusion of floating. My head was rinsed, re-soaped and rinsed again. Surely this must be the end. No—this was a cleansing to end all cleansing. Out came the plug and away went the last of my foulness. Surely the pipes must be connected with the Lhasa river and running through a boiler as big as the Potala. The master left me in a scented crystal lake and with my head safely resting on a damp towel folded over the end of the bath so that I might not slip down and drown, I fell asleep. There was no hurry. I had imagined

Roma next door in the beneficent hands of a bath mistress, sharing my ecstatic calm.

I was wakened by high-pitched soprano notes from the radio. The master was standing by my side holding a robe. I fell over the edge of the bath into it and he guided me to a divan in the other room. There he rolled me into a fresh dry robe like a papoose, with only my hands free to hold another cigarette and a fresh bowl of tea. My head was swathed in a towel turban. Roma was resting on another couch. She had been left to bath herself. She came over to pour me another cup of tea. I thanked her with a fat, flabby, scent-drunk smile. My whole being felt as boneless as sorbo rubber. 'You old Turk,' she said, 'even in Tibet men manage to get the best of it.' Before we left Lhasa for good, the bath master and I were old friends.

All I desired now was to sleep fifteen hours a night and sit out the days of a week in a deep chair with a pipe and a bottle of smooth brandy, considering the impressions which my brain was becoming too tired to put into order. During the Burma war I had seen soldiers going jungle happy after unendurable strain. In a village outside Mandalay I had once sat for an unpleasant hour watching a man, who had come to the end of his nervous tether after fighting his way down from Kohima, playing Russian roulette with a .38 revolver and no one daring to take it from him because he promised to take anyone with him who interfered. When he got tired of trying to kill himself he threw the gun on to the roof of a hut and drank himself to sleep.

I met another who spent the last two months of the campaign putting himself wherever he was most likely to be shot. He never was, but he got his closest friend killed by taking him into danger to which he was indifferent and from which he was strangely immune. I had flown the hazardous Himalayan Hump between India and China a dozen and more times, travelled in gliders over impenetrable jungle from which there would have been no way out if we had crashed into it and had been shot at from Japan to the banks of the Irrawaddy, without feeling more than momentary fright. I had suffered my first uncontrollable panic on a Bengal airfield when I was making a peaceful journey to north Burma with no Japanese fighter nearer than Indo-China or Rangoon. When a generator temporarily failed, to delay take-off, I found myself—with a voice which sounded outside myself—lying to the aircrew chief that if we didn't get away in an hour it would be too late for me to arrive at our destination. It wouldn't have mattered if I got there in another week. Only other passengers standing between me and the door prevented me from jumping out and running for my life which I was sure I was going to lose. After an hour in the air the panic went and it never recurred. Nervous collapse is unpredictable and I have observed that it usually occurs long after the events which are the cause of it.

The night after we had decided not to go overland to Chengtu we went to bed pleasantly weary. At two o'clock in the morning I wakened in terror. I got up and moved quietly into the sitting-room so as not to disturb Roma. My whole body felt paralysed and I was surprised that my legs carried me over the floor to a chair. I sat down and told myself I must have had a nightmare which I couldn't remember. I felt an irresistible impulse to shout at the top of my voice to release a tension which was bursting my head and imprisoning me in the mountains of Lhasa from which I knew there would never be any way out. I made tea and knocked over the pot which wakened Roma and brought her to my side. My hands shook and I couldn't hold a cup to my lips. The man who was supposed to be the strong one of the family was a shivering jelly of nameless fear. We talked about the children and grandchildren and Roma took me out of the room to familiar scenes at home and began naming some of the same flowers we had seen in Tibet which old George England, who helped us to look after our beautiful garden in Hampstead, would be looking after now.

Fear died with the darkness and I fell asleep again with the sun streaming through the windows. The panic didn't return.

But after I had recovered I was aware that my temper was becoming as thin as the air when I became unjustifiably irritable with our companions, but only because they and Roma, who did not appear to be at all nervously affected despite her short serious illness, told me so.

The Chinese did not have to be reminded that we were not Communists. Off and on we had argued at political loggerheads ever since we left Peking but they had been amiable discussions between people who had no disagreements about the benefits which revolution had brought to China but whose philosophical outlooks were poles apart. Now, when they told us some everyday facts which they had discovered about Tibet and in which they rightly thought we ought to be interested, I had sometimes offensively told them they should know better than to try out propaganda on me. I don't know if that was when they thought of getting some films brought to the small hostel hall but it was an inexpressible relief to everyone when we could go to the pictures in the evening—until we saw the Chinese ascent of Everest, which provoked one of the fiercest arguments of all.

It was a superb photographic production but still not as fine as that of the cameraman with the British expedition. And as a scientific adventure film it was unnecessarily spoiled by Communist jingoism. There was too much of the climbers doing it all under the glorious leadership of Chairman Mao. When an interpreter had to repeat this adulatory phrase, which is becoming the Om Mani Padme Hum of Chinese Communists, Edgar Snow used to say, 'For God's sake if you have to say it, say it deadpan and forget the expression.'

By now the praise of the Chairman evoked no more emotional response in us than a recording of 'God Save the Queen' in a British cinema. But we were disappointed when after a brief shot of some equipment which had been left on the mountain by a previous unsuccessful British expedition there was no mention of the triumphant climb by Hillary and Tenzing.

When the lights went up, Koo She-lone and Chuang Wei, who were also seeing the film for the first time, said with pride, 'Wasn't that enjoyable?'

'No,' I exploded. 'You've made a splendid achievement into a kind of political lie by giving your people the impression that the Chinese got to the top first.'

They were used to our laughing at comrades who, imagining that we were members of the Party, occasionally commiserated with us on the oppression of British workers by exploiting capitalist Imperialists but now they were shocked to silence. We walked quietly to our rooms. Koo She-lone, who was visibly upset, hurried ahead. As we passed his door he was washing his head vigorously in a bowl of cold water. We stopped on the threshold and apologised. 'We are sorry if we've been discourteous.'

Koo She-lone dried himself, and his courtesy, which had never failed to save our face in such situations, came to our rescue. 'Your criticism is very welcome,' he said.

Breakfast was never a talkative affair but next morning there was an unusual self-conscious calm disturbed only by a sucking of noodles until Roma broke into it and released the tension by saying we weren't just being stupidly patriotic and decrying Chinese achievement by criticising their Everest film. On the contrary we were complaining that the Chinese had belittled themselves by presenting their conquest of the mountain not only with patriotic pride but as Communist propaganda. Courage and endurance in scientific achievement shouldn't be exploited politically. And to pretend that the British expedition wasn't the first to reach the summit by ignoring it was falsifying history.

'I have been thinking about it,' said Koo She-lone, 'and you are right. But your criticism wasn't entirely accurate because when the success was announced I know the British climb was mentioned. It's a pity it was left out of the film.' This was pretty generous and we felt we might concede a point when She-lone felt compelled to add, 'All the same, I think it's generally acknowledged that the north side of the mountain is the hardest way up.'

But if the Chinese had begrudged British success, some British newspapers and mountaineers seem also to have been inspired by political prejudice when they implied that the Chinese might not be telling the truth when they claimed to have climbed Everest. Their unwillingness to accept the Communists' word was based on the fact that they said their men couldn't photograph themselves on the summit because they reached it in darkness. One would have thought this explanation was the most convincing proof of their integrity. Dishonest climbers who had failed in their objective, would surely have produced a picture, if that was all doubters required. I could take a photograph on the top of Helvellyn or Scafell any day and say it was exposed on a Himalayan peak without anyone being able to disprove it. But when the Chinese were being scientifically honest they were suspected of political duplicity. And when the Chinese Everest film came to England the distributors told us they couldn't get it shown in any commercial cinema.

At any rate the next film—*Tadpoles in Search of their Mother*—completely restored harmony, for we were all anxious for them to find her after their perilous adventures amongst the monsters lurking in the weeds of the pond waiting to devour them.

A great deal of modern Chinese literature, where heroes and heroines are political puppets dressed in human clothes, is excessively dull and reads like those nineteenth-century Sunday School tales of good children whose unbearable priggishness we were supposed to emulate in our own infancy. It is all very elevating but one longs for some of the characters to do wrong, like it and refuse to repent. You may have to seem to enjoy behaving with Puritan decorum and unfailing devotion to The General Line, or whatever line you are supposed to be following in China at the moment, but if you can't be your real mixed-up self in real life, you can be as human as you like in the fairy tale world of Chinese opera, ballet and film which is more beautifully idealistic than any in the world.

Walt Disney in his most lavish flights of fancy has not produced a more glorious riot of colour or achieved a technical brilliance more breathtaking than the film of the Monkey King. Life is austere and very earnest in China today but when Chinese Marxists take time off for romance they let themselves go with extravagant abandon. They don't

enjoy themselves by halves—or at least they do—because when we had
sat through this epic fantasia for nearly three hours it came to an unex-
pectedly abrupt end. It was explained that this was only the first part
of the film. The second, which might take another year or two to
complete, was still in the studios.

But the next night we sat through another two hours of an enchanting story, filmed in exquisite colour, which seemed to contain a
part of every fairy tale ever told, in which kings, princes and princesses
were the saviours of freedom against tyranny so that the audience
might have wondered why there was any need for Communists at
all.

A short cartoon devoted to the adventures of a party of pigs
restored the proper political balance. Most of them behaved with a
sense of social responsibility to their neighbours. But the moral of the
tale was that greed destroyed the greedy and this was dramatically
demonstrated by a sequence showing a fat porker who with his brothers
had found a field full of melons but not being content with one small
one had taken an armful. When he was crossing a narrow bridge over
a stream he overbalanced under the load and all his lovely fruits were
lost in the water while his more sensible companions trotted home
safely with one apiece.

When we were in Peking we had read of a company of young
Tibetans who had taken the great theatres of China's principal cities
by storm. With one or two exceptions they were the sons and daughters
of former serfs who had been taken to Shanghai to be trained by one
of the country's leading producers. A play telling the story of the
wedding journey of the Princess Wen Cheng was written for them.
They rehearsed it for two years and then went on tour. Soon after we
arrived in Lhasa they came to perform for their own people in a great
new theatre opposite the Potala.

There had always been troupes of actors in Tibet who travelled
about the country with folk and religious dramas but there could have
been nothing to compare with the splendour of this presentation. If it
could be brought to England and put on at the end of the Shakespeare
season at Stratford-on-Avon it would fill the Memorial Theatre for
the whole winter. We tried to think of a production which could match
its elegant décor, the lovely and striking contrasts of costumes and
blends of colour and could remember only one which had made such
a vivid and delightful impression. This was *Much Ado About Nothing* at
Stratford, designed by a Spaniard, and directed by John Gielgud, in
which Diana Wynyard had played Beatrice with Anthony Quayle
as Benedick.

Princess Wen Cheng was acted in Tibetan so that we could not understand a word of it but Koo She-lone persuaded a local linguist to translate a synopsis into Chinese and then to English so that we could follow the action. Chinese audiences are usually talkative even on the most important theatrical occasions and no one is disturbed if people in the next row engage in discussion about the merits of the cast or author. The Tibetans sat in reverent and awed silence before this magnificent spectacle, until one of the characters made a joke which convulsed his companions on the stage. Then, as though their chests had been bursting to let go, the stalls and the pit joined in with a vast roar of laughter. From then on, the spectators were part of the show, encouraging the heroes and heroines with polite noises of approval and discouraging the villains, who were hindering the princess on her way to marry the Tibetan king, with grunts of resentment. There was a cast of about forty, but with ingenious switches of parts and costumes we had the impression that we had seen three or four hundred moving about the great stage.

The author's technique was entirely Shakespearean in manner—the time between longer scenes being filled in with characters continuing the business of the play on the apron while the sets were being changed. When the situation demanded it, the same set was used for different acts, the change in place and atmosphere being conveyed by the disguise of furniture with different drapes. The procession of the Princess and her retinue into Lhasa brought the house down. It was a medieval tapestry come to life. The royal litter was followed by a train of brilliantly dressed lords and ladies with a great retinue of servants bearing gifts for the king, caskets of jewels, bales of blazing silks, casks of wine and the carcasses of pigs, sheep and deer. The comical hit of this scene was an actor, formerly a serf himself, who, to the enormous amusement of the audience, staggered around beneath an immense barrel, obviously a present to the royal couple from his obese lord who, burdened only by his own bulk, was badgering him to go faster. This situation was hugely appreciated by everyone for to most of the people in the theatre it had the familiarity of personal experience.

The youth who played King Songsten Gambo was for all the world a younger Laurence Olivier delivering his lines and moving with the sure authority of the English actor in *Henry V*. It was a remarkable achievement for one who had never been inside a theatre three years before.

Perhaps it wasn't so surprising that the actress playing Princess Wen Cheng, who was the daughter of a serf in Lhasa before she and her family were liberated, should have carried herself with such natural and easy dignity, for most Tibetans, however poor, seem to possess it. But it was very moving to imagine her, the king and their companions in this astonishing company as they had lived a few years ago and to see them now bowing to the audience, some of whom had tears in their eyes as they clapped and stamped their feet in wild applause at the end of the performance. For this was not only superb entertainment, it was a proud occasion for every Tibetan there who shared in the triumph.

A group of the principal actors and actresses came to a tea party to tell us about their new lives. The king, who was twenty-four, had been a peasant boy until he was chosen to go to Shanghai. Now he was filled with enthusiasm for the theatre but didn't wish to devote all his life to acting. He was preparing to write an historical play about his own people and one day hoped to produce for the new Tibetan theatre. The princess, who was eighteen, and a beautiful nineteen-year-old girl who acted the part of her slave, were the children of former household serfs. The principal villain of the piece, a seventh-century Tibetan Iago, was a lama until he was twenty. He had lived in a monastery since he was eight. The oldest member of the company, who played the T'ang emperor, father of Princess Wen Cheng, was thirty. Until 1959 he was a serf of a high official in the Dalai Lama's government. This actor would have been an outstanding success in any country. Under the old social order he would have swept floors and done general labouring work for the rest of his life. The youngest member was a merry pretty girl of fifteen. When her father and mother, who were both serfs, died, she was left destitute. A travelling Chinese Army theatre troupe adopted her and asked the director to take her to Shanghai when the Princess Wen Cheng group was being formed.

On Sunday, when these players had a night off, the theatre was taken over by singers, dancers and musicians. There were farmers from the Loka grain-growing area, an army group and a newly formed professional Tibetan company whose members came from all over the country. This was one of the gayest most exciting performances we had seen anywhere in the world. And the price of a seat was a penny. But even this big theatre couldn't hold all who wished to come so the music was relayed through loudspeakers for those outside to enjoy.

We spent a lazy morning drifting about the lovely Dragon King Lake beneath the Potala in an old rowing boat and dozing in the shade of the Dalai Lama's Pavilion on a small island. Two young soldiers, spending an idle day off duty who were attracted by our curious appearance, asked our Tibetan interpreter from what part of the world we came. One was a Han, the other a Tibetan of nineteen. They were

We met these merry youngsters gathering firewood for their mothers

Wherever we went with our cameras we were followed by hordes of children who had never seen Europeans before

OPPOSITE

above: The Great Jewel—The Boundless Light—His Serenity The Panchen Lama

below: Tibetan housewife

A boy lama of Sera Monastery

intrigued when told that we were English for neither had ever heard of England.

I said to the Tibetan lad: 'I am surprised you are in the Chinese Army. Why did you join it?'

He looked at me with a wondering expression and replied: 'I don't understand. We have to defend our country, don't we?'

'Of course,' I said, 'but many people from my part of the world think your enemies are the Chinese and you should defend it with your people who are still fighting against them.'

The boy stared with astonishment as he heard these words. Then he laughed and turned to his Chinese comrade, apparently to tell him what I had said.

'Well,' I asked the interpreter, 'what does he answer to that?'

The interpreter, who maintained an attitude of completely detached independence when he was translating so that his voice sounded like a replay of a tape-recording, for the first time appeared to be embarrassed, 'Well,' he said, 'he doesn't agree with you.' I insisted on the precise words. 'You will understand,' he answered, 'that he doesn't mean this offensively because he is puzzled but he has just asked his friend if he thinks you are mad.'

It was plain that if I pursued my inquiries I should only convince the Tibetan private that I was. He didn't look or sound as if had been forced into the Army by a Communist press gang. Compared with the dejected Chinese peasant youths I had seen being hauled at the end of a rope to Chiang Kai-shek's barracks in Kunming nearly twenty years ago, he was as smart as a British Guardsman.

The saddest creature we met in all Tibet wasn't a human being at all but the Dalai Lama's elephant, and he was the only creature who had not been freed from bondage. We found him in a yard near the lake chained by his front feet to a stout stake outside a tall stable which had been specially built for him by the thirteenth Incarnation. He had endured this captivity for eighteen years since the King of Nepal had sent him to Lhasa as a present for the god-king.

With another elephant he had walked across the bleak plateau from the Himalayan frontier, but his companion had died and he had lived alone ever since with an old half-blind Tibetan and his son who had spent the last eighteen years feeding him and sitting in the yard with him. We asked his keepers why they didn't loose him and take him for a walk. 'Ah,' said the old man, 'it would be too dangerous. He has become rather bad-tempered.' After nearly 6,600 days and nights of this intolerable boredom he might have been excused if he tried to push over the Potala with his great head, if only he could break out of his cruel bonds. If ever a citizen of Lhasa deserved a happier life in his next incarnation, he did and for his sake we wished Buddhist belief could be true.

When we walked out of the Dragon King Park we came into a leafy lane where two old men were shuffling round a chorten saying their devotions. If I had not been afraid, after my conversation with the soldiers, that our interpreter would be sure I had now lost my reason, I should have asked them to include the old elephant in their prayers. Instead I murmured an Om Mani Padme Hum of my own for him, in the hope that it might be caught up with the invocations flying off to the gods from their spinning prayer wheels.

We visited the carpet factory which, apart from the local electricity power station, is the only industrial plant in Lhasa. We had hoped to buy a rug which would be light enough to carry in an aeroplane with the rest of our luggage but the smallest and cheapest was £30 and with the duty payable in London, which would probably be as much again, we couldn't afford it with another 15,000 miles travelling before us.

The factory was a group of antique timber buildings where 120 men and women also produced knitwear and striped aprons on wooden hand looms. Formerly, we were told, carpets were made by craftsmen in their own homes for the royal palaces, government offices and nobles' houses. Now they are sold to official institutions since no private customer could afford them. The largest with bold highly coloured flower and animal designs would probably sell for £200 or £300 in Europe but until production is mechanised there is no hope of a sufficient quantity being available for export, and the power station doesn't generate enough electricity to operate heavy machinery.

But if the factory was primitive, the conditions of the workers were more up to date. As in the rest of China they worked eight hours a day, six days a week. Wages were low—about £7 to £8 a month, but they paid no rent for their homes and they could buy a substantial midday meal in the canteen for a few pence. And like their small children, who spent the days in a nursery which was part of the establishment, where they were also fed for next to nothing, they were all surprisingly well dressed. Originally there were only a few skilled workers here and the majority are still apprentices. The designers are Tibetan but the manager has come from China where he has spent all his life in the textile industry.

Before the Chinese arrived, most consumer goods were made in cottages by individual families but now workers are being encouraged to form themselves into groups to speed up and increase production. Among the first to pool their labour and resources were the Lhasa bootmakers and only a few bespoke tradesmen can now be seen working on their special pitches in the streets. Their first co-operative had been set up on the ground floor of a dark dilapidated house, the like of which hasn't been used as a workshop in England since the days of Dickens. There were no windows and what little light there was came in through the door. But against a wall girls were busy with six bright-new sewing machines. These had been bought, from China, two at a time, out of the first profits which had been ploughed back into the business after the workers had taken their share.

An old man who told us he had been making boots for nearly fifty years explained that admission to this co-operative was decided by a vote of all the members. There had been room for a few apprentices but adults must be experienced and conscientious craftsmen; otherwise the high standard of workmanship on which their reputation and sales depended would decline. When they had worked as individuals they were proud of their traditional skills. Now they were operating as a team they must be sure that this sense of personal responsibility was not lost. He was happy to say that after a few odd men out had returned to their private businesses, the rest had settled down and with increasing profits they would be able to buy more machines. He talked like a medieval guildsman. He and his companions were obviously enjoying this first experiment in Socialism in a society which they were helping to create. They had always been necessary. Now they felt important and their labour had acquired a new dignity.

The old man was also relishing the authority which his experience gave him amongst his younger companions who looked to him for guidance. This was probably more satisfying to him than the increase in income which the co-operative had brought him, for like all the rest before the liberation he had been a serf. As a specialist tradesman he had been better off than a peasant and he told us he had not been maltreated. In fact his former owner, who was about the same age as himself, was still in the city where, because he could read and write and was good with figures, he had found a job with the local government. He was one of the co-operative's first customers and there was no ill-feeling between them.

This workshop made footwear for everyday use but its pride were the beautiful boots with yak-hide soles and cloth uppers, decorated with bright-coloured hand-stitched traditional designs of flowers and foliage. It also supplied local monasteries with the special boots favoured by Lamas which are so heavy and thick-soled that their wearers lift their feet as if weights are attached to them and walk with the exaggerated movements of Peking opera characters. These boots also increase the wearer's height and give him an immensely important appearance.

We spent the next week wandering slowly through the countryside in the Lhasa-Shigatse area, filming, taking still pictures and giving our brains a rest from facts and figures before we returned to the city. Then we went to see how education was getting on.

18

LEARNING FROM LAMAS

To impress us with their achievments both Chinese and Tibetans who supported the new order sometimes exaggerated the disadvantages of the old, but more often than not we found the younger Communists were not so much trying to deceive us with propaganda as being themselves deceived by their own ignorance of the past. For example, while the great majority of Tibetans were illiterate, more could read and write than some of our informants would have us believe. Some of them were recent arrivals themselves and before they came had probably read less about conditions in Tibet than ourselves. Frequently, to their surprise, we were able to tell them more about the history of the country than they knew. But when we asked to look into any particular situation they made no attempt to divert our attention only to those things they wished us to see and which they thought would reflect credit on them. So when we wanted to see schools, they didn't select them for us but left us to make our own arrangements.

Before the Chinese came, some of the wealthier families had sent sons and daughters to be educated in Darjeeling and some boys went to Rugby but this experiment was not repeated. One of them wanted to be a mining engineer but his ambitions were frustrated by religion. Making deep holes in the earth was forbidden, presumably because the demons who were believed to live underground might escape through them. Rich nobles and landlords arranged for their children to be taught to read and write and occasionally allowed children of their serfs to be taught as well.

Some young monks were educated in the three Rs in the monasteries so that they could read the Scriptures and keep accounts but there was no state system of education. In a country largely devoted to agriculture, where most people were peasants and, apart from religious writings, there was virtually no literature, there was no need for it.

The stability of feudal society was dependent on the ignorance of the people.

But political ideology apart, mass education is as essential in the new Tibetan Socialist state as it was undesirable and unnecessary in the old culture. The Director of Culture and Education, Mr. Liu, has one of the most formidable jobs in the country in providing it.

'I have heard,' he said, 'that some foreigners criticise us for invading Tibet and taking their country away from the Tibetans. As an educationist, this strikes me with peculiar irony for my task is to help Tibetans to make Tibet worth living in. If there hadn't been an invasion of education from the interior, there wouldn't have been any at all.

'When we first came we started from scratch. There were no buildings, teachers and no-one capable of organising an education system. The nobles and landlords didn't want one and naturally the lamas were opposed to secular teaching which they feared would undermine their authority. Progress here has been comparatively slow but until 1960, after the governing aristocracy had made it clear by the rebellion that they were opposed to any kind of social reform, rapid advancement was impossible.

'For the first eight years, during which the policy of the Peking Government was to encourage Tibetan leaders to adapt themselves to the idea of social change, we relied entirely on persuasion to convince them that education was desirable, but in a serf society a national system designed for all children was unthinkable. It was only after the serfs were freed that we were also free to plan it.

'As you know, there is still a serious shortage of well qualified teachers in China so you can imagine the problems we face here. There is no compulsory education in Tibet so far because we can't compel parents to send their children to schools which aren't there, to be taught by teachers who don't exist. But where we have been able to provide facilities, children go to school when they are eight and nearly 40 per cent of infants of this age are now receiving some kind of instruction, even if only in the three Rs. Fortunately thousands of monks who left the monasteries have taken up teaching as a profession. Usually their only qualification is that they can read and write, although some are proficient at arithmetic and others are excellent musicians and dancers. But this simple knowledge was all we required to get primary education started. Some petty noble-women are also now working as teachers.

'We have been able to establish five middle schools and forty-one state primaries. This education is completely free. But 1,300 primaries have been formed and are financed and managed by parents themselves.

The government provides the buildings, usually old houses formerly belonging to landlords of great estates and sometimes barns or old temples which have not been used for religious purposes for many years. Some very small government grants are also available. The culture and education department advises on organisation, but apart from this they are responsible for running their own affairs.'

We went first to Dege (Good Luck) Street People's Primary School in the city. This was started at the end of 1959 by a group of parents who formed a committee after being told there would be no hope of government education for their children for many years. The local authorities allowed them to use an ancient farm house and its surrounding grain stores, byres and stables as class-rooms. We were received by a tall handsome Tibetan. Nawang Puchiung was the first teacher to be appointed and had seen the school grow from a small group of infants and a staff of one—himself—to a thriving institution with 332 pupils, seven masters and three mistresses.

Nawang Puchiung is thirty-eight. When he was fourteen his parents entered him as a monk of the White Sect, one of the oldest in Tibet, at Tsarong Monastery. 'I remained there for twenty-one years,' he said, 'but left after the rebellion with which I had no sympathy. First I obtained work as a clerk in the Lhasa telegraph office. Some of the people in this district knew me and when they wanted to start a school, asked if I would come to teach reading, writing and arithmetic. They couldn't afford to pay me much but they had been given some land, seized from the previous owner who took part in the rebellion, on which they grew food so they could provide me with meals. In addition they all subscribed as much as they could afford towards my salary of twenty-one yuan a month [just under £3], and of course I was given a rent-free room.

'The men repaired and decorated the buildings in their spare time and their wives cleaned them. We had no furniture and books but we had a blackboard and some chalk and the children were used to sitting on the ground so we had the essential equipment for making a start.

'Then more parents became interested and subscribed more money. Seeing that we were in earnest, the local government made a grant of £3 10s a month. Within a year we had more than 150 pupils and it was possible to employ three other former lamas anxious to become teachers. The small voluntary parents' committee wasn't big enough now to do all the necessary work of collecting subscriptions, seeing to the buildings and all the other work of management, so a second was formed.

'Now, including myself, we have five former lamas on the staff, one Living Buddha, three women and one layman. It has also been necessary to form a third committee. We teach a four-year course in the Tibetan language and arithmetic.'

Nawang Puchiung guided us up a steep narrow stone stairway to a small staff-room where we were joined for tea by his colleagues. He explained that he wasn't the headmaster because he was the first to come here. In fact there was no Principal. The curriculum was simple and all the teachers, who had equal status, decided the time-table and arranged the classes by mutual agreement. They also received the same salaries. There were no fixed fees. Parents paid into the common fund what they could afford according to their wages and family circum-stances. Contributions ranged from about 1s to 3s a month.

We asked, 'May we be introduced to your colleague who is a Living Buddha?'

Nawang Puchiung pointed to a short sturdy man who, like the other masters, wore a rough brown gown and large wide-brimmed black trilby hat. With an embarrassed smile this muscular Incarnation said, 'Well, I used to be a Living Buddha, but I'm not now.'

This was a surprising statement. We asked, how could an Incar-nation, who according to Buddhist belief had achieved perfection in his previous life but returned to earth from his god-like state to help his brethren towards heaven, cease to be himself.

'I got married,' said the Buddha.

'You mean it's impossible for a husband to be a god to his wife?' we asked, not quite sure that the question wasn't in bad taste. We needn't have worried. The joke was received with loud laughter, in which the former Buddha joined.

We asked, 'If you can cease to be an Incarnation by getting married do you know how you become one in the first place?'

The young man answered: 'No, I don't know that. I think the Kambu of my lamaserie declared that I was a Living Buddha when I was a boy. I don't know how that came about but I had a better life than some of the lamas who weren't Incarnations. But I would rather have my wife and two children and be a schoolmaster. It's a more interesting life.'

'But you are still a Buddhist and not a Communist?'

'Yes,' he said, 'we are all Buddhists but that doesn't mean that everything done in our religion was right. I think of all of us have realised during the past few years that a great deal was wrong. At any rate I feel I am doing something really useful now for the first time.'

Did Nawang Puchiung feel the same about this new life and his renunciation of the old?

Chensel Phodrang, favourite summer palace of the Fourteenth Dalai Lama
in the Norbulingka from which he fled by night in 1959. He was told this
building with other palaces in the Jewel Park was reduced to ruin by
Chinese gunfire soon after he left. We found it intact with all its contents
meticulously preserved

The holy of holies of Tibet. The altar of The Jo, which legend says was brought to Lhasa in the seventh century by the Chinese Princess Wen Cheng as a wedding gift to her husband the King of Tibet

'I don't feel I have renounced anything,' he said. 'In the monastery you devoted your time to helping yourself towards perfection. I am finding it more satisfying helping our children so they will have an opportunity of happier lives than most Tibetans used to know.'

Were there no regrets about the passing of the old society? Did they all welcome the news that the Hans were coming to bring revolution to Lhasa?

'No,' said Nawang Puchiung, 'like most people, at first I was very much afraid. We had been told that they would destroy our religion and kill the lamas, even if they didn't shoot or make slaves of everyone else.'

'And nothing of the sort happened?'

'No,' said Nawang Puchiung. 'They left us alone. Soldiers didn't even come to our monastery.'

'But many people fled from the city even in those early days so what drove them away?'

'Well,' he replied, 'they believed that even worse things would happen to them. My mother was terrified because she and her neighbours had been told that the Han soldiers ate human flesh and drank human blood.[1] She would have gone away with some of them but she was too old to walk far.'

'So within a week or two when everything was peaceful you were not alarmed any more?'

'We were not alarmed but we were not peaceful in our minds. I thought perhaps they were waiting a little before they took drastic action against us because they didn't want to make trouble for themselves immediately. It was two years before I began to believe they didn't intend to destroy us.'

'But you were the most religious country in the world and the Han Communists have no religion. You speak another language and all your traditions are different. Have you no feeling that you are being made into a subject race?'

As these words were translated one of the former lamas, who had listened intently to our conversation, asked: 'May I say something?— I feel that life is more independent for Tibetan people now. Our children won't grow up to be serfs and will be the equals of the Hans in education and opportunities.'

Now the dialogue with Nawang Puchiung and his colleague was interrupted by all the teachers talking excitedly amongst themselves.

---

1. Kuomintang propagandists invented the story of Communist Cannibalism. Chou En-lai was said to be fond of human flesh.

L

Then one of the women addressed our interpreter. 'They would like to ask,' he said, 'if you are against that?'

We explained that wherever we went in Tibet, we were trying to discover people's real feelings. Naturally the Hans would speak well of themselves. Tibetans in high places might also be expected to speak well of them because their positions would depend on it but we were more interested in the opinions of those who had no political authority and no special political convictions.

There was an embarrassed silence as they considered these words. Another of the women who had not spoken but had busied herself pouring tea for everyone replied, 'All we can do is to show you what we are doing and you can decide if it is good or not.'

It was a deserved rebuke for what they must have considered ill-mannered doubts of their honesty.

They had modestly explained that we mustn't expect too much. The standard of education wasn't high because they themselves were only capable of teaching their own language and some simple arith-metic. The tension was broken by a chubby ruddy-faced infant who put her head round the door to speak to one of the mistresses. When she saw our white faces her mouth dropped open, words gurgled in her throat and she vanished with a groan, which became a high-pitched gabble as she reached the bottom of the stairs and was apparently telling some companions what she had seen. We went down to join them.

It was playtime and the yard, formerly the farm midden, was filled with children. Some of them were barefoot. But they all had large satchels, made of plastic material or cloth or knitting, slung on their backs. These were apparently a status symbol in Tibetan schools and we hardly saw a child without one.

The ancient buildings had been patched up where loose masonry had threatened to fall into the playground and square holes had been cut here and there to form windows in which there was no glass. But the entire establishment looked as though it had been hit by a bomb and left to rot for a few years until someone had thought of making use of it again. The classrooms in the main part were substantial and airy enough and there were rough desks in some of them but Dothe-boys Hall was a palace compared with the old stables and byres where most of the pupils sat on earth floors. There were no chairs or desks here. Each child sat on the earth floor and rested his slate on the back of his neighbour sitting in front of him. After four years of straining their eyes in this gloom, lighted only by holes in the walls, they would probably need to wear glasses for the rest of their lives. But at any rate they would be able to read and write with their aid.

It was this or nothing for these infants who were as poorly dressed as any we had seen in England in fifty years but who were as bright and cheerful as any we had seen anywhere in the world. This was not surprising for slum children are often as gay and lively as their surroundings are depressing. But every one of these appeared strong and healthy. Most of their parents were illiterate. This school which they had created was the passionate and inspired expression of their desire to give their children knowledge which they had been denied. He would have been a dull-witted, cold-hearted visitor who could not share their enthusiasm.

Nawang Puchiung told us that all the pupils would go on from here to junior schools. From there a few, but only a few, because facilities were limited, would pass into middle (or grammar) schools. This was the highest education which could now be provided in Tibet. The most brilliant scholars would go to universities in Sian, Chengtu, Kunming and Peking with state scholarships.

In one classroom we found children teaching themselves. It was explained that the master had gone off on an important errand. He had left a sentence written on a large blackboard. Each child went up to it in turn and, tracing the words with a pointer, called them out to the others who repeated them in unison. When they had all had a turn as teacher they called out the sentence together, reading it from their slates on which they had written it with sticks dipped in home-made ink. When lessons were done, the whole school assembled in the open for us to take photographs. But every time a camera was levelled a small girl, whose hair was piled on top of her head and tied into a plume with bright red ribbon, ran out from the crowd and stood in front of it. With her lips tightly pressed together she stretched herself taut to her full diminutive height, staring intently up into the lens. When we moved to avoid her, she moved until she was square on again. A mistress came to my help and picked her up.

'She lives next door,' she said. 'She isn't old enough for school yet but she is here every day to ask when she can come.'

When the eager frustrated scholar was assured that her picture had been taken and she was now really a schoolgirl like all the rest, she trotted cheerfully home.

There is still plenty of inequality in Tibet. Compared with his fellow citizens, the Panchen Lama lives like a millionaire, but Tibetans would probably be surprised if he didn't and because he is the highest of all Incarnations left in the country they will think it right and proper that a new palace is being built for him. Since they can't eat more than two or three meals a day or live in several houses at the same time,

Apei and the nobles who have remained have suffered little personal inconvenience. They have given up their vast estates and hundreds or thousands of serfs but they are still as well off as men ought to be in any society. Tibetans won't resent this either because their common sense tells them that heads of government can't be expected to live like peasants any more than Abbots of monasteries can do their work if they have to live in dormitories with the rest of the community.

But the most striking inequalities are to be found in education where at first sight they are most disturbing because one feels that children at any rate should start their lives with equal opportunities.

The 518 pupils of Lhasa's first state primary, which was founded in 1952, are as poor as the children of Dege Street, but although their school doesn't bear such an auspicious name—it is known as No. 1—they and their parents are much luckier and their chances of higher education are incomparably better.

The buildings are simple but they are well lit and furnished with a chair and desk for each child. There are twice as many teachers—eleven Tibetans and nine Chinese—and they are more experienced so that the curriculum can be wider and more advanced. For example, Chinese is taught as a second language so that, when they have been through Middle School, children who attain a sufficiently high standard in other subjects will have no difficulty in studying in Chinese universities. There are also classes in elementary science, history, geography, music, painting and physical culture. It is not surprising that more than 90 per cent of the pupils are expected to qualify for higher education. Against this competition, which is inevitable in present conditions, 5 per cent of the 'Lucky' Street boys and girls will be fortunate if they can stay at school after they are twelve.

When we looked at these children in their smart surroundings our hearts went out to the infants sitting in the gloom of the earth-floored stables, straining their eyes to read the letters on the slates resting on their companions' backs.

But if these conditions must create some injustices they are at any rate an improvement on the inequality which existed before when the vast majority of Tibetans were equal because none of them had any education at all.

The Headmaster, who also told us he was a member of the Communist Party, said he was largely engaged in organisation and administration but he also taught political history to the older children. In the curriculum this subject was described as 'moral science'. If the Headmaster was as poorly informed as Mr. Chiang Tsu-ming, the

Deputy Director of the Foreign Affairs Bureau, it certainly wouldn't be scientific.

As in all other schools, the Tibetan teachers were either former lamas or members of noble families. From all accounts Tibetan women exercised a dominant influence in their own homes but in the old society they could take no part in public affairs which were controlled by a male priesthood from which they were excluded. For them Communism is synonymous with sex equality which has given a new interest and importance to their lives.

Yang Jing Zhuo-ga, who teaches arithmetic and the Tibetan language at No. 1 primary, is a petty noblewoman whose family was formerly prosperous and she is still better off than most. She is married to a nobleman whom she has known since childhood and who now works as a civil servant. She is not a Communist and takes a pragmatic view of the new political situation and her own position.

As far as outward observance of religion is concerned, she might be described as a 'Sunday Buddhist', for whom, like the people we saw at Drepung, and many Christians, visiting shrines on festival and holy days has been part of the familiar pattern of life since she was born. She is not deeply devout but her attitude to life remains religious. It could hardly be otherwise. She said that her intelligence, especially since she had come to know some simple facts of science, rejected belief in the influence of demons on the material universe which she had accepted as part of the natural order when she was a girl. They weren't just ghosts to her then. They were as physical as Father Christmas, bringing nightmares instead of presents.

But however consciously free from childish fears and superstition this charming and intelligent woman appeared to be, like the old lama doctor Ah Wang Chu-Tza, at the traditional hospital, the memories of evil spirits would probably always echo in the winter gales blowing round her house.

It is impossible for any foreigner to share the feelings of Tibetans who grew up in a world where a devil in a rock could be more real than the rock itself. One could only imagine that perhaps the emotional shocks which some of them must have experienced during the sudden transformation of their country would be like those of a twelfth-century European finding himself miraculously resurrected in France or England today.

But whatever inner conflicts might have disturbed Yang Jing Zhuo-ga—and she would also have been less than human if she did not also sometimes feel nostalgia for her former comforts and security—she had found a new interest and purpose in life, more satisfying than the old.

'People in my position,' she said, 'had little to complain about in the old society. The women in the family supervised domestic arrangements but the work was done by household serfs. We took no part in public affairs which were conducted entirely by men.

'Our principal interest was dress and social entertainment. It wasn't until I began to work that I looked back and thought how dull it must have been. When the Hans came and all kinds of social services were started, women suddenly became very important because they were needed to help in running them. Some of my friends interested themselves in the medical and welfare organisations. Then this school was opened and I was asked if I would like to teach. I had no qualifications except that, like my brother and sisters, I could read and write and was fairly good at arithmetic because my father had seen that we were taught when we were young, but that was all that was required.

'Of course everyone wasn't unhappy in Tibet under the old system. All serfs weren't treated cruelly. My mother wouldn't have allowed me to treat a servant badly but we took our world for granted. Some had been reincarnated as serfs and others as nobles like ourselves. It didn't occur to anyone that there could be any other kind of society.

'Now when I see how intelligent my pupils are, I realise what a hard and dreary world it would have been for them if there had been no changes.'

I asked Yang Jing Zhuo-ga if she still believed in reincarnation. She answered with a smile, 'If I am to be reincarnated, I hope I am reincarnated as a teacher so that I can go on with this work.'

Like Chinese children, who seem to possess an inborn discipline which has to be more painfully acquired in the West, Tibetan infants appear to be almost unnaturally well behaved but this is not through fear of physical retribution if they misbehave for in Tibet, as in all schools throughout China, corporal punishment is now forbidden. Presumably in China filial piety is just a habit formed by the centuries-old custom of respecting one's elders. The Chinese may thank Confucius for inventing good manners. Perhaps Tibetan parents would put down the tractability of their offspring to the stick and the fear of devilish torments which were invoked when they were naughty. At any rate, one result of both systems of education is that fewer teachers seem able to teach greater numbers without difficulty than in the West where it is said that children cannot be taught effectively in groups of more than forty. Sixty was the average size of a class in Lhasa. When we asked one master why there need be so many, he replied that unfortunately the classrooms weren't big enough to hold any more.

Lhasa's No. 3 primary school is for boarders. Many of the pupils here are orphans of serfs. They continued to live with their owners when their parents died but when serfdom was abolished they were homeless. They were free with nowhere to go. The remainder are the sons and daughters of parents who are both at work in the city or whose jobs take them away from it during the week. These go to their own homes at weekends.

The most privileged children in all Tibet must be the 368 pupils of Lhasa's first and only middle, or grammar school, situated in beautiful peaceful gardens from which the only other building to be seen is the Potala Palace.

Certainly Mrs. Wang, who founded it eleven years ago, is one of the most remarkable headmistresses in the world. She volunteered to come with her husband who was appointed to be the first Director of Education. In those days there was no road into Tibet beyond Kanze in Szechuan. They came there by car and then started walking, and occasionally getting lifts on ponies, over 1,000 miles to Lhasa. It took them more than three months travelling at an average height of 13,000 feet to cross fourteen of the highest mountain ranges in the world and twelve great rivers, including the Yangtze, Mekong and Salween, before they reached the city.

This intrepid woman, who if she had been born in England would have been in demand as a university college principal, agreed to work in Tibet for ten years. She and her husband, who now have two children, told us they can't now think of leaving and have decided to spend the rest of their days there.

All the girls and boys are boarders and, as everywhere else in China and Tibet, are taught in mixed classes. Three hundred and twenty are the children of Tibetans. The parents of a few are government officials, but the majority come from poor homes. The forty-eight Han children who are here are all the sons and daughters of Chinese officials or professional and technical specialists.

They come at twelve and leave when they are eighteen. There is a staff of fifty teachers. The majority are former lamas and noblemen and women who instruct the younger pupils. The seniors are taught most subjects by more highly qualified Chinese. The curriculum is almost identical with that of any English grammar school and, as in all other educational establishments in China, there is special emphasis on science. The senior classes study physics.

We are often asked by European friends who are sceptical of Chinese advances, how their education compares with our own. One can only judge this by comparing the knowledge of a Chinese educated child with a European of his own age. The son of our surgeon friend Joshua Horn in Peking has attended Chinese schools there since he was a small boy. He is interested in a scientific career but since he reads, writes and speaks Mandarin as fluently as his Chinese companions and is completely at home there, he is faced with a difficult choice in deciding whether to go on to a Chinese university or take a degree in England. Recently he went to discuss the situation with a science tutor at Cambridge who, to his surprise, told him he was a year ahead of any English senior sixth-form boy in physics.[1]

Mrs. Wang said that some Tibetan children seemed to have a special aptitude for mathematics and, all in all, irrespective of their backgrounds, were as quick to learn as the quickest children she had ever taught. Those who were able to go on to Chinese universities would have no difficulty in holding their own. The unfortunate Tibetan boy who went to Rugby and wanted to be a mining engineer but was forbidden by the priests to make deep holes in the earth, was born a generation too soon.

'With all the necessary facilities,' said the Headmistress, 'Tibet could be literate in a generation. But it is going to take a good deal longer because even if we had the buildings we shouldn't have enough teachers. We hope we are training some of them now. Of course Tibetans should have their own university in Tibet but it will be many years before we shall be able to produce enough advanced students to justify it. The Hans are now predominant in these specialist fields but if any progress is to be made here, our presence is essential.'

Two beautiful young Tibetan girls, wearing long silk gowns tied at the back with broad coloured sashes, brought us buttered tea and dishes of hot new potatoes which the boys had grown in the school gardens. A tall young Tibetan who introduced himself as the music master asked if we liked tsampa. We told him we had never tasted it, upon which he hurried off to get some and give us our first lesson in mixing barley meal with buttered tea and kneading it into balls with the thumb and two fingers. If you pour in too much buttered tea, the result is a wet adhesive mess which sticks to the hand like glue. If you pour too little the meal refuses to congeal and is too dry to swallow.

With the master at our side slowly demonstrating the technique, we made an edible job of it. Left to his own devices, Koo She-lone finished up like a slapstick comedy act, his hands and wrists gloved with a soggy porridge. The more he tried to remove it, the more evenly he spread it until his fingers looked as though they were encased in plaster

1. He has since decided to continue his studies in Peking.

of Paris. When he tried to wipe the sweat off his forehead with the back of a hand he smeared more of the terrible mixture on the lenses of his glasses so that he was half blind. The delighted girls watched this pantomime for a few moments and then took pity on him. They came to his rescue with a bowl of cold water and washed him clean. He never made another attempt and neither did we. Although it was pleasant and nutritious, otherwise Tibetans couldn't have survived on it, it was filling rather than palatable. No wonder they preferred meat when they could get it. Better to sin than to suffer this tasteless diet. Later a hospital doctor told us that a large proportion of patients were treated for stomach trouble.

The Headmistress said the boys and girls were developing a taste for Chinese cooking, not the least of the benefits which the Hans have brought to this land.[1] We would prophesy that as the standard of Tibetan living rises, the consumption of tsampa will proportionately decrease until with the gods and demons it is part of a forgotten past, like porridge which Scotsmen surely eat only out of a sense of defiant patriotism.

The Tibetans whose impressions of the old and new world would have been most interesting were schoolchildren, but there were none old enough to remember the past before the Chinese came. For some of the senior pupils the rebellion was a faint, fading confusion of noisy, frightening days when they were kept indoors out of danger. Some of the orphans were the sons and daughters of men killed in the fighting. But the Chinese were not visiting their rebellious 'sins' on their children, who would not have understood the bitter irony of their fathers' deaths in a revolt which, if it had succeeded in freeing Tibet from the Communist Hans, would have bound their own future in Tibetan serfdom.

While we drank our buttered tea and finished our tsampa we were entertained to an informal concert by the school orchestra, conducted by the ex-lama master who had taught the children centuries-old folk-tunes of the country. Girls and boys sang solos and then we went outside into the sun where we filmed a dance troupe. We found our best pictures after lessons were over, when we took the children unawares playing basket-ball, Tibetan draughts and shuttlecocks, which were the most popular form of entertainment amongst the older pupils. An enchanting scene was a group of youngsters who were dancing a pattern of intricate, precisely executed movements round a Chinese teacher playing a gay tune on an accordion. When they tired themselves

1. The nobles of Tibet always preferred it.

out and flopped on the grass the musician introduced himself as Tao Chiang Sung.

He told us he taught Mandarin to a class of forty-nine thirteen-year-olds. He had nothing to do with the music department but had taught himself the accordion to amuse himself in his spare time.

Then he must be quite an expert choreographer to have instructed the children in such an involved form of dance?

'No,' he said, 'I don't know anything about it. These boys and girls made up all these movements themselves. They are always adding to them and leaving some out so if you came again tomorrow they would not be the same. I'm glad you like it. I think it's much more interesting than repeating formal steps which they have learnt by heart.' In dance form this was the equivalent of improvised jazz and it was just as refreshing and exciting.

When we returned to England an executive of one of the biggest newspaper organisations in the world looked at some of the photographs we took here and said plaintively, 'They are rather disappointing, aren't they?'

'Perhaps they are a bit over-exposed here and there,' we said. 'The light was so intense it was sometimes difficult to judge.'

'Technically,' he replied, 'they are first class. But the children look so happy. They give such a different impression from the kind of thing we expected.'

19

THE MONK'S STORY

We invited some teachers to supper. While most of us haven't the experienced ears of Professor Higgins so that we can place a man a few miles from his birthplace by his accent, the tones of a Marxist student are unmistakable if he speaks in a whisper. There could be no mistake about the political convictions of Mr. Chiang Tsu-ming. When he spoke of politics and history, the Panchen Lama talked like a gramophone record which he could probably have intoned backwards without stumbling over a word. But none of these teachers, nor any other Tibetans we met, spoke jargon.

So, Chuen Tse didn't tell us that he had become a teacher because he had revolted against the oppression of the people which was represented by the feudal ecclesiastical power of Drepung where he was formerly a lama. He hadn't entered the monastery with a religious vocation only to discover when the Communists 'liberated' him that the Buddhism of Lamaism was a primitive superstition. He had been bored with the life of a monk from the time his parents made him one.

He said he didn't need any Chinese or Tibetan to tell him that the claims of most of his superiors to spiritual superiority were a fiction. He had lived with them and the humblest monk knew that 300 Living Buddhas of Drepung weren't incarnations of perfect spirits. They or their parents had paid for their Living Buddhaships and Chuen Tse was surprised that everyone didn't understand this, although it would have been indiscreet for anyone to say so publicly. To accuse a personally obnoxious Incarnation of purchasing his holiness would invite a flogging. This young man was most astonished when we referred to monks exploiting the people.

'Yes,' he said, 'it's true that the monasteries lived on the work of their serfs and the gifts of the people. But you are mistaken if you think that all monks lived rich idle lives. Also you shouldn't imagine that all high lamas were dishonest men. Some were truly holy. But a great many monks were as poor as the poorest peasants themselves and worked as hard to keep themselves alive.

'The poorer were in fact usually fed by the monastery for only three months of the year. For the rest they were given food by their families. If this wasn't enough they worked as farm labourers or pedlars in the towns and villages. During the first month of the year when the Great Prayer Festival was held, they had a better chance than at other times of receiving or exacting alms from the people. The most fortunate would find landlords for whom they would perform religious services. In return for these and for work on the land they received shelter and keep.

'When living in the monasteries, monks spent their mornings in the chanting house, reciting prayers, and learned the Tibetan langu-age in the afternoons. When they could read and write they studied the Scriptures. Flogging was the usual punishment for failure to pay attention to lessons. Out of 7,000 monks at Drepung, the majority were almost illiterate. There were about 500 rich lamas. Some of them had their own estates and owned serfs who worked them. Some of the more prosperous had their own houses in the monastery and their own staffs of monk servants. Noblemen who became lamas lived as com-fortably at Drepung as did their families at home. For them, as for many others, religion was a profession. The monasteries also ran prosperous trading companies which did business with China, India and other countries.'

Did Chuen Tse believe that the Dalai Lama was a god?

'We were told that he was,' he replied. 'I remember a Ge Shi [a middle scholar] who taught me the Scriptures, once saying, "Since the Dalai Lama knows all, we can ask him how many people are in a room before he enters it and he will give us the correct answer," but I never heard that the Dalai Lama or any other Incarnation was ever asked such a question and I don't think I ever really believed he could possess such powers. But then I was never a very religious person. When I was young I prayed to the gods because I was afraid of devils and demons. But, looking back, I think that, like other children, I only believed in them with my imagination but not really with my mind.'

We had heard that homosexuality was encouraged in monasteries to preserve chastity. Was that true?

Chuen Tse said it was generally accepted; this had also provoked trouble through jealousy between rivals. He had heard that on one occasion it had led to murder in Drepung.

Discipline was maintained in the monasteries by 'Iron Bar', or police lamas who also bought their positions for which there was great competition so that they occupied them for only limited periods after which they made way for others. Besides carrying heavy bars with which they beat monks who offended them, they also used thick leather whips, and monks had been known to die from the injuries inflicted by them. During the Great Prayer in Lhasa the entire city was in the charge of 'Iron Bars' and woe betide any who came into conflict with them.

Chuen Tse's grandmother had also been told that the soldiers of the Chinese Communist Army might eat her. Although the government hadn't then decreed that monks could continue the religious life or abandon it, he left Drepung in 1957 and married because he believed the authorities wouldn't dare to take action against him if he appealed to the Chinese for protection. In fact his departure was ignored.

It was not surprising that our other guests who were all formerly monks of Drepung or Sera—Tue Ji Zhan Tui, and Giangba Tan Ta—preferred their lives as teachers and family men—they were all married with children—if their lives in the monasteries were as dull and uneventful as they had described. And we had no reason to doubt them for we could still see monks living in the same way at any lamaserie in Tibet.

And whenever we visited them and learned from them the nature of their way of life and the world they had made, we could think of no words which more accurately described it than those of Aldous Huxley who had never been there.

'In moments of complete despair,' he wrote, 'when it seems that all is for the worst in the worst of all possible worlds, it is cheering to discover that there are places where stupidity reigns even more despotically than in Western Europe, where civilisation is based on principles even more fantastically unreasonable. . . . The spectacle of an ancient and elaborate civilisation of which almost no detail is not entirely idiotic is in the highest degree comforting and refreshing. It fills us with hopes of the ultimate success of our own civilisation; it restores our wavering self-satisfaction in being citizens of industrial Europe. Compared with Tibet, we are prodigious. Let us cherish the comparison.'[1]

Huxley's informant was a Japanese monk, Kawaguchi, who spent three years in Tibet in the early days of this century.

We did not have to suspect our former lama visitors of being treacherous apostates or victims of Communist subversion when they

1. Aldous Huxley: *On the Margin* (Chatto and Windus, 1923).

deplored their past and welcomed their present condition. More than fifty years ago, Kawaguchi had used stronger language about this spiritual kingdom than Chinese Communists would consider polite. He learned Tibetan and walked from the Himalayas to Lhasa where he hoped to find an enlightenment unrevealed to those living beneath the roof of the world. He pretended to be a Chinese, and in the three years he stayed there came to know the Dalai Lama and the ecclesiastical and lay nobility. He also made friends with the lowliest. When he came away the best he could say of them was that:

'The Tibetans are characterised by four serious defects, these being: filthiness, superstition, unnatural customs (such as polyandry) and unnatural art. I should be sorely perplexed if I were asked to name their redeeming points.'

He then listed the latter as the fine climate in the vicinity of Lhasa and Shigatse, their sonorous and refreshing voices in reading scripture, the animated style of the catechisms and ancient art.

Communist philosophy would have been anathema to the Japanese monk, but he wouldn't have been at all surprised by the views of the new schoolteachers. He would have been more likely to have suspected that they weren't Tibetans at all but Chinese impostors brought to school to deceive us, for these lively minded young men bore no resemblance to the inhabitants of the monasteries he had known.

If, as Chuen Tse had said, religion was a profession, it was also an immensely profitable business. Drepung was the biggest landlord in the world. It owned 185 manors and 25,000 peasant serfs, as well a, 300 great pastures and 16,000 herdsmen. But the vast yield in grains meat and wool, which serfs paid as rent for their holdings, was not enough.

20

LOSER PAYS ALL

There was a saying in Tibet that there were as many taxes as hairs on a yak. A complete list would fill several pages of this book. You were taxed on getting married and on the birth of each child. When you died your children paid another for your departure from the world. A woman who plaited her hair in two braids paid tribute for the second. A man paid for wearing an ear-ring. If you hung a prayer flag over your cottage it must be blessed by a priest who demanded a fee for the service and if you put one up unblessed, you could be fined. The sacred Scriptures weren't free either, and those who could read them weren't allowed to do so until they had paid for the privilege. As if going six miles round the Lingkor on your hands and knees to expiate your sins didn't tax your strength enough, a tax was due for that holy exercise as well. Piety must be paid for on all occasions. Parents paid a special tax to a monastery when a boy was entered as a monk and if permission was granted for him to leave, another was demanded before he could go. You paid taxes for wearing new clothes, owning a flower pot or putting a bell on an animal.

Even the weather wasn't to be had for nothing. You could be taxed for the sunshine which fell on you and the crops; and for rain, snow, wind and hail. But if you planted a tree in your yard you couldn't escape the sunshine tax by sitting in the shade—you paid for the protection of the tree as well.

If you were sent to prison that wasn't punishment enough. You paid a tax for losing your freedom and another when you came out for regaining it. If you were sentenced to be mutilated you were taxed according to the severity of torture—so much for one eye gouged out, more for the loss of two eyes. If you couldn't get a job or were work-shy and became a beggar you paid for your idleness. If you wanted to go to another town or village where you might find work you paid a passage tax.

You were taxed for keeping a dog (which might also explain why the towns were plagued by stray animals), a cat, horse, sheep, donkey or chickens.

You couldn't enjoy a religious festival tax free. You paid for singing, dancing, chanting, drumming, drinking and ringing a bell. We gathered there were about eighty special religious taxes but we never did get round to writing them all down.

These were all personal matters. But there were still payments to be made for those who had levied the taxes. You contributed to the food expenses of the county officials, and if they decided to hold a banquet, you paid your share of that as well. One of the most resented taxes was the enforced provision of animals and drivers for officials travelling from one district to another. Compared with the monastic tycoons of Tibet, who made an art of extortion, the Mafia are clumsy amateurs. They didn't miss a trick. When grain was distributed the serfs' share was short measured so that they were fortunate if they received more than 40 per cent of their due.

And when their pastors had emptied their pockets, they lent them enough to keep them alive and charged a minimum of 20 per cent interest on the loans. The maximum might be 50 per cent. A fourth of the income of Drepung was 'earned' by this usury.

The monk financiers were endlessly resourceful. A traveller from the city might envy the life of herdsmen caring for the flocks on the wide open grasslands beneath the splendid snow mountains. But they too were hobbled with debt from which they were not permitted to escape if their monastic or lay lords could help it. Yak and sheep were leased to them in return for specified quantities of butter and wool each year. These animals were usually old and unproductive and if they died before they could yield the wool and butter rent, it was still demanded by the priest proprietors. A variation of this arrangement was that a borrower must pay rent to the owners in the form of lambs or calves which were bred from the leased stock. If the ewes or cows were barren, or if they or their young died, the borrower was still liable for payment. But if he couldn't meet his obligations, what then? The monastery financiers took that possibility into account. The debtor paid with all he had left which was his limited freedom as a serf. He became a slave for as long as the monastery demanded. Sometimes this was for the rest of his life.

There was no business with which the monastic counting houses weren't concerned. They were as skilled in retail trading as in whole-sale exploitation. The Chinese sold black brick tea to Tibet at a profit

A lama of Kumbum in a temple courtyard

Worshipper at the feet of The Jo, Jokhan Cathedral

but the travelling salesmen of Drepung, Sera, Gaden and all the other religious companies made a bigger one by re-selling it.

One of the best jobs in Tibet was that of a monastic inspector who visited the ecclesiastic properties. These officials paid heavy premiums to their superiors for their appointments. They went round the estates like mobile grocery shops, stocked with goods which tenants were compelled to buy at black-market prices because they couldn't get them from anyone else. So they would be offered tea, tobacco or snuff in return for butter worth twenty or thirty times more.

It has been said that serfs were also compelled to supply lamas and monks with women for their pleasure but perhaps one must allow for some Communist prejudice in these stories. Rape is one of the most popular of all propaganda weapons. Lamas who went with one monastery inspector to visit Drepung estates told Chinese Communist officials that at one place all the women in sixty families had been violated by him and his retinue of monks. But apparently they didn't say how many men had been concerned in this horrific, not to say formidable, sexual achievement. Their spontaneous potency sounds too much like the exaggeration with which Tibetans delight to embellish their stories, and in the absence of evidence by the women it isn't necessary to believe it to be convinced that monastic inspectors didn't treat their serf tenants courteously.

Tibetans are also very ready to tell listeners what they think they would like to hear. They regard this as a part of good manners and certainly Chinese Communists are not loath to believe the worst of lamas and monks of whom, for good reasons, they have a poor opinion. But this kind of mass atrocity is as likely as tales of the slaughter and torture of tens of thousands of Tibetans which refugees found it necessary to tell to people in India whose sympathy they required, and who they rightly thought would welcome horror if it was told against the Chinese.

We had an amusing experience of the Tibetans' willingness to be helpful to visitors when we suggested we should like to see people who were said to have been mutilated on the orders of lay and ecclesiastical lords.

We spent half a morning visiting various houses in Lhasa where we were introduced to people said to have been injured by their serf-owners or cruel landlords. One had a twisted leg but he could have broken it falling downstairs. Another had a finger missing, but he could have chopped it off cutting wood. A third looked a bit bent and battered but we had seen many old English folk worse crippled with arthritis. When we said politely that they weren't really bad

M

enough to be filmed or photographed, our guide cheerfully agreed that they could be worse. He knew we weren't impressed and didn't attempt to convince us. He thought we wanted to see some beastliness and he had done his best to produce it. When we did meet Tsereh Wang Tuei, the herdsman who had been blinded for stealing sheep, we didn't need a Chinese or Tibetan Communist public-relations man to persuade us that he had been tortured. His injuries weren't of the kind to be inflicted accidentally.

The truth about Tibet was dramatic enough, told by people with no political axes to grind.

21

WITHIN THE ROSE FENCE

At Sera (Rose Fence), the second biggest monastery in the world, we found the most underprivileged of all Tibetans. No government in the world could provide education for everyone in this twelfth-century country within a few years. It would have been a considerable achievement to put 20 per cent of the child population into schools. The new administration had succeeded in making some kind of instruction possible for nearly 50 per cent, even if this was only in the three Rs.

We were greeted by the Abbot and his senior assistants, dressed in fine quality gowns with the usual sumptuous gold embroidered undercoats and splendid boots. On our way to their apartments we passed through a great courtyard. Beside a stone furnace in a wall used for burning prayers to the gods were three small boys. As we approached they turned to run and then seeing their way of escape barred by a group of elderly lamas who had gathered to watch us pass by, stood frozen in their tracks like frightened scarecrows. Their bodies were barely covered by strips of filthy brown rags. Their feet were black with encrusted dirt but when we smiled at them they grinned back, displaying even white teeth. As we puffed our way up a steep stony incline to the Abbot's house we turned to take another look at them and caught one mimicking us by blowing out his cheeks and making grunting noises. An old lama pretended to go for him and he fled over the wall with a whoop followed by his two companions.

We asked the Abbot. 'To whom do they belong?'

'Have you not seen boy lamas before?' he replied. 'They belong here.'

There were 110 of these children at Sera. The youngest was nine and the oldest—the lad who had mimicked us—was thirteen. Twenty-five had come since the rebellion of 1959 and the social and religious reform. They were studying to be priests. Some had been given by their parents and others who were orphans had been offered by relatives.

The Abbot said they were being taught to read and write the Tibetan language and the Scriptures—that was all. This was the usual instruction given in monasteries.

Was flogging forbidden for these boy lamas? One of the assistants who explained that he was the chairman of the democratic reform committee interrupted to say that although the religious life of Sera continued as before, the behaviour of the community was in accordance with the civil law of the country. No physical punishment was permitted in any circumstances.

Did we imagine we caught a faint gleam of disapproval for new-fangled notions of religious discipline in the eyes of the Abbot? Did he welcome the new ways?

'I was used to the old ones,' he said, 'but the new ones work quite well.' He had come to Sera when he was seven years old and he had always been flogged when he was naughty.

A psychiatrist might conclude that in these celibate communities the use of whips and sticks provided a vicarious sexual satisfaction. When we asked the Abbot why flogging seemed to be so popular, even for trivial offences when verbal admonition might have done just as well, he replied blandly, 'It was the lama's privilege.' Compared with the opulent appearance of the Abbot and his colleagues, the boy novices were destitute beggars. While religious freedom had been proclaimed for everyone, the only Tibetans who were bound to the monastic life, whether they liked it or not, were these children. We suggested that although they were doubtless receiving proper religious education they might perhaps be more suitably clothed. Couldn't the monastery provide them with decent gowns and shoes?

The Abbot smiled at our concern: 'You know what boys are,' he said, 'if they wore their best clothes every day they would ruin them.' The best that could be said for this answer was that the Abbot hadn't dressed the boys in their party best to show us how different things were since the monastery had been reformed, but the more likely explanation was the obvious one—there weren't any better clothes for them to wear than the rags in which we found them.

Sera was the great military monastery of Tibet. In *Lhasa the Holy City* F. Spencer Chapman wrote: 'Drepung, containing a larger pro-portion of Mongolians, Kalmuks and other aliens, has a reputation for being pro-Chinese, while Sera has a more patriotic record'—a curious statement in view of the fact that Chinese Emperors, who feared the political power of Drepung above all other monastic corporations, limited the population to 7,700 monks by special edict.

We didn't have to ask the Abbot if it was true, as the Dalai Lama wrote from hearsay, that the Chinese had subjected his monastery to 'useless wanton devastation' during the 1959 rebellion. Any major damage to these ancient walls would have been impossible to conceal with repairs. We found no signs of a fierce or prolonged battle in which Communist artillery battered the monk defenders into surrender.

The Abbot would not be here now if he had taken part in the fighting but he was at Sera during the uprising.

'I think,' he said, 'that the ecclesiastical leaders and nobility—though not all of them—could not face the fact that their authority would have to be surrendered eventually. The Peking Government had given them time to introduce reforms. They chose to believe that the people would side with them in defeating the Communists.

'There had always been arms at Sera but not enough to oppose a modern army. More rifles and ammunition were brought from the stores in the Potala long before the revolt in March 1959, so although it was said that the Chinese had begun the attacks, it looked to some of us as if it was going to be the other way about. Many of us told those who tried to persuade us to take part that, whatever their feelings, it was hopeless to think trained soldiers could be defeated and since they had not interfered with us we could see no reason for provoking trouble. The leaders of the revolt in Sera persuaded many of our community to join them by telling them we could destroy the enemy by magic.

'There is a grindstone here which was used in rituals for grinding out evil spirits. Some of the rebel monks mixed red powder with water and put it in the machine. When the dyed liquid ran out they said, "This is the blood of our enemies and this is how we shall destroy them."

'In fact there wasn't much shooting. As the soldiers came across the plain and approached the walls, some monks fired at them with rifles. Chinese officers used megaphones to shout to them to surrender because resistance was useless and if they had to attack the monastery with big guns great damage would be caused for no purpose. They sent two or three shells over the roofs and they exploded in the hill behind us. When they heard the explosions and realised how hopeless it would be to continue, the rebellious monks gave in. I believe a few hid themselves in alleyways and buildings and went on sniping. Several were killed and others wounded but in a few hours everything was peaceful again.'

As at Drepung and all other religious houses which took part in the insurrection, the cash of Sera in gold and silver was confiscated. The monastic lands were taken over by the government excepting those required for the support of the community. No religious furniture was removed and if one had not known that the vast majority of monks had left when, like all other lamaseries, Sera was disestablished, one would not have known from external observation that any change had taken place.

We later asked the Tibetan Deputy Secretary General of the Provisional Government and second-in-command to Apei about the boy lamas.

'I am a Communist,' he said, 'so you will not expect me to be in sympathy with religious practices in which I no longer believe. But I was brought up as a devout Buddhist. Until long after I was adolescent I didn't question any of the religious beliefs which I was taught. I accepted them implicitly. That is why I know it is impossible to abolish religion by force. The boy lamas at Sera and other monasteries are a proof that we aren't trying to do so.

'When the government decreed after the rebellion that monks should be free to continue or renounce the monastic life, none could object to that because no one could argue that a man should be a priest against his will. The people might have been surprised that so many decided to leave. They might regret that they weren't so devout and devoted as they had imagined but they were grown up and their decision was their own affair. No one had compelled them to make it. But if the government had removed all the boy lamas, then the people would surely have said, "Now the Communists are really out to destroy our religion because they are making certain that when all the older ones are dead there will be no more lamas." So it is true that while freedom of religion has been decreed for everyone, the only Tibetans who remained bound to the monastic life are these children. But this is an inescapable dilemma if you do what we have been trying to do in Tibet since 1951. I can tell you that when the People's Liberation Army first came here the serfs who were told they had come to bring freedom were surprised that they weren't made free. Instead, for eight years they remained in serfdom. The nobles kept all their lands and riches and so did all the monasteries. There was no revolution. The Peking Government took over the defences of the country and the foreign policy—there was no dispute about that. They also built hospitals and started schools. They tried to persuade landlords to reduce interest on loans and the government to reform taxation. They hoped that the feudal system would be transformed peacefully and a direct clash with the aristocracy avoided. But the ecclesiastical and lay lords just couldn't surrender their power voluntarily. This has been broken but religion remains and it will remain as long as there are people who believe in it. I personally doubt if a majority of the boy lamas will remain in the monasteries when they grow up. There will undoubtedly be many who will continue to have a genuine devotion to the religious life, but I hope I am not being cynical when I say that I think others will be more attracted to bicycle wheels than prayer wheels when they can choose between them.'

We asked, 'When will they be able to choose?'

'At eighteen they can do as they please.' He promised that he would go to the monastery himself to see that the boys were better clothed.

When we related this experience to Foreign Minister Chen Yi in Peking, he asked, 'What would you have done about the novices?'

We said that since they had been put in Sera without being asked if they wanted to be there or not, we should have given them the chance of going to ordinary schools. Chen Yi laughed. 'You are not Communists,' he said, 'but in that case you would be more revolutionary than I.'

22

HOLIDAY IN JEWEL PARK

According to the Dalai Lama, on 20th March 1959, forty-eight hours after he fled from Lhasa, the Chinese Communist Army shelled the Norbulingka all day and then turned their artillery on the city, the Potala, the Jokhan Temple and neighbouring monasteries. Thousands of bodies were seen inside and outside the Jewel Park. Some of the main buildings and all others were damaged except one chapel. By the end of this day, when the Norbulingka was a smoking ruin full of dead, the Chinese entered it, and that evening they were seen going from corpse to corpse examining the faces, apparently to see if they had killed the god-king. When they discovered that he was not there, alive or dead, they continued to shell the city and monasteries and mercilessly slaughtered thousands of Tibetans armed only with sticks and knives and a few short-range weapons.

On 2nd October 1962, when the anniversary of the People's Republic of China was celebrated in Tibet with a public holiday, the Norbulingka was thrown open to all the citizens. Thousands of men, women and children in gay-coloured clothes were wandering about among flower-beds filled with dahlias and vivid blooms as big as the hats, trimmed with fur and gilt braid which some of them were wearing. The gold roofs of palaces burned against a flawless sky above the mountains etched into the horizons. Little dogs, like those which lie on marble tombs in English churches at the feet of their lords and ladies, trotted at the heels of their Tibetan masters and mistresses who wouldn't have looked amiss in Chipping Campden high street 600 years ago. In a row of stone cages in the shade of a wall, black bears, which had been the pets of the Dalai Lama, hung with razor-sharp claws on the iron bars hungrily watching picnic parties eating their lunches and grunting urgent appeals for a share.

A group of shabby, down-at-heel, shaven-headed monks who had come out of their dark cloisters to enjoy a day in the sun, sat by the edge

Monk actor

Ancient mystery play being
performed at 551st anniversary
of Drepung Monastery

Roma Gelder in the stalls

Pa Tei Chiang Chu, the deaf-mute monk of Kumbum

Tibetan urchin at Drepung festival play

of a wooden stage on which, beneath an enormous canopy slung between tall trees, a troupe of beautiful girls and handsome young men were performing folk-dances. Suddenly the crowd standing near them swayed apart, dividing into two lanes, making way for five High Lamas splendidly attired in russet, gold and silver. Between them was a small, chubby faced boy of eight or ten, even more magnificently dressed, who strutted over the grass like a bantam cock in white thick-soled boots decorated with embroidered birds and flowers. They stayed for a few moments watching the performance and then departed by the way they had come without looking to right or left. They appeared to be unaware of our existence. A spectator told us the boy was a Living Buddha who had come to the Holy City on a pilgrimage from his monastery on the borders of Mongolia.

In other parts of the gardens, orchestras were playing traditional music and on a wide lawn before a house which had been occupied by the Thirteenth Incarnation, a great audience was enjoying a Peking opera.

The Dalai Lama has written a poignant description of his last hours in Chensel Phodrang, his favourite palace in the Norbulingka. Disguised as a Tibetan soldier and with a rifle slung over his shoulder, he made his way through the darkness to the River Kyi, which he and his party crossed in coracles. On the other side, horses were waiting to carry them on their long journey over the mountains to India. His mother and sister were disguised as men.

It was in the gardens of the Jewel Park that the peasant boy from the poor village in Chinghai who had become the 'divine' ruler of his country had spent his happiest hours. Perhaps those who told him that this lovely sanctuary had been blasted by Chinese Communist guns into a graveyard for all his people he had left behind there, hoped this would convince him he had escaped death or capture by leaving the city. Perhaps they thought he might find exile unbearable unless he could be persuaded to believe that unimaginable horror was being inflicted on his countrymen and that his flight was necessary so that he would be preserved to regain Tibet from its pitiless conquerors.

Children were playing on the steps of Chensel Phodrang when we visited it. If the Dalai Lama returned to his lovely home today he would find it as he left it five years ago. His private apartments, like the rest of the building, are in meticulous order. His bed is made up. His personal possessions remain untouched by any but those who are taking care of them. A butter lamp burns perpetually before his photograph. His clock remains stopped at the time where it ran down soon after his departure. No visitors are permitted to sit on his furniture or handle anything which belonged to him. With a shocked expression one of the monk attendants ordered a Chinese driver who was carrying our heavy camera gear and rested for a moment on a couch, to get up at once.

We were told that windows were broken during brief fighting when some Tibetan rebels tried to hold the palace as a fortress from which they fired on anyone who approached it, and there were bullet marks in the outside walls. There were no signs of serious damage. A photograph which we took of the exterior is indistinguishable from that published on page 70 of the Dalai Lama's autobiography and might have been taken on the same day.

We asked a gardener, 'Was it rebuilt?' He didn't understand what we were talking about. We explained we had been told that the palace was destroyed in 1959. He shook his head and smiled, describing the shape of the façade with his hands. 'You can see for yourself,' he said.

Where walls are not decorated with murals, they are covered with painted wooden panels and some are lined with delicately carved gilt-framed glass cases containing Buddhas and fragile religious vessels. It would have taken master craftsmen years to have reconstructed them and to have matched new paint and painted wood so that it was indistinguishable from the old.

The Dalai Lama's bed, ornately decorated and gilded, with a richly painted canopy, was in fact a bunk so short that it would have been impossible for a normal-sized man to stretch himself full length in it. The only pieces of modern furniture in the palace were a bath, imported from a well-known English firm, which stood alone in another small room with a water closet. The W.C. waste was connected up but there were no pipes attached to the bath.

Visitors are allowed to see the more public rooms in the palace only on festival days and then the carpets are rolled up. None, excepting authorised officials, are permitted to enter the private apartments and we were the first to photograph them.

We asked the senior lama in charge of them if he expected the Dalai Lama to return. He looked sadly round the private sitting-room and replied: 'I think it was wrong for them to take him away, for no one else may live here. Nothing is changed so if he comes back he will find we are keeping it for him as he would wish.' Then he asked, 'Do you know him, sir?' We told him we had not been to see him at his new home in India. 'Then if you do,' said the Lama, 'you can tell him that when he wishes to come back, we shall be ready to receive him.'

We said we were sorry if he felt that we had intruded on his master's privacy and we understood that if he had been there we should not have been allowed to see where he lived. The Lama glanced at our Chinese companion and said, 'He would not object to your coming.' His eyes as plainly said that the invitation would not have applied to Chinese visitors. After we had taken many photographs he invited us to sit down. When we asked him to sit beside us he politely declined saying, 'I should not feel comfortable.' For him the room was still filled with the presence of the Dalai Lama, whose portrait looked down on us in the light of the butter lamp which his faithful attendant kept burning.

In a quiet part of the Norbulingka gardens and approached by a footbridge over a charming ornamental lake is the god-king's private summer house. Ducks, which he feared the Communist soldiers would eat, still swim in the clear water in which masses of vivid blooms surrounding the banks and adorning the terrace and windows, are reflected. Our lunch had been sent up from the guest house and, to our embarrassment, had been laid out on tables in the exquisite little house whose wide open doors looked out on to the terrace. We were thankful to shelter from the hot sun and rest on cushioned benches but we were disconcerted by the appearance of men and women who stood at the foot of the steps making deep obeisance towards us, muttered prayers, spun their prayer wheels and ran their rosaries through their fingers.

Our hosts who had arranged this alfresco meal for our convenience had obviously no intention of giving offence and perhaps none was taken by the Tibetans who came to bow to the Presence in whose place we were sitting. But for the first time we felt like arrogant usurping conquerors who had no right to be there.

When we returned to Peking we told Chen Yi that some older pious folk might be deeply offended by such a casual, if unintended, disregard of their feelings for the sanctity of this place. We suggested that in future guests should be entertained more discreetly. We should have been quite happy to eat on the grass in the shade of a tree. We enjoyed our tea in the privacy of another of the Incarnation's palaces. All the other palaces of his previous bodies in the Norbulingka remain intact. Some were being redecorated when we were there. Each bore a golden wheel of life over the entrance and the roofs were resplendent with symbols which had been regilded. One had been converted into a museum filled with priceless treasures and unique Tibetan curios which had belonged to the Dalai Lamas. These were displayed in newly made glass cases. A special request had to be telephoned to the Minister who was responsible for them, before one object was allowed to be removed so that we could photograph it. The museum officials explained that for any of them to be damaged would be disastrous, for they were irreplaceable.

But if we were disconcerted by the people who came to bow before us at the summer house, Roma was entirely confused by the attentions of little boys and girls and men, who followed us with excited curiosity when we walked through the gardens. Until now she had worn slacks, which were more convenient for climbing up and down the steep steps and narrow stairs of monasteries and travelling round the countryside. But when she saw this was going to be a blazing hot day, she had put on a thin skirt to keep cool. Obviously some Tibetan males had never seen female legs before, those of their own women and girls being covered to the ankles, and Roma's caused a sensation. They were transfixed by her 'nakedness', so that as they walked alongside us, staring at her nylon-clad legs, they bumped into people approaching from the opposite direction. Then one small boy, more daring than the rest and overcome by curiosity, darted forward, flicked her skirt up to the knee and tried to pop his head underneath to see what was beyond it. This was the signal for more timid companions to see what they could discover. Roma was brought to a standstill, holding her clothes tightly about her until Koo She-lone, assisted by a sturdy Tibetan matron, came to her rescue and shooed away her innocent tormentors, who, unabashed, continued to study her fascinating anatomy from a distance.

23

TOMB AT THE TOP

After four weeks living at 12,000 to 13,000 feet we were ready for the 400-foot assault on the Potala, a few minutes stroll at sea-level, an exhausting climb in Lhasa. There is a steep dirt road at the back of the palace over which cars can travel nearly to the top but the soft edge had been washed away by rain and we had to walk. Even now, fairly well acclimatised to the altitude, we had to rest every hundred yards and when we reached the gate at the entrance to the first court-yard, we sat down for five minutes before making the last steep ascent up precipitous narrow stone stairways and almost vertical wooden ladders to the top. From the Dalai Lama's promenade we overlooked the city lying like a doll's village in the wide valley 6,000 feet below the surrounding snow-peaked mountains which for centuries were the rim of the world to most of the inhabitants.

Presumably Tibetans don't suffer from vertigo for there was no wall or guard rail between the edge of the terrace and the hamlet of Sho, which was immediately below us, so that if we had slipped over the edge we should have fallen straight into the middle of its roofs.

The golden pinnacles of the Jokhan and Ramoche temples and blue-green tiles of the Turquoise Bridge in the middle distance flashed in the sun but in this incomparable landscape these were the only out-standing buildings amongst the drab mud-coloured flat-roofed houses which from this height gave Lhasa the appearance of a pioneer shanty town in the American West. Apart from the large new concrete theatre and government offices, the city's architecture has remained almost unchanged since Thomas Manning described it 150 years ago. He found nothing striking or pleasing. Everything to him seemed mean and gloomy and even the mirth of the inhabitants appeared dreamy and ghostly.

Manning was a martyr to indigestion, and physical discomfort obviously soured his pleasure at being the first Englishman to see the

Holy City so that he remembered only overcast and rainy days. Otherwise his description of Lhasa as gloomy is inexplicable, for when the sun shines here, more brilliantly than anywhere else in the world, it is a paradise of colour and light.

All the same, his impressions were probably closer to those of Tibetans themselves than those of more romantic travellers who perceived an attractive quality in their lives, of which he was unaware.

Looking on this scene from the summit of the Potala we thought how strange it was that different eyes could receive such diverse images of the same places and people. Alan Winnington, the Communist journalist, was so carried away by the view that he wrote that if he had to select one with which to spend the rest of his life it would be this. For Landon, Lhasa was a dirty, petty place. The common people did not wash, their houses were by our standards filthy and they lived in a state of serfdom, 'but what delightful folk nevertheless'.

On the whole, Chapman decided that although the administration of Lhasa—which had been ruled by the ecclesiastical Lords from this palace—was corrupt, it was efficient. It is perhaps understandable that at these altitudes, visitors should be given to dizzy speculations but we were unable to follow the Secretary to the Head of the British Mission to his conclusions.

In whose interests was corruption efficient?

The people, he said, were used to a certain amount of extortions but if the traditional limit was exceeded, their natural independence asserted itself and there was trouble. There was an appeal to a higher authority and the rapacious official was punished. Chapman did not tell us what was the traditional limit of extortion nor how serfs could assert independence which as serfs they did not possess.

Tibet, he observed, was in the position of European countries in the Middle Ages and added gratuitously that this was a position which in many ways 'we' were bound nowadays to envy. Tibet, he acknowledged, was run by the monasteries and noble families. But there was no unemployment, no underlying feeling of insecurity and, except for those who chose begging as a profession, no real poverty.

Unemployment could hardly be a problem in a society where if a man ran away from work he was dragged back to it by the man who owned him. There could hardly be any sense of insecurity in the secure bondage of serfdom by which one was protected from the hazards of freedom.

There could be no more appropriate place for reading Chapman's book than in these surroundings, but as we compared his descriptions with what we were now seeing, we could not imagine what he found us bound to envy in a system in which, he said, half the population lived parasitically on the working laymen, who had little hope of salvation.

We found him more incomprehensible when we returned to England and the film we had made in Tibet was shown on television. Mr. Chapman did not see it but on the hearsay of friends who did, objected[1] to our 'suggestion' that the Chinese had brought benefits to the Tibetans. These, of course, included medical services and schools which our cameras had not suggested but photographed. We referred Mr. Chapman to himself by repeating his own descriptions of monastic parasites and a corrupt social system. He complained that in all justice we could not refute his present views, that a sturdy, cheerful, self-reliant nation living at peace with its neighbours was now oppressed and denied the right to democratic government (*which had never existed in the country*),[2] by quoting his words of more than a quarter of a century ago. One had only to look at Hitler's Germany to see how much a country could change in very much less than twenty-five years.

He could hardly have chosen a more unfortunate comparison for before Germany was changed six million Jewish men, women and children were gassed and tortured to death, and the most frightful war in history, in which millions of others perished, had to be fought to defeat the Nazi tyranny whose leaders committed suicide or were executed or imprisoned for their crimes against humanity.

A hundred and forty-five years after Manning wrote of the conditions in which he found the Tibetans, Mr. Chapman found their surroundings the same. But he assumed that in the twenty-five years between his own departure from Lhasa and our arrival, the parasitic serf-owning clergy and nobility were transforming their medieval society into a modern democracy under the leadership of an 'enlightened and cultured' Dalai Lama whose programme of reforms (*of which no one in Lhasa had ever heard before 1951*)[3] would have been carried out but for the obstruction of the Chinese. Indeed it was impossible for the Chinese to have obstructed any reforms proposed by the Dalai Lama, for when they arrived he was a minor and had no political or executive authority.

When he first left Lhasa for Yatung in face of the Chinese advance, as much treasure as could be loaded on to a thousand pack animals went with him. Indian newspapers reported that this was worth about

1. In a letter to the *Daily Telegraph*.
2. Authors' italics.
3. Authors' italics.

four million dollars and there was one wild guess of 100 million. But no one will ever know the real value, for the Indian Government admitted it without customs examination. Certainly more than a hundred times as much was left behind, but when we walked through the old treasuries there was none to be seen. The Chinese have confiscated the fabulous store of jewels, gold, silver and precious objects which successive Dalai Lamas have collected through the centuries and have not disclosed their value. But, apart from these private possessions, all the priceless religious furnishings and sacred images of the palace remain undisturbed.

It is impossible for the camera to photograph or for words adequately to describe the magnificence of the Potala, which rises 440 feet above the plain and stretches more than 900 feet across the Red Hill on which it stands. It is the only distinguished building in the world whose splendour is so isolated from any other structure and there is none other which so completely commands the eyes which are drawn to it wherever one may stand in the city, or from the furthest points in the valley from which it is visible.

Its immense height is also enhanced by the walls which slope inwards from their base and by the optical illusion produced by the windows which, as in all other Tibetan architecture, narrow towards the top so that they appear to recede further from one's view, the higher they are placed.

The lower half of the colossal façade, which faces south over the valley, is of whitewashed stone. The middle section of the upper half, which projects from two flanking white wings built on a lower level, is deep crimson. From the centre of the façade hangs a vast 'curtain of heaven' woven from yak hair, eighty feet deep.

Beneath the eaves of the topmost roof and running its entire length is a deep maroon band of dyed twigs, cut flush to the stonework and bordered by a strip of white, embossed with four huge gold monograms which glow in the full light of the sun as if they are on fire. Against the background of splendid mountains the marvellously wrought golden canopies over the tombs of departed Dalai Lamas shine in a sky of such deep and unblemished blue that if one looks into it for more than a few moments it turns to indigo and one is temporarily blinded by its glare.

As the structure appears heightened by the inward sloping walls and receding windows so the breadth is increased by an immense stone stairway of 250 broad steps, wide enough for several horsemen to ride abreast, which crosses the façade from south to north-west,

Tsereh Wang Tuei, former serf of Drepung, who was blinded and mutilated
for stealing two sheep from his monastic lords

Tibetan grammar school teacher

turns sharply to the north-east to cross it again and as it approaches the entrance, turns to the north-west once more.

In this matchless setting the palace looks as if it grew naturally out of the ground instead of being built by men. But when it rains and the sky and mountains are hidden by grey cloud it becomes a monstrous prison and the most forbidding building on earth.

If Landon sometimes described Britain's Imperial mission as though he were reporting for *Chums* or *The Boy's Own Paper*, he was a faithful observer of the Tibetan physical scene. He was so deeply moved by this majesty that he wrote:

'Lamaism may be an engine of oppression, but its victims do not protest; and there before one's eyes at last is Lhasa. It may be a barrier to all human improvement; it may be a living type of all that we in the west have fought against and at last overcome, of bigotry, cruelty and slavery; but under the fierce sun of that day and the white gauze of the almost unclouded sky of Lhasa, it was not easy to find fault with the creed, however narrow and merciless, which built the Potala palace and laid out the green spaces at its foot. In this paradise of cool water and green leaves, hidden away among the encircling snows of the highest mountain ranges of the world, Lamaism has upraised the stones and gold of Lhasa, and nothing but Lamaism could have done this thing. To Lamaism alone we owe it that when at last the sight of the farthest goal of all travel burst upon our eyes, it was worthy, fully worthy, of all the rumour and glamour and romance with which in the imaginings of man it has been invested for so many years.'

But when he went inside he had to add:

'It must be confessed, though the words are written with considerable reluctance, that cheap and tawdry are the only possible adjectives which can be applied to the interior decoration of this great palace temple. Part of it is fine in design, most of it is commonplace, all of it is dirty.'

It remains as Landon found it except that the Chinese have cleaned it up.

No one has ever seen the 1,000 rooms of which the Potala is composed and probably no one ever will; most of them are the same, dark, cheerless, malodorous. There is no water supply nor sanitary system. The toilets, including that of the Dalai Lama, which is a small windowless, airless closet leading off his private audience chamber, are holes in the floors, open to cesspits in cellars more than 400 feet below.

The palace includes a small monastery once inhabited by 170 monks. Apart from their individual religious duties, they were concerned with the care of shrines and attendance upon the Dalai Lama himself.

N

The priest population of the building was probably never more than four or five hundred men, but an army of serfs and monk servants was required to supply them with all their needs. All food and drinking water and butter and water for innumerable holy vessels and lamps had to be carried up the 250 steps. A lama who had lived here for most of his life, told us that in former days the great stairway was filled with a never-ending procession of porters so that it must have given an impression of a gigantic escalator in perpetual motion.

It is believed that forty or fifty of the Potala monks followed the Dalai Lama to India. One is known to have been killed in the fighting during the rebellion when a group of lay rebels locked themselves in the palace. Thirty still live there. The remainder have gone to join the community at the Jokhan, or have returned to their homes. The building, like all other 'royal' establishments, is now a museum, for whose preservation and maintenance a Chinese curator is responsible.

Two elderly quiet-faced lamas were in charge of the private apartments of the Dalai Lama, which no one may enter except by permission of the Lhasa Government. Perhaps he will never return, for although he could not be deprived of his religious authority, he could only do so as a political subject of the Chinese. Nevertheless, although it may be an impossible journey for him to make, the way back is being kept open for him so that his home is preserved exactly as he left it. The day will also come when the fourteenth Incarnation must depart to the 'Honourable Field'. When he does, he may decide to rest there in eternal peace but, according to Buddhist belief, if he decides to be reincarnated once more in a human body, no earthly power can prevent him. The Chinese could discourage his discovery but they will have to think hard before they meddle in such miraculous matters. Or course it will always be possible for them to select a suitable candidate and presumably there would be no difficulty in persuading the High Lamas entrusted with the discovery of a fifteenth body to approve the Chinese choice according to the prescribed formula.

Mr. Chiang Tsu-ming, the Deputy Director of the Tibet Foreign Affairs Bureau, would be outraged by the suggestion and Prime Minister Chou En-lai and Foreign Minister Chen Yi would deprecate it, but a dilemma may one day confront the Peking Government.

It is also possible that if the present Dalai Lama lives for another fifty years, when all the older people will have died off, the new generation educated in the ways of Communism will have lost interest in Chenrezi and other incarnate gods. In the meantime the Chinese are doing nothing to lead any Tibetans to believe that the Dalai Lama is not welcome to come home when he likes. To permit them to enter his chambers, to which no mortals other than his personal servants and priest officials were admitted, would be as good as telling them that he would never return.

Perhaps because we were foreigners, the attendant lamas did not resent our intrusion and although they refused to sit down themselves on the lion-skin covered couches of the sitting-room because they said they still felt aware of The Presence, they invited us to rest on them and graciously presented us with long sticks of black incense specially made for the Dalai Lama and which none other was permitted to burn.

This was the most luxurious living known to Tibetans, but there were perhaps more penalties than privileges in being a god-king and one of them was being confined through the long bitter winters at the top of this unheated fortress.

During the previous month we had spoken with more of his countrymen than he would meet personally for as long as he lived. It was necessary for his Ministers, High Lamas and personal staff to approach him more informally, but others were not permitted to meet him face to face or to regard him with more than a brief glance as they bowed before him.

When he went through Lhasa in procession or travelled from the Potala to the Norbulingka, hefty monk policemen armed with heavy staves lined the streets and whacked anyone smartly over the head who was so bold as to stare rudely into the Incarnation's palanquin, in which he was concealed behind yellow curtains.

The floor of the sitting-room was covered with beautifully coloured carpets. Three of the walls were decorated with charmingly painted panels of real and legendary animals, birds, religious scenes and symbols and golden deities in ornately carved cases. On a long shelf was a row of plain silver bowls containing holy water.

The roof, like the roofs of all palaces and temples in Tibet, was supported by pillars clothed in highly coloured and richly decorated scalloped tapestry. This form of decoration had intrigued us ever since we arrived and now we learned for the first time that it was not there primarily for aesthetic pleasure but to protect the wood of the pillars from splitting in the intense cold.

The Dalai Lama's own seat was a couch behind a heavily carved table on which his gold and jade drinking cups still stood in their accustomed places. These were the gifts of Chinese emperors to a previous body.

The Incarnation's bedroom was guarded by a heavy door, like those of medieval castles, with elaborate metal hinges and an immense lock. From the centre hung a thick rope bound with multi-coloured strips of silk, attached to the gilded head of a legendary beast. The bed was an elaborately carved bunk like that in the Norbulingka Palace. When we expressed surprise that it was so short we were told it was necessary for its occupant to sleep in a Buddha-like position, prescribed by ritual, with knees bent. This sounded a fanciful explanation but there may have been some truth in it for in a bare room next door was an iron hospital cot. Perhaps when he had retired for the night and his retainers had gone, the young 'god' changed beds to get a decent night's rest.

The principal bedroom also contained a large case of Buddhas and the walls were close panelled with paintings of religious figures, landscapes, birds, beasts and flowers.

The great private audience chamber roof, like the sitting-room, was supported by pillars clothed with tapestries and here the capitals were carved with natural scenes. The Dalai Lama's throne stood on a broad dais behind which was a wall composed of religious images. The throne was flanked by large porcelain vases filled with artificial flowers as incongruous in this setting as pots of aspidistras in the galleries of Hampton Court.

And here the Chinese had installed electricity. Hanging between the pillars was a long flex at the end of which a bulb was covered with a white china kitchen shade. It was as comically shocking as if the attendant lamas had suddenly gone into a 'Knees up, Mother Brown'.

Not that the Tibetans themselves hadn't also introduced strange incongruities. We were photographing a wall painting of Tibetan nobles in another throne room when, amongst portraits of Cabinet Ministers, including Apei in ceremonial robes with his hair tied into a bun on top of his head, we found ourselves staring at Edward Prince of Wales (Duke of Windsor), who looked at us with the chocolate-box Prince Charming smile which had turned over every flapper's heart when we were children.

We asked a monk if he knew who he was. No, he said, but perhaps he was some foreign religious dignitary or noble. Most likely, the artist copied the prince's head from a photograph in an old magazine for there were other unidentifiable foreign characters mixed up with the local aristocrats.

There are many chapels in the Potala but they are of no special interest, being replicas of nearly all monastic shrines. One of the most important contains life-size statues of King Songsten Gambo, the Princess Wen Cheng, and his Nepalese wife with their cooking-pot which legend says they used when they lived on the Red Hill a thousand years before the Potala was built by the 'Great Fifth'.

On this storey is also the Yik Tsang (nest of letters), the Secretariat of the Dalai Lamas. Here documents are stitched into rolls of cloth and filed by hanging them in any spare space on pillars, furniture and walls. Before the main doors of the more important chambers hang long cylinders of tiger-skin, symbols of justice and ruling power.

The bodies of all Dalai Lamas, except the Sixth, who was deposed, and those murdered in childhood, are embalmed in the Potala and the canopies of their tombs which rise over the roof are the crowning splendour of the palace. The most splendid of all, and the last to be made, contains the remains of the Thirteenth.

Sheathed with 300,000 ounces of solid gold, this rises seventy feet through three storeys to join the canopy at roof level. The base standing in a room forty feet square contains personal possessions of the departed Incarnation, precious gifts from the priesthood and laity, grain, tea and religious objects. In a great sphere above, the body sits in the posture of the Buddha.

The corpse was preserved by rubbing it with a salty solution coated with clay and thickly lacquered with pure gold leaf. This human statue was then clothed in costly robes and enthroned. Placed around it are the departed god's favourite scriptures, books and writing materials. From the spherical tomb rises a cone which soars to the underside of the roof of the palace where it is surmounted by a bell on which the rising sun and moon are engraved. The entire structure is studded with turquoise, amethysts, lapis lazuli, sapphires, onyx, coral, diamonds and rubies.

Of all buildings on earth, the Potala demanded interior decorators whose imaginations matched the inspiration of its architects but the ecclesiastical lords who ordered it to be made were not satisfied with the perfect symmetry of this tomb and its jewelled decoration. They embellished it with large silver balls hanging from the ceiling and an altar at its foot crowded with finely wrought gold and silver holy-water vessels, porcelain vases and exquisitely designed butter lamps jumbled up with every kind imaginable of tawdry religious bric-à-brac so that the whole shrine had been given the appearance of a fairground shooting gallery. A row of rifles for potting at the balls would hardly have seemed out of place. We had not been so shocked since we had walked into Siena Cathedral to be confronted with an enormous banner slung across the nave bearing a crudely painted picture of a young girl in a flannel nightdress lying in an iron cot. If we had not been told that she was a saint about to be officially canonised we should have assumed the canons were short of cash and had allowed a local junk-dealer to put up a poster advertising secondhand beds.

24

CLOUDS OF CONFUSION

We remained friends with our Chinese Communist companions despite our ridicule of their more tendentious propaganda, for example that they had freed Tibet from foreign invaders, including our own countrymen. Translated from jargon, this could only make sense if they were suggesting that with the Americans we should have liked to prevent them from entering the country if we could. This was true and in so far as it was a continuation of Lord Curzon's attitude to China, the Chinese could regard us as unregenerate if frustrated Imperialists whose interest in Tibetan independence, as always, was less concerned with the welfare of the Tibetan people than with our own security.

It would have been less confusing to everyone if the Peking Government had said so instead of trying to justify the occupation of a country over which they had exercised no control since 1911, by announcing that they and the 'Lhasa local government' had agreed to 'unite and drive out the aggressive imperialist forces from Tibet' so that the Tibetan people could return to the big family of the motherland.

Argument collapsed in laughter when we reminded our friends, who regarded our attempts to be objective as incorrigible British chauvinism, that by this kind of political sophistry, the Chinese Communists did not convince anyone of their integrity any more than on another occasion the Governor of Shantung convinced his friends of his erudition. The illiterate old warlord, being anxious to demonstrate his concern for learning brought a professor of foreign languages to the provincial university. He invited him to dinner and introduced him to his other guests by saying, 'Now here we have a very accomplished man who speaks the English of six different countries.'

The Chinese reoccupied Tibet for three reasons. They were the

first Chinese Government since the collapse of the Manchu dynasty
with sufficient strength to do so and reassert the sovereignty which had
not been seriously questioned until the British invented suzerainty to
justify their own interference in Tibetan and Chinese affairs.

Generalissimo Chiang Kai-shek, recognized by the United States
—and the United Nations—as President of all China, would do the
same if he could regain control over the mainland. The State Department has not found it possible to rebuke him for his claim that Tibet
is part of China. There is no conflict between him and Mao Tse-tung
over this matter.

Secondly, the Communists considered it necessary to protect their
furthest western frontier against possible encroachment.

The third reason was given to us by Foreign Minister Marshal
Chen Yi. Since China is a multi-national state in which there is a
population of fifty million minorities and two million of these are
Tibetans living in Sinkiang, Kansu, Chinghai, Szechuan and Yünnan
under the rule of Peking, the government could not permit more than
a million others to exist as serfs without denying the purposes of the
revolution and abandoning its responsibilities.

If Peking had been less tortuous in self-justification and reasserted
China's sovereignty without announcing that her army had been
invited by the Dalai Lama's government to occupy Lhasa and reunite
Tibet with 'the motherland' when, in fact, the 'liberators' had been
met with armed resistance, their subsequent claims to have introduced
long-needed reforms might have been regarded with less scepticism,
and the wild charges of genocide made by some Tibetan refugees
might not have been so unquestioningly believed.

Instead the Communists have justified themselves by quoting
the 17 Article Agreement signed by Apei and four other representatives of the Dalai Lama in Peking on 23rd May 1951, expecting the
world to believe that this was a freely negotiated treaty. We have the
word of Apei, former member of the Dalai Lama's Cabinet, Commander-in-Chief of the Tibetan Army and present Secretary-General
of the Tibetan Government, that it was not, despite the fact that he
has told different stories to different people.

He told the Dalai Lama that he had been defeated by the Chinese
and was a prisoner. Therefore, in the face of the overwhelming power
of the People's Liberation Army he sought authority, which he received, to negotiate peace terms.

Robert Ford, who was employed by the Tibetan Government as a
radio operator at Chamdo, has written that when they discussed how he
should leave Tibet in the event of defeat Apei told him—'You do not

Tibetan theologian, the High Lama Tu Teng Ka Tsung

Tibetan youth wearing portrait brooch of Fourteenth Dalai Lama

A village schoolgirl

Johkan Buddha decorated with Hatas (good-luck scarves)

need to worry. We shall not give the Chinese permission to send troops into Tibet. If they enter by force we shall resist. If necessary, of course, we shall evacuate Chamdo and retreat on Lhasa. There will be no local surrender as long as I am in Chamdo.'[1]

This is how one would have expected the Tibetan Commander to behave and there is no reason to doubt Ford's account of this conversation. But eleven years later in Lhasa, Apei decided to tell us that although he had been ordered to oppose the Communists, he had no intention of fighting them and began to disband his forces as soon as he arrived at the border. There was no heavy fighting so there was no question of battle being won or lost.

These contradictions apart, would the People's Liberation troops have advanced into Tibet if the Tibetans had refused to sign the agreement? Of course they would. Peking had already announced, immediately after the defeat of Chiang Kai-shek, that this was precisely what they were going to do because Tibet was part of China.

It is true that the Chinese held their troops at Chamdo until the agreement had been signed but this delay had nothing to do with their concern for the rights of Tibetans to make their own decisions. It was dictated by political and tactical considerations. A bloodless victory would save many Chinese as well as Tibetan lives. Why provoke guerilla resistance over an enormous area which it would take disproportionate military forces to subdue when the Tibetan and lay aristocracy could be convinced that their authority would be unaffected?

The feudal lords, just as sensibly, accepted the terms which were offered to them but this did not mean they would not have repelled the Communists if they had been able to do so.

But the Tibetan rulers were naive if they thought the agreement was anything more than an armistice, for none with their wits about them could have supposed that the Communists would permit a separate and feudal society to exist within a national Socialist state. They openly defied the agreement by armed rebellion in 1959 because they could not continue to uphold it without destroying their own power. The Peking Government did not keep to it in its entirety because some of its provisions contradicted their own intentions.

It promised that:

'The central authorities will not alter the existing political system in Tibet. The central authorities also will not alter the established status, functions and powers of the Dalai Lama. Officers of various ranks shall hold office as usual.'

1. Captured in Tibet (Harrap).

According to the common use of words, this could only mean that the Communists would not abolish serfdom or the political arrangements by which a small minority of lay lords and the monasteries not only ruled, but owned the country and most of the people in it.

This undertaking was re-emphasised in Article 7, which, after undertaking that the 'religious beliefs, customs and habits of the Tibetan people shall be respected and lamaseries protected', stated: 'The central authorities will not effect any change in the income of the monasteries.'

Since monastic income was entirely dependent on the labour of serfs, this could only mean that either the serfs would remain bound to their owners or if the Central Government freed them it would continue to guarantee to the monasteries the wealth they had produced.

Article 10 was more vague, saying that agriculture, livestock raising, industry and commerce should be developed step by step and the people's livelihood 'shall be improved step by step in accordance with the actual conditions in Tibet'.

How could the conditions of serfs be improved if their owners and landlords were to retain their privileges and income, unless the Central Government was going to alter those conditions which it had promised to preserve? As though to remove any uneasiness on the part of the serf owners the first sentence of Article 11 was reassuring. It said:

'In matters related to various reforms in Tibet there will be no compulsion on the part of the central authorities.'

This was immediately followed by the salutary warning that:

'The local government of Tibet should carry out reforms of its own accord and when the people raise demands for reform they shall be settled by means of consultation with the leading personnel of Tibet.'

In accordance with Article 15 the Central Government was to set up a military and administrative committee and a military area command. Local Tibetan members of the committee would include 'patriotic elements from the local government of Tibet, various districts and leading monasteries and—the name list shall be drawn up after consultation between the representatives designated by the Central People's Government for appointment'.

Patriotic elements would naturally be those Tibetans who could be relied upon to support any changes proposed by Peking and therefore demanded by 'the people'. The necessity of submitting all names proposed for the committee to the Chinese made it clear that none who would not be reliable supporters of Communist policies would be accepted.

There could hardly be reasonable objections to Chinese insistence that those who had supported Chiang Kai-shek, or were pro-American or pro-British, should sever relations with their friends who opposed Peking. It was also essential, if Tibet was a part of the Chinese Republic, for Peking to conduct its foreign policy.

The Dalai Lama has written that the 'Preparatory Committee for the Tibet Autonomous Region', of which he was appointed Chairman and whose purpose was to prepare the country for regional autonomy, was a mere façade behind which the Communists exercised complete control of Tibet. The majority of members were Tibetans but, like all others, they were approved by Peking. Basic policies were in fact decided by a body called the Committee of the Chinese Communist Party in Tibet, which included no Tibetans. The Dalai Lama therefore had no real political or administrative authority.

But if the Chinese in their anxiety to 'liberate' Tibet peacefully had diplomatically—but sometimes not convincingly—concealed their real intentions of transforming the country, the Tibetan leaders, who could not have been as obtuse as some of them now pretend, were also ambivalent in their attitude to their 'liberators'.

If events from 1951 to 1959 are clouded in confusion, none has helped to confuse us more than the Dalai Lama himself by his contradictory accounts of the Chinese occupation and the Tibetan rebellion.

No one but he can say what he kept secretly in his mind during those years, but he made no secret of his admiration for Mao Tse-tung four years after the Chinese Communist leader had ordered his army to 'invade' Lhasa.

25

HYMN TO MAO

In the central shrine of the Buddhist Temple of Broad Charity in Peking hangs this hymn to Mao Tse-tung, written in the Dalai Lama's own hand and presented by him when he visited the capital in 1954. It reads:

'The great national leader of the Central People's Government, Chairman Mao, is the Cakravarti born out of boundless fine merits. For a long time I wished to write a hymn praying for his long life and the success of his work. It happened that the Klatsuang-kergun Lama of Kantsu Monastery in Inner Mongolia wrote me from afar, saluting me and asked me to write a poem. I agreed to do so as this coincides with my own wishes.

The Fourteenth Dalai Lama Dantzen-Jaltso
at Norbulin-shenfu Palace, 1954.

O, the Triratna,[1] (Buddha, Dharma and Sangha) which
    bestow blessings on the world,
Protect us with your incomparable and blessed light
    which shines for ever.

O! Chairman Mao! Your brilliance and deeds are like
    those of Brahma and Mahasammata, creators of the
    world.
Only from an infinite number of good deeds can such a
    leader be born, who is like the sun shining over the
    world.

Your writings are precious as pearls, abundant and
    powerful as the high tide of ocean reaching the edges
    of the sky.

1. Triratna—Trinity of Buddha, Dharma (the Law) and Sangha, the congregation of believers.

O! most honourable Chairman Mao, may you long live.

All people look to you as to a kind protecting mother,
they paint pictures of you with hearts full of emotion,
May you live in the world forever and point out to
us the peaceful road!

Our vast land was burdened with pain, with shackles and
darkness.
You liberated all with your brilliance. People now are
happy, full of blessings!

Your work for peace is a white jewelled umbrella, giving
shade over heaven and earth and mankind.
Your fame is like golden bells on the umbrella, ringing
and turning forever in the sky!

Our foe, the bloodthirsty imperialists, are poisonous
snakes, and messengers of the devil furtively crawling,
You are the undaunted roc which conquered the
poisonous serpent. To you be power!

The cultural and industrial constructions which make
the people prosperous and defeat the enemy's armed
forces are like a vast sea;
These constructions develop continuously until they shall
make this world as full of satisfaction as heaven.

The perfect religion of Sakyamuni (Buddha) is like a
Moonlight pearl lamp shining bright.
It is like a perfumed pearl ornament which we wear
without prohibition. O! Of this we are proud.

Your will is like the gathering of clouds, your call like
thunder,
From these comes timely rain to nourish selflessly the
earth!

As the Ganges River rushes precious and to all the earth
The cause of peace and justice will bring to all peoples
boundless joy!
May our world gradually become as happy as paradise!
May the torch of our great leader, be lit forever.

May the powers of the benevolent Bodhisattvas, the
resourceful Dharma-Protector and the truthful words
of the Maharishis make these good hopes true.

This hymn probably astonished Mao Tse-tung, who is used to extravagant adulation, as much as it may now embarrass and dismay its author. But unless the Dalai Lama suggests that this is the traditional manner in which Tibetan kings praise their conquerors and that the hymn is no more than a formal address, he can hardly protest that his situation required him to make such genuflections, nor that the man who gave him 'the impression of kindness and sincerity', demanded praise comparing him with the creator of the world.

However, from exile eight years later he recalled that soon after delivering this eulogy to the Communist leader, who had liberated his country from 'burdens of pain' and 'shackles and darkness', he was disillusioned.

On his way home to Lhasa from Peking he found mounting bitterness and hatred of the Chinese who had grown increasingly ruthless. The resentment of Tibetans against their 'liberators' was boiling. The ink of the poem of praise was hardly dry before he was discovering that Mao's government was destroying religious freedom in China. Buddhist monasteries were being starved to death and allowed to decay.

But obviously not the Temple of Broad Charity in Peking which was built before Kublai Khan and restored to perfection by the Communists.

When he reached Lhasa, the Dalai Lama found that his Cabinet was still on tolerably friendly terms with the Chinese. The hostility of the people seemed to have died down and given way to complacency. The city was quiet and peaceful. But then he added, the citizens didn't know of Chinese repressions in the border areas and the full force of the bitter resentments of their countrymen hadn't spread to the centre of the country.

Four sentences later in the memoirs, the Cabinet wasn't even prepared to be courteous to China's Deputy Premier and Foreign Minister. Marshal Chen Yi was coming to inaugurate the new Preparatory Committee for the Autonomous Region of Tibet. Not unnaturally, since there could be no working relationship if the head of the Tibetan Government was not on speaking terms with Peking's representative, he expected the Dalai Lama to receive him. But the Cabinet wouldn't agree.

The Dalai Lama felt this was no time for standing on his dignity but with a staggering unconsciousness of the situation, even for a young man untutored in politics, he wrote in his autobigraphy:

'If it would please the Marshal and help to give the Committee [of which he was designated the first Chairman] a better start, I thought it worth it; so I went.'

Which perhaps explains why two years before the Dalai Lama's memoirs were published, Chen Yi told us that after his talks in Lhasa, he concluded that the Dalai Lama and his nobles had no intention of carrying out reforms if they could help it. Perhaps the old soldier-statesman, who was also a poet, was too cynical an observer—and maker—of history to mistake poetic emotion for political intention. At any rate he seems to have known the Tibetan rulers better than they then knew themselves.

The Dalai Lama has recalled these days by describing 'popular' resentment against the actions of the Preparatory Committee over which he presided and spontaneous demands for its abolition. But he doesn't say exactly what was resented, or how serfs who had never been permitted to express political opinions came to voice them now.

Doubtless the nobility thought any social and economic changes in Tibet of which they were unquestionable rulers were unnecessary.

As the Dalai Lama has written, outside the monasteries this was a feudal society. There was 'inequality of wealth between the landed aristocracy at one extreme and the poorest peasants at the other'.

It was difficult, he explained, to move up into the class of aristocracy but not impossible. For instance, through bravery a soldier could be given hereditary land and a title.

So, the only hope of the odd Tibetan to improve his condition was to wait for a war in which he might be brave enough to earn a title and a piece of land if he was lucky enough to survive? The Dalai Lama hasn't given us any other example of civilian opportunities for advancement but says that promotion in the monasteries was demo-cratic. According to him the reincarnation of High Lamas could also be said to have a democratic influence because, like himself and his brother, Thubten Jigme Norbu, they often chose to be reborn in humble families.

The chance of a Tibetan peasant boy becoming a Dalai Lama, or the rich Abbot of a great monastery, was about as remote as an English farm labourer winning a fortune on the football pools.

In the Fourteenth Incarnation's opinion, the material life of the Tibetan people (except in the monasteries) was very much like the life of a peasant class in any other country. Three paragraphs later he writes that during his education—which wasn't completed when the Chinese first came to Tibet—he learned very little of any other social system 'but our own'. And although he could speak of a popular demand for the abolition of the new Preparatory Committee because the people were well satisfied with their traditional government, in another breath he could say the Tibetans in general thought of their feudal system as a natural state of affairs and *never gave a thought to any theories of government*.[1]

But although he knew nothing of politics or the world, he remembered, from India, that as he grew up he began to see how much was wrong with Tibetan society. Inequality in the distribution of wealth was not in accordance with Buddhist teaching and 'in the few years when I held effective power in Tibet I managed to make some fundamental reforms'. He recalls that he appointed special committees of lay and monk officials and monastic representatives to consider them.

So it was the Chinese Communists who frustrated social and economic improvements in Tibet because they wanted to introduce their own.

But when were his years of effective power during which the Dalai Lama persuaded his Cabinet and high officials to introduce tax and land reforms?

When the Chinese came to Tibet he was only sixteen. The country was ruled by a Regent. In the face of the Chinese advance he was hastily invested with full powers which normally would have come to him two years later, but he had no time to exercise authority before the state oracle advised that he should go to Yatung near the Indian frontier over which he could escape to Mr. Nehru's protection if his life was felt to be in danger. When he returned to Lhasa it was already occupied by Chinese troops and officials and from that time according to his own story he had no real control over events.

There is no record of reforms instituted by him or his local government during the period between his return to the capital from Yatung and his departure for a tour of China in 1954, nor in the time after he returned from Peking and his final flight to India. Because according to him there was nothing he could do.

It is not impossible that in suppressing rebellion human beings should behave with the savagery described by the Dalai Lama, who learned of it by hearsay. But we do not require evidence from Peking that the Chinese People's Liberation Army is one of the best disciplined and behaved in the world.

Describing the successful war which the Communist soldiers fought against the Japanese, the Councillor of the United States Embassy in Chungking wrote to the Secretary of State:

'This total mobilisation is based upon and has been made possible by what amounts to an economic, political and social revolution. It has

1. Authors' italics.

A reading class at Dege (good luck) Street People's Primary School

A primary school pupil

OPPOSITE

above: A Tibetan actress—daughter of a former serf

below: Youngest member of the first Tibetan drama school

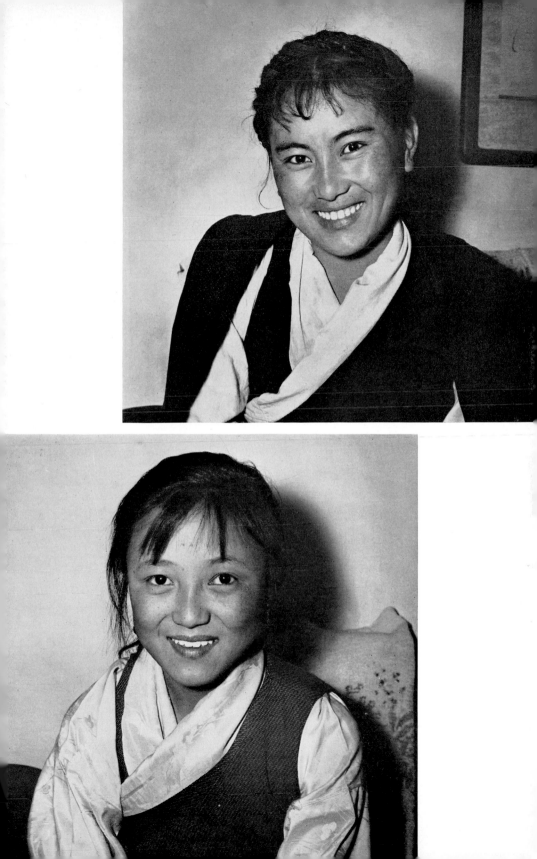

Matron and orphan at old folks' and children's home, Tsai Gon Tang village

Woman of old folks' home wearing clothes confiscated from house of a noble who took part in 1959 rebellion

improved the economic condition of the peasants by rent and interest reduction, tax reform and good government. It has given them democratic self-government, political consciousness and a sense of their rights. It has freed them from feudalistic bonds and given them self-respect and a strong feeling of co-operative group interest. The common people, for the first time have something to fight for.'

After being imprisoned by them without trial for five years, Robert Ford, who was captured in Tibet, cannot be expected to entertain friendly feelings for the Communists. But he has written that when they came 'there was no sacking of monasteries. They made it clear they had no quarrel with religion, nor with the Tibetan people, who were treated correctly.'[1]

Despite the tremendous supply problem, he added, the advance units of the Army didn't live off the country. They carried a week's emergency rations. They had strict orders to respect persons and property and make friends with the people 'by all possible means'. Brotherhood was the keynote and no Chinese troops in Tibet 'had ever behaved so well'.

---

1. Not perhaps unnaturally after the treatment he received Mr. Ford ascribed this good behaviour to Chinese political cunning.

26

REBELLION IN LHASA

If throughout the Dalai Lama's memoirs one reads 'people' for 'government, monasteries and nobility' it will appear that the struggle of the ecclesiastical and lay lords to preserve their power was also the struggle of Tibetan serfs to preserve a freedom they didn't possess. Ironically, the Chinese may have helped to provoke rebellion not by oppressing the serfs but by tolerating serfdom too long in their anxiety to avoid conflict with the feudal establishment.

If immediately on their occupation of the country they had abolished the feudal system it is possible that the revolt would never have taken place for then the serfs could have welcomed them as liberators from their bondage. In fact the Communists observance of that part of the 17 Article Agreement stipulating that reform should not be enforced but proceed step by step, also enabled the feudal rulers to identify themselves with the people, for they could now tell them that the Communists, like all previous Chinese 'invaders', were interested in the conquest of the country for their own ends and had no concern for the welfare of the common folk—otherwise why had they left them as they were.

The Dalai Lama has recalled that when he went to Peking to see Mao Tse-tung, the people were unwilling that he should go because they feared he might not be allowed to return. He hasn't explained how the people, who were never consulted about his movements, expressed their apprehensions, nor why anyone should imagine that the Chinese should wish to kidnap the god-king who in his public statements had proved to be Mao's most valuable ally in Tibet. The man who was about to publish his hymn of praise to the Communist leader, whom he wished might live for ever, could hardly have feared he might be made a prisoner in Peking. However, he says, the citizens were sad and depressed to see him depart, but they let him go. He came back safe and sound.

In 1956 he visited India. The Chinese obviously trusted him to return to Tibet, as he had trusted them with his freedom when he went to China two years earlier. They were justified in their confidence, but only just.

When he met Nehru, he told the Indian Premier that he was afraid the Chinese meant to destroy Tibetan religion. He now therefore pinned all his hopes on Delhi and explained that he wished to stay in India until his country could regain its freedom by peaceful means.

Mr. Nehru advised him to go home, saying that 'nobody had ever formally recognized our country's independence'[1] and it was useless to try to fight against the Chinese.

Having also received assurances from Chou En-lai, who was visiting Delhi at the same time, that complaints against Chinese in Tibet would be reported to Mao Tse-tung and the causes removed, he returned to Lhasa.

There he was told that terrible atrocities were being committed in the east and north-east. The Chinese were using artillery and bombers against guerillas and totally destroying monasteries and villages, whose inhabitants were suspected of helping them. Lamas and lay leaders of the people were being imprisoned, tortured and killed. Sacred images and other holy objects were being smashed, derided or stolen. Blasphemous proclamations were being published.

In an effort, he says, to save his people from further suffering, th Dalai Lama now asked the Cabinet to send a mission to the rebels to ask them to lay down their arms with a promise that if they fulfilled his wishes no action would be taken against them. The mission, of two lay officials and three monks, ignored his instructions and joined the guerillas.[2]

1. Authors' italics

2. The Chinese Government claim that Tibetan Lords who accompanied the Dala Lama to Peking in 1954 began to organise armed rebellion among the Khampas in eastern Tibet on their way back to Lhasa, was dismissed as Communist propaganda by the nobles in exile, who protested that Tibetan revolts were inspired by Chinese oppression of the people. Surkhang Wang-chuk-Galeh was a member of the Tibetan cabinet for 18 years. He accompanied the Dalai Lama to Peking in 1954. In an interview with *The Guardian* in November 1963 this nobleman who was described by that newspaper as 'the key figure of the 1956-9 Tibetan revolt' boasted that he first laid plans for rebellion among the Khampas when travelling with the Dalai Lama through Kham on their way back to Lhasa. In 1958, said Surkhang, he persuaded the Dalai Lama to feed and equip the Khampas from secret arsenals, making the revolt nation-wide. We have only Surkhang's word for it that the Dalai Lama was in fact engaged in this deception. If he was not, attempts by the Tibetan nobles to implicate him bear out the Chinese contention that he was their victim in a situation over which

Now came the final crisis.

On 1st March 1959 the Dalai Lama was in the Jokhan Temple for the Monlam Festival celebrations when he received an invitation to a theatrical entertainment at the Chinese Army camp from the Commander, General Tan Kuan-san, who asked him to name a convenient date. He replied by saying he would attend a performance on 10th March.

He has now written that the Chinese, who insisted he should go without an armed escort, informed the commander of his personal bodyguard that he would be received at the camp entrance by unarmed Chinese soldiers.

A rumour spread through the city that the invitation was a plot to kidnap him. It would be impossible to understand why the Chinese should resort to such senseless action but for the Dalai Lama's explanation that 'there was another fact which made the people all the more certain that a trap had been laid to abduct me'.

This fact was that the Chinese National Assembly was to be held in Peking in April and the Chinese had asked him to attend. There was nothing remarkable, let alone sinister, in this invitation since the Dalai Lama was Chairman of the Tibet Preparatory Committee and since 1954 when he had attended the first session of the National Assembly, which met to discuss the new Chinese constitution, he had been the leader of the Tibetan delegation.

But he now recalls that knowing the mood of the people he had tried to avoid accepting the invitation and had not given a definite answer. Without waiting for it the Chinese had already announced in Peking that he was going.

This made the people in Lhasa very angry and naturally they concluded that the invitation was a ruse to fly him to China against his will.

If he had not made up his mind whether to go or not, how could the people of Lhasa know what he was thinking? How could they have learnt that he had tried to avoid accepting the invitation because he was aware of their 'mood'? How could they know that his acceptance had been published without his consent if the announcement had been made only in the Chinese capital?

Naturally he would discuss his intentions with his Ministers and

---

he had no control. In his autobiography describing his part in the events from 1951 to 1959, the Dalai Lama does not anywhere state that he personally took part in organising rebellion, let alone that he secretly armed the Tibetan rebels, nor have the Chinese at any time charged him with such duplicity.

senior officials but since when did they report private discussions
in the Norbulingka Palace to the people, unless they now made it
their business to broadcast their fears for the Dalai Lama's safety, who
was assuring everyone around him that he was in no danger from the
Chinese? How were 30,000 people, three-quarters of the population
of Lhasa, persuaded to surround the Norbulingka shouting in furious
anger: 'The Chinese Must Go,' 'Leave Tibet to the Tibetans'?

Why were people, who had seen him go 1,500 miles to Peking
and return safely, now afraid for him to make a brief journey from one
part of the city to another?

Since he had decided that the fury of the crowds was uncontrollable,
the Dalai Lama sent three Ministers to General Tan to explain that he
could not attend the theatrical performance. Anxious, he says, to
avoid a ruthless massacre of Tibetans, which he feared would result
from a clash with the Chinese forces, he ordered an announcement of
his decision to be made to the people but most of them still refused to
disperse.

According to his envoys, the Chinese General was in a towering
rage and used language never spoken in polite society. He threatened
drastic measures to crush opposition to Chinese rule.

The Ministers, says the Dalai Lama, tried to counsel patience and
told the General not to make the situation worse by retaliation. They
assured him that the government would do everything possible to
prevent foolhardy Tibetans from provoking armed conflict. The
General, with good reason as it soon turned out, was not reassured for
the Dalai Lama has reported that on the same evening, about seventy
members of the government ('mostly junior officials') together with
leaders chosen by the crowd and members of his own bodyguard, met
in the Norbulingka grounds to support a resolution declaring that
Tibet no longer recognized China's authority.

Apparently realising that this amounted to a declaration of civil
war, the Dalai Lama sent instructions to the leaders telling them it was
their duty to reduce tension and not to aggravate it. His orders were
ignored.

By the following day, the people were becoming more difficult
to control. They posted six guards near the Cabinet office inside the
Norbulingka and told Ministers they would not be allowed to leave.
The Cabinet once more appealed to the rebel leaders to ask the people
to disperse and they promised to do so. But barricades had already been
put up to the north of Lhasa on the highway to China.

The Chinese military commander informed the Cabinet that if
they did not order their removal they must accept responsibility for

the consequences. Again the Cabinet sent for the rebel leaders and 'advised' them to pull down the barriers. They flatly refused.

The Dalai Lama was distressed by a step which he feared would lead to disaster. The rebels now appointed men to guard his palace which they said they would not leave unprotected. This time he sent for the seventy insurgent leaders. He told them that General Tan had not compelled him to accept his invitation. He had in fact been consulted and given his consent before the invitation was formerly issued. He assured them he was in no personal danger from the Chinese. They agreed it was impossible to disobey his orders but ignored them just the same.

They left the Norbulingka and established headquarters in the hamlet of Sho at the foot of the Potala. From there they repeated their demand that the Chinese must evacuate Tibet.

On 16th March they reported to the Dalai Lama that the Chinese were bringing all their artillery within range of the Norbulingka. Chinese civilians repairing telegraph lines were said to be taking readings for range finding. The Dalai Lama admits that the people didn't know much about guns and might have been wrong.

By the morning of the 17th it seemed to him and his Cabinet that the situation was desperate. The fury of the people against the Chinese could not be restrained. The Cabinet wrote to Apei (Ngapo Ngawang Jigme), Secretary-General of the Preparatory Committee, who had been personally conveying messages between them and the Chinese and was at the Chinese camp, asking the Army commander not to use force to disperse the crowds but to wait until they had appealed to them once more to go home. The Ministers also asked Apei if he would help them to take the Dalai Lama to the Chinese camp for protection.

The Dalai Lama remembers that a special code was sent with this letter asking Apei to use it in his reply because the 'popular guards round the Norbulingka Palace were censoring any letters addressed to him or the Cabinet'.

Apei answered by saying the Cabinet's proposal to escort the Dalai Lama to the Chinese camp was welcome and he would reply in detail later.

But while his letter was being discussed there came the boom of two heavy mortar shells which were heard to splash in a marsh outside the north gate of the Norbulingka.

With this 'warning of death' says the Dalai Lama it was decided that he must escape from Lhasa. He and his Ministers consulted the leaders of the rebellion who agreed that his flight must take place without the people knowing. During that night he, his mother, sister and small brother left the city on their long journey to India.

Memories of this critical week were written by the Dalai Lama in India. But he left behind him in Lhasa a day-to-day record of events as they occurred, written in his own hand. This was contained in a series of letters written to General Tan in reply to letters from the Chinese commander.

When the Chinese published them, he complained that they had only done so to support their own propaganda, to prove that he wanted to seek shelter in the Chinese headquarters but was kept a prisoner in the Norbulingka by a 'reactionary clique' and was abducted to India against his will.

What else did he expect Mao Tse-tung's Government to do in face of accusations that their Army commander endangered his life? The Dalai Lama now protests that he wrote these letters to gain time for anger to cool and for him to urge moderation on the rebellious people. He says he also decided to write in a way which he hoped would calm down General Tan and that he could only do this by 'seeming' to accept his sympathy and welcome his advice.

He explains that he could not approve of the people's violence but appreciated their affection which was the real cause of their anger against the Chinese (*despite the fact that he had personally assured them he was in no danger from them*).[1] He was sure their actions could only lead to disaster and he felt he must prevent them bringing about their own destruction. Then he adds: 'and although my letters to the Chinese general were written to disguise my real intentions, I felt and still feel that they were justified'.

The Chinese could not be expected to know that he was only 'seeming' to accept and welcome General Tan's sympathy and advice. They could only read what he wrote and believe that he meant what he said.

If it was not holding him under duress to post guards at the doors of his palace to prevent him and his Ministers from moving in and out when he and the Cabinet had told the rebels they weren't wanted or needed there, how should this action be described?

If the members of the Tibetan Cabinet were not asking the Chinese commander to take the Dalai Lama under his protection when they wrote to Apei asking him to find a way of getting him to the Chinese camp, what were they doing?

The Chinese claim that the Dalai Lama was physically abducted from Lhasa against his will doesn't have to be accepted to believe that he may not have been as free to make the decision to escape as

1. Authors' italics.

he thinks he was, although his letters gave them some reason for their conclusion.

But if it is untrue that the Dalai Lama was forcibly taken away, it appears true from his own letters that the rebels who convinced him that his life was in danger made it difficult, if not impossible, for him to remain. And quite clearly by the night of 17th March 1959, he was persuaded that if he stayed he might be killed . . . not by General Tan Kuan-san, who had made it unmistakably clear to him that he was concerned for his safety, but by his own people whose behaviour despite his appeals to them to disperse peacefully was making armed conflict with the Chinese inevitable and unavoidable. What was the evidence which finally convinced the Dalai Lama that he must escape?

Apei had written a personal message, enclosed with General Tan's last letter, saying: 'If Your Holiness with a few trusted officers of the bodyguard can stay within the inner wall [of the Norbulingka] and hold a position there and inform General Tan Kuan-san exactly which building you will occupy, they will certainly intend that this building will not be damaged.'

From this the Dalai Lama says he concluded that Apei knew that the Chinese intended to destroy his palace and the crowd but wanted to do so, if they could, without also killing him. But this warning was necessary for the Dalai Lama's protection if the rebellion broke into open war and, to defend themselves, the Chinese felt compelled to storm the Norbulingka. The Chinese were not at this time threatening to fight the Tibetans. The leaders of the Tibetan rebels had declared that the Chinese must leave Lhasa and Tibet and if they carried out the threat to expel them, bloody conflict was certain.

The only other evidence of a Chinese intention to attack was the sound of mortar shells being fired and splashing into a marsh. For people who, according to the Dalai Lama, didn't know much about artillery, this was astonishingly accurate detection.

On 10th March 1959, after hearing from his Ministers that the Dalai Lama could not leave the Norbulingka to attend the theatrical performance in the Chinese camp, the Chinese commander wrote:

'Respected Dalai Lama,

It is very good indeed that you wanted to come to the Military Area Command. You are heartily welcome. But since the intrigues and provocations of the reactionaries have caused you very great difficulties, it may be advisable that for the time being you do not come.

Salutations and best regards,

Tan Kuan-san'

The Dalai Lama replied on 11th March:

'Dear Comrade Political Commissar Tan,
I intended to go to the Military Area Command to see the theatrical performance yesterday, but I was unable to do so, because of obstruction by people, lamas and laymen, who were instigated by a few evil elements and who did not know the facts; this has put me to indescribable shame. I am greatly upset and worried and at a loss what to do. I was immediately greatly delighted when your letter appeared before me—you do not mind at all.
Reactionary, evil elements are carrying out activities endangering me under the pretext of ensuring my safety. I am taking measures to calm things down. In a few days, when the situation becomes stable, I will certainly meet you. If you have any internal directives for me, please communicate them to me frankly through this messenger.
The Dalai Lama,
written by my own hand'

On the same day General Tan wrote to the Dalai Lama:

'To Dalai Lama:
The reactionaries have now become so audacious that they have openly and arrogantly engaged in military provocations. They have erected fortifications and posted large numbers of machine guns and armed reactionaries along the national defence highway (the highway north of the Norbulingka) thereby very seriously disrupting the security of national defence communications.
On many occasions in the past, we told the kasha[1] that the People's Liberation Army is in duty bound to defend the country and to ensure the protection of communications related to national defence; it certainly cannot remain indifferent to this serious act of military provocation. The Tibet Military Area Command has sent letters therefore, to Surkong, Neusha, Shasu and Pala asking them to tell the reactionaries to remove all the fortifications they have set up and to withdraw from the highway immediately. Otherwise, they will have to take full responsibility themselves for the evil consequences. I want to inform you of this. Please let me know what your views are at your earliest convenience.
Salutations and best regards
Tan Kuan-san'

1. Cabinet

The Dalai Lama replied on 12th March:

'Dear Comrade Political Commissar Tan,
    I suppose you have received my letter of yesterday forwarded to you by Ngapo (Apei). I have received the letter you sent me this morning. The unlawful activities of the reactionary clique cause me endless worry and sorrow. Yesterday I told the kasha to order the immediate dissolution of the illegal conference[1] and the immediate withdrawal of the reactionaries who arrogantly moved into the Norbulingka under the pretext of protecting me. As to the incidents of yesterday and the day before, which were brought about under the pretext of ensuring my safety and have seriously estranged relations between the Central People's Government and the local government, I am making every possible effort to deal with them. At eight thirty Peking time this morning, a few Tibetan army men suddenly fired several shots near the Chinghai-Tibet Highway. Fortunately, no serious disturbance occurred. I am planning to persuade a few subordinates and give them instructions.
    Please communicate to me frankly any instructive opinions you have for me.

                                                    The Dalai'

    General Tan answered on 15th March:

'Respected Dalai Lama,
    I have the honour to acknowledge receipt of your two letters dated March 11 and March 12. The traitorous activities of some reactionary elements among the upper social strata in Tibet have grown to intolerable proportions. These individuals, in collusion with foreigners, have engaged in reactionary, traitorous activities for quite some time. The Central People's Government has all along maintained a magnanimous attitude and enjoined the local government of Tibet to deal with them in all earnestness, but the local government of Tibet has all along adopted an attitude of feigning compliance while actually helping them in their activities, with the result that things have now come to such a grave pass. The Central People's Government still hopes that the local government of Tibet will change its wrong attitude and immediately assume responsibility for putting down the rebellion and mete out severe punishment to the traitors. Otherwise the Central People's Government will have to act itself to safeguard the solidarity and unification of the motherland.

    1. Underground Tibetan Resistance Movement.

In your letter, you said: "As to the incidents ... which were brought about under the pretext of ensuring my safety and have seriously estranged relations between the Central People's Government and the local government, I am making every possible effort to deal with them." We warmly welcome this correct attitude on your part.

We are very much concerned about your present situation and safety. If you think it necessary and possible to extricate yourself from your present dangerous position of being held by the traitors, we cordially welcome you and your entourage to come and stay for a short time in the Military Area Command. We are willing to assume full responsibility for your safety. As to what is the best course to follow, it is entirely up to you to decide.

In addition, I have much pleasure in informing you that it has been decided that the Second National People's Congress will open its first session on April 17.

Salutations and best regards,
Tan Kuan-san'

The third and last letter of the Dalai Lama to General Tan was written on 16th March. It reads:

'Dear Comrade Political Commissar Tan,

Your letter dated the 15th has just been received at three o'clock. I am very glad that you are so concerned about my safety and hereby express my thanks.

The day before yesterday, the fifth day of the second month according to the Tibetan calendar, I made a speech to more than seventy representatives of the government officials, instructing them from various angles, calling on them to consider seriously present and long-term interests and to calm down, otherwise my life would be in danger. After these severe reproaches, things took a slight turn for the better. Though the conditions here and outside are still very difficult to handle at present, I am trying tactfully to draw a line separating the progressive people among the government officials from those opposing the revolution. In a few days from now, when there are enough forces I can trust, I shall make my way to the Military Area Command. When that time comes, I shall first send you a letter. I request you to adopt reliable measures. What are your views? Please write me often.

The Dalai'

27

NO RING OF TRUTH

When the Chinese discovered that the Dalai Lama had gone they made no attempt to pursue him. There was only one way for him to go—to India. The routes in this wild country over which it was possible to travel by horse were well known. There would have been no difficulty in overtaking his party, including his mother, other elderly people and children, who couldn't be expected to ride like cavalrymen. In fact his movements were followed by observation aircraft and his arrival in India was reported by Peking radio before it was known in Delhi.

The Chinese Foreign Minister, Marshal Chen Yi, gave one good reason why no attempt was made to capture the Dalai Lama when he told us:

'It is certain that the rebel escort would have resisted any attempt to contact him. They wouldn't have hesitated to shoot at our soldiers and if their fire had been returned the Dalai Lama might have been accidentally wounded, if not killed. We didn't wish him to go. We believe he was taken against his better judgment, expressed in his letters to General Tan which accurately described the situation and his personal dilemma. We had no reason to harm him. His own account of the rebellion proved his innocence of personal complicity in the rebellion whatever he may have said or been reported to have said since—unless he now wishes to accuse himself of eight years of deception.'

According to Chinese military records, confirmed by the Dalai Lama, who has not reported that any fighting took place when he was in Lhasa, the rebellion flared into war at 3.40 a.m. on 20th March, forty-eight hours after he was clear of the city.

The Chinese commander told Peking that the rebels then opened fire from the Potala, the Norbulingka and Iron Hill. During the preceding week, he had confined his troops to barracks in accordance with instructions from his government not to retaliate against demonstrations, however provocative, unless he was directly attacked. It was not until 10 a.m., six hours and twenty minutes after the first rebel shots, that he received a radio message from Peking authorising him to take counter-action.

The Dalai Lama was told by refugees said to have escaped from Lhasa, that by the end of this day the Norbulingka was a smoking ruin full of dead. We have already described how we found his own palace residence—Chensel Phodrang—intact as he left it, as well as all the other palaces of previous Bodies.

There was no atrocity story too lurid for Western newspapers to believe or invent. Lamas had been slowly tortured and hung by the heels from temple bells. We searched for those bells in Lhasa but found none big enough to carry the weight of a cat. According to the imaginative journalists the Panchen Lama was first murdered, then abducted to Peking, now enthroned by the Chinese as the Fifteenth Dalai Lama in the Potala. No nonsense was too nonsensical to accept.

But the Dalai Lama's correspondence with General Tan Kuan-san had not been published then.

The Chinese have not criticised the Dalai Lama, let alone denounced him, because they have no evidence that he was responsible for the rebellion. They have only his own evidence, supplied by himself, that he was an unwilling victim of it. They did not invent the story that he was a prisoner of his own people. He told them so himself.

The rebellion in Lhasa lasted forty-eight hours, during which more than 7,000 Tibetans surrendered to about 1,500 regular Chinese troops.

The city hospital records show that fewer than a hundred injured rebels were treated, the majority being walking wounded. It was estimated that about 1,500 had run away but the exact number can never be known. Also a great many wounded would not go to the hospital unless they were taken as prisoners. From reports of Chinese units engaged in the fighting, it was estimated that the total number of Tibetan casualties was not more than 600 and fewer than half were killed.

It took only three hours and one company of infantry, supported by machine-gunners, to take Iron Hill, the highest point in the city from which all Lhasa could be commanded by artillery. By seven o'clock in the evening the Norbulingka, where there were 3,000 rebels, had capitulated. The most stubborn fighting was at the Ramogia Monastery. By nightfall the only rebel forces in action were in the Potala and the Jokhan. They had both surrendered by the following day.

Had the rising been well organised and as popular and spontaneous as the exiled government claims, the result could have meant the over-whelming defeat of the Chinese. For when it was all over, the rebels were found to have abandoned about 20,000 shells and seventy-nine guns and machine-guns, more than 10,000 rifles and nearly ten million rounds of ammunition.

In the Loka area, the granary of Tibet, in the south-east, the revolt lasted two weeks longer and it was estimated that more than 12,000 men were involved. By the end of April nearly 5,000 had surrendered. In this guerilla fighting, as in most of the scattered engagements in Lhasa itself, few on either side were killed.

The 1959 revolt was the end and not the beginning of rebellion in Tibet.

The Chinese admit that as early as 1955–6 10,000 Khampas and other guerillas were resisting the occupation of their country by the Chinese forces.

In 1958 there was an outbreak in Kansu and Chinghai. The Chinese claim to have discovered documents proving that this was inspired by the monasteries and landlords who resisted any interference with their authority and particularly any reduction in rents and taxes. They also resented the abolition of monastic prisons and courts, which had tried monastery serfs.

It ought not to be surprising that stories of atrocities by the Chinese in Tibet are so readily accepted. The twentieth century has witnessed more barbarous behaviour than any other. For those who remember Italians killing defenceless Ethiopians with poison gas, the murder of millions of Jews in Hitler's gas-chambers, Russian confessions of the murder and repression of millions of innocent people by Stalin, no human abomination is too monstrous to believe. It is only when we can't bear to contemplate man's beastliness, perhaps because in moments of appalling self-revelation it appears as a nightmare reflection of part of our own nature, that we refuse to recognize it.

But the behaviour of the Chinese, like that of everyone else, is not a matter of belief but of fact.

During our journeys we discovered no fact to justify the accusation that they are oppressing, let alone destroying the Tibetan people. Instead we saw how they had improved their condition. We could not judge this from our personal experience because we were not there before the Communists arrived. But it was not necessary for us to accept the word of the Communists that they were responsible for the improvement to be convinced of it. We came to this conclusion by comparing descriptions of Tibet by previous Western travellers, some of whom now condemn the Chinese for committing genocide, with what we saw. The oppressions and exploitations which they had found were no longer to be seen.

But if the serfs welcomed the Chinese, why did so many resist them and why did 20,000 escape to India with their owners?

The Chinese claim that, out of a population of one and a quarter million, fewer than 30,000—including the Khampas—joined in the revolts. It was estimated by Chinese Army commanders that 7,000 of those who fled to India had taken part in actual fighting.

They were told that the Communists lived on human flesh, that they and their families would be tortured and murdered if they were caught. These were good reasons for becoming refugees. Since they had been warned what would happen to them if they were taken prisoner their assumption that those left behind were tortured and killed is not surprising.

But how, if their stories were unreliable, did they convince a committee of lawyers that they were true?

An attempt to answer this question has been made by Miss Lois Lang-Sims, the first organising secretary of the Tibet Society of the United Kingdom, who went to India to meet refugees.[1]

She wrote a summary of the report of the committee of the International Commission of Jurists, highlighting religious martyrdoms and especially the accusation that the Communists had compelled crowds of Tibetans to watch and take part in the torture and execution of lamas and stole babies from their mothers to deport them to China.

She found she was never able to discover in these stories the 'ring of authenticity' which was to be found in accounts of Nazi persecutions of Jews. Taken collectively, she said, 'They convince me as being in general true and yet I remain, against my own will, faintly doubtful of each individual statement.'

During her third visit to India the uneasiness which she had already felt when she contributed her 'impassioned' summary to the Tibet Society's 'hand out' increased. For now, although an object of her journey was to collect more stories from refugees, she says, '*I failed to obtain one which I could conscientiously pigeon-hole as "authentic"*.'[2]

She explained she had learned by experience when talking through an interpreter ('as the members of the inquiry committee presumably had to do in each instance') how impossible it was to assess whether an informant was describing something which actually happened to himself.

1. *The Presence of Tibet* (Cresset Press 1963).
2. Authors' italics

Miss Lang-Sims wrote that the ordinary Tibetan was by nature truthful and honest. But to rely on this without also recognising that 'his view of "truth" bears no relation to what the west would regard as valid evidence, is dangerous. The Tibetan peasant has been accustomed from his cradle to accepting legend and fairy tale as literal truth.'

From China the Dalai Lama is seen as a tragic figure, not because he is a young king who has lost his kingdom, for in fact he was more possessed than possessing, but because now his life as a Tibetan in exile can only have purpose as long as he can believe that his people are suffering the cruelties which torment him. It is to be hoped that the day will also come when he will know, as we saw, that this image of his country is as illusory as the happy Shangri-la which existed only in the imaginations of those who have never been there and in which no Tibetan ever lived.

Roma's Chinese nurse in Lhasa

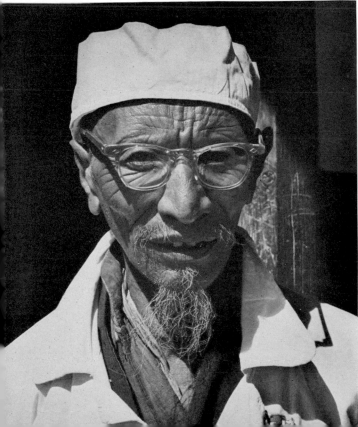

Ah Wang Chu Tza,
Dean of the traditional
lama hospital, who is
still sometimes worried
by evil spirits

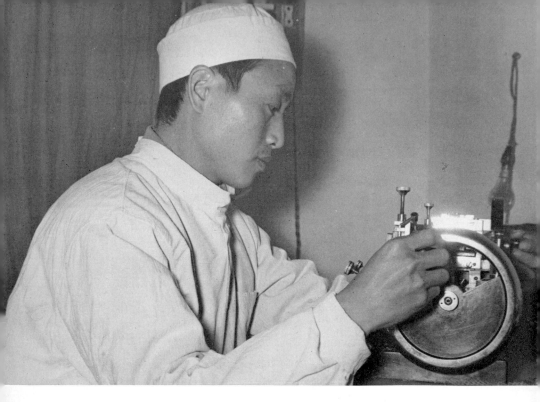

Pathologist—new Lhasa hospital

Surgeon—new Lhasa hospital

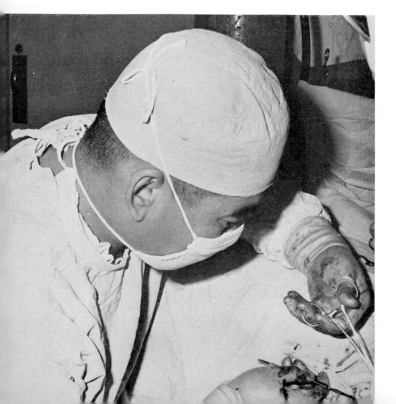

28

LHASA IN LONDON

When we saw the last sunlight shining on the golden roofs of the Potala as we left for the eastern grasslands on our way back to China, we should have seen the last of the Holy City in this 'incarnation'. In a few years we should be too old to ascend again to breathless heights. But if we could never return to these heavenly scenes we could take some of Lhasa home in a string bag. Almost a year to the day since we went to the Norbulingka for the last time, flame-coloured dahlias from the Dalai Lama's palace bloomed in our London garden.

When we had arrived five weeks earlier the Tibetan uplands were a carpet of flowers from the Chinghai road to the feet of the snow mountains. Thousands of small mouse-hares scurried about the grass searching for food and great herds of horses and ponies, for whom there was no shade in the treeless landscape, found refuge from the burning sun in the water meadows by the river. Bridges and long stretches of road had been washed away by floods which had piled up in the steep gorges and burst over the banks, which became shallower as the river came into more level ground, drowning the valley. Lorries over which the waters had swept in their first frantic leap were stranded, engulfed in mud.

Now the mountains were drained dry and the sun had baked the earth to a brown desert. But heavy transport was already tearing off the crust so that we drove through a dusty curtain a hundred miles thick.

All the flowers were dead. The mouse-hares had gone to their winter sleep. The birds of prey had flown to look for their livings round the lowland farms. Only yaks which could survive the high Tibetan winter and thick-coated horses remained with the herdsmen and their families in their hamlets of black yak-hair tents which would keep out the cold of an antarctic blizzard.

These were the last Tibetans to say goodbye to us. The men rode over on their fiery ponies followed by their women and children to wave us on our way.

As our aircraft climbed swiftly out of the airfield the ice-bound horizon was lost instantly beneath a canopy of snow turning slowly to red in the first light of dawn.

Koo She-lone dropped his oxygen mask on to his chin and leaned over to us. 'Well,' he said, 'do you think you found what you expected?'

I told him, 'There was once another tired journalist in a bar who was asked by a companion if he always wrote the truth. He said: "I've found the truth. I'm looking for something better."'

'Some people at home will expect us to tell them we found something much worse.'

APPENDIX I

CONVENTION OF 17th MARCH 1890 BEWEEN GREAT BRITAIN AND CHINA RELATING TO SIKKIM AND TIBET, 27th AUGUST 1890

WHEREAS Her Majesty the Queen of the United Kingdom of Great Britain and Ireland, Empress of India, and His Majesty the Emperor of China, are sincerely, desirous to maintain and perpetuate the relations of friendship and good understanding which now exist between their respective Empires; and whereas recent occurrences have tended towards a disturbance of the said relations, and it is desirable to clearly define and permanently settle certain matters connected with the boundary between Sikkim and Tibet, Her Britannic Majesty and His Majesty the Emperor of China have resolved to conclude a Convention on this subject, and have, for this purpose, named Plenipotentiaries, that is to say:

Her Majesty the Queen of Great Britain and Ireland, his Excellency the Most Honourable Henry Charles Keith Petty Fitzmaurice, G.M.S.I., G.C.M.G., G.M.I.E., Marquess of Landsowne, Viceroy and Governor-General of India;

And His Majesty the Emperor of China, his Excellency Sheng Tai, Imperial Associate Resident in Tibet, Military Deputy Lieutenant-Governor;

Who, having met and communicated to each other their full powers, and finding these to be in proper form, have agreed upon the following Convention in eight Articles:

I. The boundary of Sikkim and Tibet shall be the crest of the mountain-range separating the waters flowing into the Sikkim Teesta and its affluents from the waters flowing into the Tibetan Mochu and northwards into other rivers of Tibet. The line commences at Mount Gipmochi on the Bhutan frontier, and follows the above-mentioned water-parting to the point where it meets Nepal territory.

II. It is admitted that the British Government, whose Protectorate over the Sikkim State is hereby recognised, has direct and exclusive control over the internal administration and foreign relations of that State, and except through and with the permission of the British Government neither the Ruler of the State nor any of its officers shall have official relations of any kind, formal or informal, with any other country.

III. The Government of Great Britain and Ireland and the Government of China engage reciprocally to respect the boundary as defined in Article I, and to prevent acts of aggression from their respective sides of the frontier.

IV. The question of providing increased facilities for trade across the Sikkim-Tibet frontier will hereafter be discussed with a view to a mutually satisfactory arrangement by the High Contracting Powers.

V. The question of pasturage on the Sikkim side of the frontier is reserved for further examination and future adjustment.

VI. The High Contracting Powers reserve for discussion and arrangement the method in which official communications between the British authorities in India and the authorities in Tibet shall be conducted.

VII. Two joint Commissioners shall, within six months from the ratification of this Convention, be appointed, one by the British Government in India, the other by the Chinese Resident in Tibet. The said Commissioners shall meet and discuss the questions which, by the last three preceding Articles, have been reserved.

VIII. The present Convention shall be ratified, and the ratifications shall be exchanged in London as soon as possible after the date of the signature thereof.

In witness whereof the respective negotiators have signed the same, and affixed thereunto the seals of their arms.

Done in quadruplicate at Calcutta, this 17th day of March, in the year of our Lord 1890, corresponding with the Chinese date, the 27th day of the second moon of the 16th year of Kuang Hsu.

LANSDOWNE,

Signature of the Chinese Plenipotentiary

APPENDIX II

CONVENTION BETWEEN GREAT BRITAIN AND TIBET. SIGNED AT LHASA, 7th SEPTEMBER 1904

WHEREAS doubts and difficulties have arisen as to the meaning and validity of the Anglo-Chinese Convention of 1890, and the Trade Regulations of 1893, and as to the liabilities of the Thibetan Government under these Agreements; and whereas recent occurrences have tended towards a disturbance of the relations of friendship and good understanding which have existed between the British Government and the Government of Thibet; and whereas it is desirable to restore peace and amicable relations, and to resolve and determine the doubts and difficulties as aforesaid, the said Governments have resolved to conclude a Convention with these objects, and the following Articles have been agreed upon by Colonel F. E. Younghusband, C.I.E., in virtue of full powers vested in him by His Britannic Majesty's Government, and on behalf of that said Government, and Lo-Sang Gyal-Tsen, the Ga-den Ti-Rimpoche, and the representatives of the Council of the three monasteries Se-ra, Dre-pung, and Ga-den, and of the ecclesiastical and lay officials of the National Assembly on behalf of the Government of Thibet:—

I. The Government of Thibet engages to respect the Anglo-Chinese Convention of 1890, and to recognise the frontier between Sikkim and Thibet, as defined in Article 1 of the said Convention, and to erect boundary pillars accordingly.

II. The Thibetan Government undertakes to open forthwith trade marts to which all British and Thibetan subjects shall have free right of access at Gyantse and Gartok, as well as at Yatung.

The Regulations applicable to the trade mart at Yatung, under the Anglo-Chinese Agreement of 1893, shall, subject to such amendments as may hereafter be agreed upon by common consent between the British and Thibetan Governments, apply to the marts above mentioned.

In addition to establishing trade marts at the places mentioned, the Thibetan Government undertakes to place no restrictions on the trade by existing routes, and to consider the question of establishing fresh trade marts under similar conditions if development of trade requires it.

III. The question of the amendment of the Regulations of 1893 is reserved for separate consideration, and the Thibetan Government undertakes to appoint fully authorized delegates to negotiate with representatives of the British Government as to the details of the amendments required.

IV. The Thibetan Government undertakes to levy no dues of any kind other than those provided for in the tariff to be mutually agreed upon.

V. The Thibetan Government undertakes to keep the roads to Gyangtse

229

and Gartok from the frontier clear of all obstruction and in a state of repair suited to the needs of the trade, and to establish at Yatung, Gyangtse, and Gartok, and at each of the other trade marts that may hereafter be established, a Thibetan Agent who shall receive from the British Agent appointed to watch over British trade at the marts in question any letter which the latter may desire to send to the Thibetan or to the Chinese authorities. The The Thibetan Agent shall also be responsible for the due delivery of such communications and for the transmission of replies.

VI. As an indemnity to the British Government for the expense incurred in the dispatch of armed troops to Lhasa, to exact reparation for breaches of Treaty obligations, and for the insults offered to and attacks upon the British Commissioner and his following and escort, the Thibetan Government engages to pay a sum of £500,000 (equivalent to 75 lakhs of rupees) to the British Government.

The indemnity shall be payable at such place as the British Government may from time to time, after due notice, indicate, whether in Thibet or in the British districts of Darjeeling or Jalpaiguri, in seventy-five annual instalments of one lakh of rupees each on the 1st January in each year, beginning from the 1st January 1906.

VII. As security for the payment of the above-mentioned indemnity, and for the fulfilment of the provisions relative to trade marts specified in Articles II, III, IV, and V, the British Government shall continue to occupy the Chumbi Valley until the indemnity has been paid, and until the trade marts have been effectively opened for three years, whichever date may be the later.

VIII. The Thibetan Government agrees to raze all forts and fortifications and remove all armaments which might impede the course of free communication between the British frontier and the towns of Gyangtse and Lhasa.

IX. The Government of Thibet engages that, without the previous consent of the British Government:-

(a) No portion of Thibetan territory shall be ceded, sold, leased, mortgaged or otherwise given for occupation, to any Foreign Power;

(b) No such Power shall be permitted to intervene in Thibetan affairs;

(c) No Representatives or Agents of any Foreign Power shall be admitted to Thibet;

(d) No concessions for railways, roads, telegraphs, mining or other rights, shall be granted to any Foreign Power, or the subject of any Foreign Power. In the event of consent to such Concessions being granted, similar or equivalent Concessions shall be granted to the British Government;

(e) No Thibetan revenues, whether in kind or in cash, shall be pledged or assigned to any Foreign Power, or to the subject of any Foreign Power.

X. In witness whereof the negotiators have signed the same, and affixed thereunto the seals of their arms.

Done in quintuplicate at Lhasa, this 7th day of September, in the year of our Lord, 1904, corresponding with the Thibetan date, the 27th of the seventh month of the Wood Dragon year.

| (Thibet Frontier Commission.) | F. E. YOUNGHUSBAND, Colonel, British Commissioner. | (Seal of the Dalai Lama affixed by the Ga-den Ti-Rampoche.) |

(Seal of British Commissioner.)

| (Seal of Council.) | (Seal of Dre-pung Monastery.) | (Seal of Sera Monastery.) | (Seal of Ga-den Monastery.) | (Seal of National Assembly.) |

In proceeding to the signature of the Convention, dated this day, the representatives of Great Britain and Thibet declare that the English text shall be binding.

| (Thibet Frontier Commission.) | F. E YOUNGHUSBAND, Colonel, British Commissioner. | (Seal of the Dalai Lama affixed by the Ga-den Ti-Rimpoche.) |

| (Seal of Council.) | (Seal of Dre-pung Monastery.) | (Seal of Sera Monastery.) | (Seal of Ga-den Monastery.) | (Seal of National Assembly.) |

AMPTHILL,

Viceroy and Governor-General of India.

The Convention was ratified by the Viceroy and Governor-General of India in Council at Simla on the 11th day of November, 1904, subject to reduction of the indemnity to 25 Lakhs of rupees and a declaration that British occupation of the Chumbi valley would cease after payment of three annual instalments of the indemnity, provided that the Tibetans had complied with the terms of the Convention in all other respects.

APPENDIX III

CONVENTION BETWEEN GREAT BRITAIN AND CHINA RESPECTING TIBET. SIGNED AT PEKING, 27th APRIL 1906 (RATIFICATIONS EXCHANGED AT LONDON, 23rd JULY 1906)

(Signed also in Chinese)

WHEREAS His Majesty the King of Great Britain and Ireland and of the British Dominions beyond the Seas, Emperor of India, and His Majesty the Emperor of China are sincerely desirous to maintain and perpetuate the relations of friendship and good understanding which now exist between their respective Empires;

And whereas the refusal of Tibet to recognize the validity of or to carry into full effect the provisions of the Anglo-Chinese Convention of March 17, 1890, and Regulations of December 5, 1893, placed the British Government under the necessity of taking steps to secure their rights and interests under the said Convention and Regulations;

And whereas a Convention of ten articles was signed at Lhasa on September 7, 1904, on behalf of Great Britain and Tibet, and was ratified by the Viceroy and Governor-General of India on behalf of Great Britain on November 11, 1904, a declaration on behalf of Great Britain modifying its terms under certain conditions being appended thereto;

His Britannic Majesty and His Majesty the Emperor of China have resolved to conclude a Convention on this subject and have for this purpose named Plenipotentiaries, that is to say:–

His Majesty the King of Great Britain and Ireland:

Sir Ernest Mason Satow, Knight Grand Cross of the Most Distinguished Order of Saint Michael and Saint George, His said Majesty's Envoy Extraordinary and Minister Plenipotentiary to His Majesty the Emperor of China;

And His Majesty the Emperor of China:

His Excellency Tong Shoa-yi, His said Majesty's High Commissioner Plenipotentiary and a Vice-President of the Board of Foreign Affairs; who having communicated to each other their respective full powers and finding them to be in good and true form have agreed upon and concluded the following Convention in six articles:–

I. The Convention concluded on September 7, 1904, by Great Britain and Tibet, the texts of which in English and Chinese are attached to the present Convention as an annexe, is hereby confirmed, subject to the modification stated in the declaration appended thereto, and both of the High Contracting Parties engage to take at all times such steps as may be necessary to secure the due fulfilment of the terms specified therein.

232

II. The Government of Great Britain engages not to annex Tibetan territory or to interfere in the administration of Tibet. The Government of China also undertakes not to permit any other foreign state to interfere with the territory or internal administration of Tibet.[1]

III. The Concessions which are mentioned in Article IX(d) of the Convention concluded on September 7th, 1904, by Great Britain and Tibet are denied to any state or to the subject of any state other than China, but it has been arranged with China that at the trade marts specified in Article II of the aforesaid Convention Great Britain shall be entitled to lay down telegraph lines connecting with India.

IV. The provisions of the Anglo-Chinese Convention of 1890 and Regulations of 1893 shall, subject to the terms of this present Convention and annexe thereto, remain in full force.

V. The English and Chinese texts of the present Convention have been carefully compared and found to correspond, but in the event of there being any difference of meaning between them the English text shall be authoritative.

VI. This Convention shall be ratified by the Sovereigns of both countries and ratifications shall be exchanged at London within three months after the date of signature by the Plenipotentiaries of both Powers.

In token whereof the respective Plenipotentiaries have signed and sealed this Convention, four copies in English and four in Chinese.

Done at Peking this twenty-seventh day of April, one thousand nine hundred and six, being the fourth day of the fourth month of the thirty-second year of the reign of Kuang-hsu.

ERNEST SATOW

(Signature and Seal of the Chinese Plenipotentiary.)

---

1. *Authors' Note: Since by this Convention China's sovereign rights in Tibet were implicitly recognised, there was no question of her agreeing, as Britain agreed, not to annex Tibetan territory or interfere in the administration of the country.*

Q

APPENDIX IV

CONVENTION BETWEEN GREAT BRITAIN AND RUSSIA RELATING TO PERSIA, AFGHANISTAN AND TIBET. SIGNED AT ST. PETERSBURG, 31st AUGUST 1907.

His Majesty the King of the United Kingdom of Great Britain and Ireland and of the British Dominions beyond the Seas, Emperor of India, and His Majesty the Emperor of All the Russias, animated by the sincere desire to settle by mutual agreement different questions concerning the interests of their States on the Continent of Asia, have determined to conclude Agreements destined to prevent all cause of misunderstanding between Great Britain and Russia in regard to the questions referred to, and have nominated for this purpose their respective Plenipotentiaries, to wit:

His Majesty the King of the United Kingdom of Great Britain and Ireland and of the British Dominions beyond the Seas, Emperor of India, the Right Honourable Sir Arthur Nicolson, His Majesty's Ambassador Extraordinary and Plenipotentiary to His Majesty the Emperor of All the Russias;

His Majesty the Emperor of All the Russias, the Master of his Court Alexander Iswolsky, Minister for Foreign Affairs;

Who, having communicated to each other their full powers, found in good and due form, have agreed on the following:

ARRANGEMENT CONCERNING THIBET

The Governments of Great Britain and Russia recognising the suzerain rights of China in Thibet, and considering the fact that Great Britain, by reason of her geographical position, has a special interest in the maintenance of the status quo in the external relations of Thibet, have made the following arrangement:

ARTICLE I

The two High Contracting Parties engage to respect the territorial integrity of Thibet and to abstain from all interference in the internal administration.

ARTICLE II

In conformity with the admitted principle of the suzerainty of China over Thibet, Great Britain and Russia engage not to enter into negotiations with Thibet except through the intermediary of the Chinese Government. This engagement does not exclude the direct relations between British Commer-cial Agents and the Thibetan authorities provided for in Article V of the Convention between Great Britain and Thibet of the 7th September 1904, and confirmed by the Convention between Great Britain and China of the 27th April 1906; nor does it modify the engagements entered into by Great Britain and China in Article I of the said Convention of 1906.

It is clearly understood that Buddhists, subjects of Great Britain or of Russia, may enter into direct relations on strictly religious matters with the Dalai Lama and the other representatives of Buddhism in Thibet; the Governments of Great Britain and Russia engage, as far as they are concerned, not to allow those relations to infringe the stipulations of the present arrangement.

ARTICLE III

The British and Russian Governments respectively engage not to send Representatives to Lhasa.

ARTICLE IV

The two High Contracting Parties engage neither to seek nor to obtain, whether for themselves or their subjects, any Concessions for railways, roads, telegraphs, and mines, or other rights in Thibet.

ARTICLE V

The two Governments agree that no part of the revenues of Thibet, whether in kind or in cash, shall be pledged or assigned to Great Britain or Russia or to any of their subjects.

Annexe to the arrangement between Great Britain and Russia concerning Thibet.

Great Britain reaffirms the declaration, signed by His Excellency the Viceroy and Governor-General of India and appended to the ratification of the Convention of the 7th September 1904, to the effect that the occupation of the Chumbi Valley by British forces shall cease after the payment of three annual instalments of the indemnity of 25 Lakhs of Rupees, provided that the trade marts mentioned in Article II of that Convention have been effectively opened for three years, and that in the meantime the Thibetan authorities have faithfully complied in all respects with the terms of the said Convention of 1904. It is clearly understood that if the occupation of the Chumbi Valley by the British forces has, for any reason, not been terminated at the time anticipated in the above Declaration, the British and Russian Governments will enter upon a friendly exchange of views on this subject.

The present Convention shall be ratified, and the ratification exchanged at St. Petersburgh as soon as possible.

In witness whereof the respective Plenipotentiaries have signed the present Convention and affixed thereto their seals. Done in duplicate at St. Petersburgh, the 18th (31st) August 1907.

Note: The Tibetans and Chinese were not notified of the conclusion of this treaty.

APPENDIX V

CONVENTION BETWEEN GREAT BRITAIN, CHINA, AND TIBET. SIMLA 1914

His Majesty the King of the United Kingdom of Great Britain and Ireland and of the British Dominions beyond the Seas, Emperor of India, His Excellency the President of the Republic of China, and His Holiness the Dalai Lama of Tibet, being sincerely desirous to settle by mutual agreement various questions concerning the interests of their several States on the Continent of Asia, and further to regulate the relations of their several Governments, have resolved to conclude a Convention on this subject and have nominated for this purpose their respective Plenipotentiaries, that is to say:

His Majesty the King of the United Kingdom of Great Britain and Ireland and of the British Dominions beyond the Seas, Emperor of India, Sir Arthur Henry McMahon, Knight Grand Cross of the Royal Victorian Order, Knight Commander of the Most Eminent Order of the Indian Empire, Companion of the Most Exalted Order of the Star of India, Secretary to the Government of India, Foreign and Political Department;

His Excellency the President of the Republic of China, Monsieur Ivan Chen, Officer of the Order of the Chia Ho;

His Holiness the Dalai Lama of Tibet, Lonchen Ga-den Shatra Pal-jor Dorje; who having communicated to each other their respective full powers and finding them to be in good and due form have agreed upon and concluded the following Convention in eleven Articles:

ARTICLE I

The Conventions specified in the Schedule to the present Convention shall, except in so far as they may have been modified by, or may be inconsistent with or repugnant to, any of the provisions of the present Convention, continue to be binding upon the High Contracting Parties.

ARTICLE 2

The Governments of Great Britain and China recognising that Tibet is under the suzerainty of China, and recognising also the autonomy of Outer Tibet, engage to respect the territorial integrity of the country, and to abstain from interference in the administration of Outer Tibet (including the selection and installation of the Dalai Lama), which shall remain in the hands of the Tibetan Government at Lhasa.

The Government of China engages not to convert Tibet into a Chinese province. The Government of Great Britain engages not to annex Tibet or any portion of it.

ARTICLE 3

Recognising the special interest of Great Britain, in virtue of the geographical position of Tibet, in the existence of an effective Tibetan Government, and in the maintenance of peace and order in the neighbourhood of the frontiers of India and adjoining States, the Government of China engages, except as provided in Article 4 of this Convention, not to send troops into Outer Tibet, nor to station civil or military officers, nor to establish Chinese colonies in the country. Should any such troops or officials remain in Outer Tibet at the date of the signature of this Convention, they shall be withdrawn within a period not exceeding three months.

The Government of Great Britain engages not to station military or civil officers in Tibet (except as provided in the Convention of September 7, 1904, between Great Britain and Tibet) nor troops (except the Agents' escorts), nor to establish colonies in that country.

ARTICLE 4

The foregoing Article shall not be held to preclude the continuance of the arrangement by which, in the past, a Chinese high official with suitable escort has been maintained at Lhasa, but it is hereby provided that the said escort shall in no circumstances exceed 300 men.

ARTICLE 5

The Governments of China and Tibet engage that they will not enter into any negotiations or agreements regarding Tibet with one another, or with any other Power, excepting such negotiations and agreements between Great Britain and Tibet as are provided for by the Convention of September 7 1904 between Great Britain and Tibet and the Convention of April 27 1906 between Great Britain and China.

ARTICLE 6

Article III of the Convention of April 27 1906 between Great Britain and China is hereby cancelled, and it is understood that in Article IX(d) of the

Convention of September 7 1904 between Great Britain and Tibet the term 'Foreign Power' does not include China.

Not less favourable treatment shall be accorded to British commerce than to the commerce of China or the most favoured nation.

ARTICLE 7

(a) The Tibet Trade Regulations of 1893 and 1908 are hereby cancelled.

(b) The Tibetan Government engages to negotiate with the British Government new Trade Regulations for Outer Tibet to give effect to Articles II, IV and V of the Convention of September 7 1904 between Great Britain and Tibet without delay; provided always that such Regulations shall in no way modify the present Convention except with the consent of the Chinese Government.

ARTICLE 8

The British Agent who resides at Gyantse may visit Lhasa with his escort whenever it is necessary to consult with the Tibetan Government regarding matters arising out of the Convention of September 7 1904, between Great Britain and Tibet, which it has been found impossible to settle at Gyantse by correspondence or otherwise.

ARTICLE 9

For the purpose of the present Convention the borders of Tibet, and the boundary between Outer and Inner Tibet, shall be as shown in red and blue respectively on the map attached hereto.

Nothing in the present Convention shall be held to prejudice the existing rights of the Tibetan Government in Inner Tibet, which include the power to select and appoint the high priests of monasteries and to retain full control in all matters affecting religious institutions.

ARTICLE 10

The English, Chinese and Tibetan texts of the present Convention have been carefully examined and found to correspond, but in the event of there being any difference of meaning between them the English text shall be authoritative.

ARTICLE 11

The present Convention will take effect from the date of signature.

In token whereof the respective Plenipotentiaries have signed and sealed this Convention, three copies in English, three in Chinese and three in Tibetan. Done at Simla this third day of July, A.D., one thousand nine hundred and fourteen, corresponding with the Chinese date, the third day of the seventh month of the third year of the Republic, and the Tibetan date, the tenth day of the fifth month of the Wood-Tiger year.

Initial of the Lonchen Shatra. (Initialled) A.H.M.

Seal of the Lonchen Shatra. Seal of the British Plenipotentiary.

This Convention was signed by the Chinese representative but his signature was repudiated by the Chinese Government which refused to recognise it.

On 14 October 1954 the Indian Government recognising Tibet as part of the People's Republic of China concluded a trade agreement with Peking.

APPENDIX VI

THE CHINESE-TIBETAN AGREEMENT
OF 23rd MAY 1951

Text of 'Agreement of the Central People's Government and the Local Government of Tibet on Measures for the Peaceful Liberation of Tibet'.

The Tibetan nationality is one of the nationalities with a long history within the boundaries of China and, like many other nationalities, it has done its glorious duty in the course of the creation and development of the great motherland. But over the last 100 years or more, imperialist forces penetrated into China, and in consequence also penetrated into the Tibetan region and carried out all kinds of deceptions and provocations. Like previous reactionary governments, the Kuomintang reactionary government continued to carry out a policy of oppressing and sowing dissension among the nationalities, causing division and disunity among the Tibetan people. And the Local Government of Tibet did not oppose the imperialist deception and provocations, and adopted an unpatriotic attitude towards the great motherland. Under such conditions, the Tibetan nationality and people were plunged into the depths of enslavement and sufferings. In 1949, basic victory was achieved on a nation-wide scale in the Chinese People's War of Liberation; the common domestic enemy of all nationalities—the Kuomintang reactionary government—was overthrown; and the common foreign enemy of all nationalities—the aggressive imperialist forces—driven out. On this basis, the founding of the People's Republic of China and of the Central People's Government was announced. In accordance with the Common Programme passed by the Chinese People's Political Consultative Conference, the Central People's Government declared that all nationalities within the boundaries of the People's Republic of China are equal, and that they shall establish unity and mutual aid and oppose imperialism and their own public enemies so that the People's Republic of China will become a big family of fraternity and co-operation, composed of all its nationalities. Within the big family of all nationalities of the People's Republic of China national regional autonomy shall be exercised in areas where national minorities are concentrated, and all national minorities shall have freedom to develop their spoken and written languages and to preserve or reform their customs, habits and religious beliefs, and the Central People's Government shall assist all national minorities to develop their political, economic, cultural and educational construction work. Since then, all nationalities within the country, with the exception of those in the areas of Tibet and Taiwan (Formosa), have gained liberation. Under the unified leadership of the Central People's Government and the direct leadership of higher levels of People's Governments, all national minorities have fully enjoyed the right of national equality and have exercised, or are exercising, national regional autonomy. In order that the influences of aggressive imperialist forces in Tibet might be successfully eliminated, the unification of the territory and sovereignty of the People's Republic of China accomplished, and national defence safeguarded; in order that the Tibetan nationality and people might be freed and return to the big family of the People's Republic of China to enjoy the same rights of national equality as all the other nationalities in the country and develop their political, economic, cultural and educational work; the Central People's Government, when it ordered the People's Liberation Army to march into Tibet, notified the Local Government of Tibet to send delegates to the central authorities to conduct talks for the conclusion of an agreement on measures for the peaceful liberation of Tibet. At the latter part of April 1951, the delegates with full powers of the Local Government of Tibet arrived in Peking. The Central People's Government appointed representatives with full powers to conduct talks on a friendly basis with the delegates with full powers of the Local Government of Tibet. As a result of the talks, both parties agreed to establish this agreement and ensure that it be carried into effect.

1. The Tibetan people shall unite and drive out imperialist aggressive forces from Tibet; the Tibetan people shall return to the big family of the motherland—the People's Republic of China.

2. The Local Government of Tibet shall actively assist the People's Liberation Army to enter Tibet and consolidate the national defences.

3. In accordance with the policy towards nationalities laid down in the Common Programme of the Chinese People's Political Consultative Conference, the Tibetan people have the right of exercising national regional autonomy under the unified leadership of the Central People's Government.

4. The central authorities will not alter the existing political system in Tibet. The central authorities also will not alter the established status, functions and powers of the Dalai Lama. Officials of various ranks shall hold office as usual.

5. The established status, functions and powers of the Panchen Ngoerhtehni shall be maintained.[1]

6. By the established status, functions and powers of the Dalai Lama and of the Panchen Ngoerhtehni are meant the status, functions and powers of the 13th Dalai Lama and of the 9th Panchen Ngoerhtehni when they were in friendly and amicable relations with each other.

7. The policy of freedom of religious belief laid down in the Common Programme of the Chinese People's Political Consultative Conference shall be carried out. The religious beliefs, customs and habits of the Tibetan people shall be respected, and lama monasteries shall be protected. The central authorities will not effect a change in the income of the monasteries.

8. Tibetan troops shall be re-organized step by step into the People's Liberation Army, and become a part of the national defence forces of the People's Republic of China.

1. Panchen Lama

9. The spoken and written language and school education of the Tibetan nationality shall be developed step by step in accordance with the actual conditions in Tibet.

10. Tibetan agriculture, livestock raising, industry and commerce shall be developed step by step, and the people's livelihood shall be improved step by step in accordance with the actual conditions in Tibet.

11. In matters related to various reforms in Tibet, there will be no compulsion on the part of the central authorities. The Local Government of Tibet should carry out reforms on its own accord, and when the people raise demands for reform, they shall be settled by means of consultation with the leading personnel of Tibet.

12. In so far as former pro-imperialist and pro-Kuomintang officials resolutely sever relations with imperialism and the Kuomintang and do not engage in sabotage or resistance, they may continue to hold office irrespective of their past.

13. The People's Liberation Army entering Tibet shall abide by all the above-mentioned policies and shall also be fair in all buying and selling and shall not arbitrarily take a needle or thread from the people.

14. The Central People's Government shall have centralised handling of all external affairs of the area of Tibet; and there will be peaceful co-existence with neighbouring countries and establishment and development of fair commercial and trading relations with them on the basis of equality, mutual benefit and mutual respect for territory and sovereignty.

15. In order to ensure the implementation of this agreement, the Central People's Government shall set up a military and administrative committee and a military area headquarters in Tibet, and apart from the personnel sent there by the Central People's Government shall absorb as many local Tibetan personnel as possible to take part in the work.

Local Tibetan personnel taking part in the military and administrative committee may include patriotic elements from the Local Government of Tibet, various districts and various principal monasteries; the name-list shall be set forth after consultation between the representatives designated by the Central People's Government and various quarters concerned, and shall be submitted to the Central People's Government for appointment.

16. Funds needed by the military and administrative committee, the military area headquarters and the People's Liberation Army entering Tibet shall be provided by the Central People's Government. The Local Government of Tibet should assist the People's Liberation Army in the purchase and transport of food, fodder and other daily necessities.

17. This agreement shall come into force immediately after signatures and seals are affixed to it.

Signed and sealed by:

Delegates of the Central People's Government with full powers:

Chief Delegate:
LI WEI-HAN

Delegates:
CHANG CHING-WU
CHANG KUO-HUA
SUN CHIH-YUAN

Delegates with full powers of the Local Government of Tibet:

Chief Delegate:
KALOON NGABOU NGAWANG JIGME

Delegates:
DZASAK KHEMEY SONAM WANGDI
KHENTRUNG THUPTEN TENTHAR
KHENCHUNG THUPTEN LEKMUUN
RIMSHI SAMPOSEY TENZIN THUNDUP

Peking, 23rd May 1951

INDEX